FM AUDITORY TRAINING SYSTEMS

FM AUDITORY TRAINING SYSTEMS
Characteristics, Selection, and Use

Edited by
Mark Ross, Ph.D.
with special assistance from Helen Ross

Timonium, Maryland

YORK
PRESS

This book was manufactured in the United States of America. Typography by Brushwood Graphics, Inc., Baltimore, Maryland. Printing and binding by McNaughton & Gunn, Inc., Ann Arbor, Michigan. Cover design by Joseph Dieter, Jr.

ISBN 0-912752-31-9

Library of Congress Cataloging-In-Publication Data

FM auditory training systems, characteristics, selection, and use / edited by Mark Ross ; with special assistance from Helen Ross.
    p. cm.
  Includes bibliographical references and index.
  ISBN 0-912752-31-9
  1. FM auditory training systems—Congresses.   I. Ross, Mark.
RF308.F6   1992
617.8'9—dc20   92-21604
                                                                       CIP

Contents

Contributors

Arthur Boothroyd, Ph.D.
Graduate School
City University of New York
33 West 42nd Street
New York NY 10036

Diane Brackett, Ph.D.
New York League for the Hard
of Hearing
71 West 23rd Street
New York NY 10010

Chris Hawrylak Evans, M.A.
Rochester School for the Deaf
1545 St. Paul Street
Rochester NY 14621

Carol Flexer, Ph.D.
Department of Communication
Disorders
University of Akron
Akron OH 43325

Jane Madell, Ph.D.
Department of Communicative
Disorders
Long Island College Hospital
340 Henry Street
Brooklyn NY 11201

Antonia Brancia Maxon, Ph.D.
Communication Sciences
Department
University of Connecticut
Storrs CT 06268

Ellen Pfeffer, M.A.
New York League for the Hard
of Hearing
71 West 23rd Street
New York NY 10010

Mark Ross, Ph.D.
New York League for the Hard
of Hearing
71 West 23rd Street
New York NY 10010

Richard Seewald, Ph.D.
Department of Communicative
Disorders
Elborn College
University of Western Ontario
London Ontario N6G 1H1
Canada

Linda Thibodeau, Ph.D.
Department of Speech
Communication
University of Texas at Austin
Austin TX 78712-1089

Preface

The New York League for the Hard of Hearing sponsored a Conference on Frequency Modulated (FM) Auditory Training Systems on March 7 and 8, 1991, supported in part and hosted by the Chase Manhattan Bank. This book is an expanded version of the papers presented at that conference. Since the advent of FM systems about 25 years ago, they have proved to be valuable, indeed indispensable, educational, and clinical tools. Actually, the term *FM Auditory Training Systems* is now basically obsolete. Their use far transcends that of simple "auditory training" for hearing-impaired youngsters, which was their first application and the stimulus for their development. (In fact, the initial purpose of the systems was not "auditory training" but the same as it is now—namely, to transmit a distant talker's speech to a recipient.) If we use the same term now that we did 25 years ago, it is simply because no other generally accepted term to describe these systems has emerged.

When FM systems first appeared on the clinical/educational scene, I was very interested in the effect of classroom acoustics on speech intelligibility. One conclusion stressed in a chapter that I wrote on the topic (Ross 1972) was that the shorter the distance between the speech source and the recipient, the higher were the speech discrimination scores. It seemed clear that the same logic would apply for wireless FM microphones. Thus, their possible contribution to the auditory reception and development of hearing-impaired children was evident from the start (although not always realized then or, for that matter, even now). Having worn hearing aids myself for about twenty years at that time, I was quite aware and sensitive to the effects that noise had upon the reception of speech. I also knew that the simple expedient of getting closer to a speaker (or taking my body aid out of my pocket and locating it close to a talker's mouth) always improved my speech comprehension. It seemed then, and this is still true in spite of all the advances in hearing aid technology, that no better method of reducing the impact of poor acoustical conditions exists than advantageous microphone placement.

This is not an easy concept for normal-hearing people to accept. When such a person has little or no difficulty comprehending speech in a moderately noisy environment, it is not easy to fully appreciate the difficulty that hearing-impaired people may have in understanding speech in the same situation. This observation led to several studies that directly compared speech perception with and without an FM system in a regular classroom (Ross and Giolas 1971; Ross, Giolas, and Carver 1973). The results, we felt, were incredibly positive. Absolute differences in excess of 30% were common, with some children improving their *relative* scores by factors of 2 and 3. With this kind of evidence in hand, we felt that we could approach school administrators and easily convince them to purchase FM systems for the hearing-impaired children enrolled in their classes. Our subsequent experiences soon corrected this optimistic forecast; with all the good will in the world, it was difficult for school administrators to translate a difference in numbers to actual difficulty experienced by hearing-impaired children. Now, 25 years after FM systems have become available, after numerous studies and use of FM systems in schools, we still have difficulty convincing many school professionals of the potential value of FM systems. Perhaps this book will help.

In my estimation, FM systems are the most significant therapeutic tool developed for hearing-impaired children since the advent of personal and group amplification devices. Used and functioning properly, they can exploit the residual hearing most hearing-impaired children possess in a way not possible with any other device. There have been many books devoted to the consequences of congenital hearing loss and aspects of the therapeutic process. FM auditory training systems, because they have the capacity to deliver the clearest amplified speech signal into the ears and brain of a hearing-impaired person, deserve and require the same extensive coverage. Moreover, their advantages with special populations (such as learning disordered children) and with hearing-impaired adults are increasingly being recognized and accepted. As with any tool, however, their effectiveness is limited by the skill with which they are used. The purpose of this book is to present the necessary information so that practitioners will realize the full potential of FM auditory training sytems.

No edited book is going to be free of a certain amount of redundancy. Some of the information in one chapter may appear in another, albeit in a different form and for a different purpose. There is only one basic rationale for the use of an FM system (increasing the intensity level of the primary speech signal relative to the background noise, or the signal-to-noise ratio or S/N ratio) and different chapter authors refer to it in their own way for their own purposes. Comments on coupling modes and selection goals and techniques also appear in several chapters. The point of view taken in this book is that, to the extent that it occurs, the overlap is necessary to preserve the integrity of the different chapters, as well as being an aid to learning.

It should be understood that FM auditory training systems are basically radio transmitters and receivers. How radio waves are modulated by an audio signal, the place in the electromagnetic spectrum in which radio waves occur, and the variables affecting the radio wave itself are presented by Arthur Boothroyd in Chapter 1.

In the next chapter, I analyze the reasons hearing-impaired people find FM systems so necessary and helpful. Basically, this chapter describes the acoustical conditions existing in our society, the relative effects of noise and reverberation on normal and hearing-impaired people, and the role that signal-to-noise ratio plays in circumventing the effects of negative acoustical conditions. This particular theme is recurrent throughout the entire book.

The chapter on acoustical considerations is followed by a specific description of the physical components and features of current FM systems. When they first came on the scene 25 years ago, only one fitting and wearing option existed. (As a matter of fact, the first systems were unable to modify the basic electroacoustic characteristics of the speech signal.) As we see in Linda Thibodeau's chapter, FM systems are much more involved now than they were then. With additional variations in possible system components, additional problems arise that clinicians and teachers must consider when using these systems.

The desired output from the FM receiver into the ear canal can be conceptualized as a unifying theme that unites all the possible variations caused by the different physical components. After all is said and done, after all variations in microphone and coupling possibilities are considered, what is the nature of the amplified speech signal being delivered into the ear canal by the FM and/or environmental microphones? The electroacoustic product of FM systems is the topic of Chapter 4 by Richard Seewald and K. Shayne Moodie.

After we define the desirable electroacoustic product, we must select a specific unit for a specific person who then wears the unit in specific educational and environmental circumstances. In Chapter 5, Antonia Maxon describes and gives examples of correct and incorrect use of FM systems in classrooms (still the major setting in which they are used).

FM systems share with hearing aids the propensity to break down at inauspicious times (not that there is an auspicious time for an FM/hearing aid breakdown). From a clinical/educational point of view, it is probably wise to assume that the FM system *will* break down and that, therefore, frequent troubleshooting is a mandatory requirement. In Chapter 6, Chris Evans presents a step-by-step troubleshooting program for teachers and parents, leading to the time when the hearing-impaired person can take control of his or her own amplification system. Drawing on her extensive experience with such systems at the Rochester School for the Deaf, she also cautions us about potential areas of concern in which troubleshooting considerations overlap selection of specific systems.

For the last eight years, the New York League for the Hard of Hearing has fit FM systems on newly detected hearing-impaired children as their first and primary amplification device. Jane Madell discusses in Chapter 7 the rationale for this clinical practice and how families are convinced to accept the need for a relatively large amplification device. Dr. Madell explains the unique considerations involved in fitting FM systems to these very young children. First-time visitors to the New York League are always amazed to see how nonchalantly parents wear FM microphones suspended around their necks while talking to their children in and around the League.

The speech perception results obtained from this same group of children are presented by Diane Brackett in Chapter 8. Up to this point, it has been the intrinsic logic of improving the signal-to-noise ratio that has supported the practice of fitting FMs on young children. Validating data supporting this practice have generally not been available. To my knowledge, no group of comparable children has achieved speech perception scores as high as this group. Based on Dr. Brackett's results, we may have to revise our estimates of what degree of hearing loss constitutes "audiological" deafness. She also cautions us that simply placing an FM system on a child, while a necessary condition for the best auditory linguistic growth, is insufficient in itself. A well-constructed therapy program is still an indispensable ingredient for maximizing a child's potential.

One of the spin-offs of conventional FM auditory training systems is the use of the FM concept in Public Address systems. Basically, the FM microphone is used to deliver the teacher's speech to several loud-speakers located around the classroom. In Chapter 9, Carol Flexer outlines the acoustic and educational reasoning behind this practice, and reviews some research and experiences with such systems. Of all the current uses of FM systems, this practice has the potential of achieving the most positive speech perception and academic results for the largest group of children.

As suggested above, the possible contribution of FM auditory training systems transcends their traditional use with school-age hearing-impaired children (including their use with newly detected hearing-impaired infants). In her chapter, Ellen Pfeffer discusses how the advantageous microphone placement of an FM system can benefit children with minimal and unilateral hearing losses and learning disabilities, as well as adults with special listening needs.

This book, then, represents the current "state of the art" as it pertains to FM systems. The future is going to look somewhat different. Current technology is based on body-worn FM receivers, coupled to the ear with button transducers (self-contained FM systems) or through a personal hearing aid. The variables and complications produced by variations in coupling modes are described throughout the book. At the time of this writing, a new development may well significantly alter this picture. One company has developed an FM receiver completely incorporated in a behind-the-ear (BTE) hearing aid. Based on the history of the industry, where one company goes, the others are not far behind.

The acoustic options afforded by this new development seem very desirable. It is possible to use this system as a BTE hearing aid, as an FM receiver, or both simultaneously. There will be no need for different coupling modes (direct audio-input, neckloop, and silhouette), and this will eliminate one major source of electroacoustic variability. Usage options seem equally desirable. The system can be used as a conventional hearing aid until the assistance of an FM transmission is needed and desired. At that time, the FM microphone/transmitter can be added to the listening experience (such as in a lecture hall, on a noisy vehicle or street, in a restaurant, and so on). My own long-awaited wish is for the inclusion of a hand-held highly directional FM microphone with the BTE FM. The system can then be used in noisy gatherings to increase, in a convenient manner, the effective S/N ratio. The development of this new FM system is still in its infancy— unforeseen problems will undoubtedly occur—but the future path is clear.

I hope this will not be the extent of future developments in FM systems. There are other possible desirable features, such as a built-in scanner in the transmitter, which would sample the permitted radio spectrum, and retransmit the clearest one, or FM receivers that can simultaneously detect two or more frequencies (but only one person can talk at a time!). Whatever technical developments do occur in the future, we can be sure that Murphy's law will always apply: whatever can go wrong, will. The astute and sensitive clinician will never take the operation of any FM system for granted, no matter how well it seems to be designed or how glowing the testimonials. This book will, I hope, keep Murphy's law in check.

Mark Ross, Ph.D.

REFERENCES

Ross, M. 1972. Classroom acoustics and speech intelligibility. In *Handbook of Clinical Audiology*, ed. J. Katz. Baltimore: Williams & Wilkins.
Ross, M., and Giolas, T. 1971. Effect of three classroom listening conditions on speech intelligibility. *American Annals of the Deaf* 116:580–84.
Ross, M., Giolas, T., and Carver, P. 1973. Effect of three classroom listening conditions on speech intelligibility. A replication in part. *Language, Speech, Hearing Services in Schools* 4:72–76.

Acknowledgments

This book is based on a national conference on FM Systems sponsored by the New York League for the Hard of Hearing. We are indebted to a number of individuals and institutions for their assistance and cooperation.

The Gerald and May Ellen Ritter Memorial Fund helped fund the conference. The Chase Manhattan Bank provided facilities with the generous cooperation of William Menger and James Glynn. The Canteen Corporation hosted the lunch, with the arrangements being approved and made by Ray Norton, John Hine, and William Menard.

I am indebted to Robert Essman for lending me his creative imagination in our graphic needs, as he has done for other of our similar efforts. The Development office of the New York League ensured the smooth operation of the conference because of the cheerful competence of Manuel Cuenca, Joe Brown, and Justin Cristaldi.

The conference itself was the brainchild of Jane Madell, who insisted that professionals need more information about FM Systems. As she has done on other such occasions, Ruth Green, the former Executive Director of the New York League for the Hard of Hearing, not only kept little glitches from growing into big ones, but gave us her enthusiastic support during the entire process, from conference to book.

Finally, as always, I am indebted personally and professionally to my wife, Helen, who read and agonized over every word in this manuscript.

Mark Ross, Ph.D.

This book is dedicated to my children, Paula and Joel, who have always filled my life with love.

Chapter • 1

The FM Wireless Link
An Invisible
Microphone Cable

Arthur Boothroyd

Sensorineural hearing impairment is caused by damage to the inner ear and its associated nerves. Such damage affects hearing in four principal ways (see, for example, Boothroyd 1978; Davis and Silverman 1978; Ross, Brackett, and Maxon 1982):

1. *Threshold elevation*—that is, an increase, relative to normal, of the intensity level at which sound becomes audible. The pure tone audiogram is a graph of threshold elevation as a function of frequency and provides the basic means by which we categorize and quantify severity of hearing impairment.
2. *Dynamic range reduction*—that is, a reduction of the intensity difference between sounds that are just loud enough to be heard and those that are too loud for comfort. The reduction of dynamic range is caused by the fact that very loud sounds are as uncomfortable to persons with sensorineural hearing impairment as they are to normally hearing persons.
3. *Discrimination loss*—that is, a loss of the ability to hear differences among sound patterns, even when the sounds themselves are loud enough to be heard. A principal cause of discrimination loss is an inability to resolve fine detail in both the frequency and the time domains. Sometimes there is also a complete loss of audibility for high frequency sounds.

Preparation of this paper was supported, in part, by NIDRR grant #HI133E80019.

4. *Increased noise susceptibility*—that is, an increase in the interfering effects of noise beyond that which would be experienced by normally hearing persons. Increased noise susceptibility is one of the consequences of discrimination loss. The analysis and impact of this factor are discussed at more length in Chapter 2.

Hearing aids address the issue of *threshold elevation* by amplifying sound—that is, by increasing its loudness. Unfortunately, the benefits of hearing aids are limited by the other three effects of sensorineural hearing loss listed above (Skinner 1988). *Dynamic range reduction* requires that the aid's output be prevented from exceeding comfortable levels and this makes it difficult to cope with variations of speech intensity, especially those that accompany changes of distance between the talker and the hearing aid microphone (Kamm, Dirks, and Mickey 1978). *Discrimination loss* limits the wearer's ability to differentiate the sound patterns of speech after they have been amplified (Erber and Alencewicz 1976; Boothroyd 1984; Stelmachowicz 1985). Furthermore, the hearing aid does not distinguish between speech and noise, but amplifys them both equally, and leaves the wearer at the mercy of his or her *increased noise susceptibility* (Dirks, Morgan, and Dubno 1982). There are even limits to the ability of hearing aids to deal with the effects of threshold elevation. When the hearing loss exceeds 90 dB, problems of acoustic feedback make it impossible to provide enough amplification for full audibility of speech produced at conversational distances (Grover and Martin 1974). These limitations are illustrated in figure 1.

Considerable research is underway with the aim of improving hearing aid performance (Levitt 1987; Studebaker and Bess 1982; Studebaker, Bess, and Beck 1991). Better methods are being sought to tailor individual amplification characteristics to the needs of the individual wearer (Levitt et al. 1987; Engebretsen, Morley, and Popelka 1987). Improvements of automatic gain control, amplitude limiting, and amplitude compression are being explored in attempts to reduce the effects of dynamic range reduction (Braida et al. 1982; Boothroyd et al. 1988). Engineers are studying possible techniques for the automatic identification and suppression of noise (Weiss 1987; Graupe, Grosspietsch, and Basseas 1987), and methods are being sought for the elimination of acoustic feedback (Egolf 1982). More radical approaches involve the enhancement of those details of sound patterns believed to be particularly important in speech perception (Revoile et al. 1987; Guelke 1987; Gordon-Salant 1987). Much of the recent work has been spurred by the development of digital signal processing techniques that have opened up new possibilities for hearing aid design (Levitt 1987; Studebaker, Sherbecoe, and Matesich 1987). Progress is slow, however, and there may be inherent limits to the possible improvement of hearing aid per-

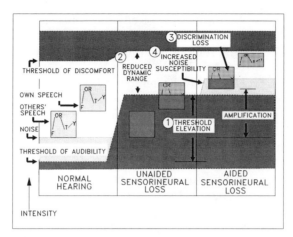

Figure 1.   This figure, in which sound intensity is represented vertically, illustrates the four main effects of sensorineural hearing impairment and the ways in which they limit the benefits of amplification. The input is an utterance of the word "forty"—chosen because it includes the weak fricative "f" and the strong vowel "aw." For persons with normal hearing, self-generated speech and the speech of others lie comfortably between the thresholds of audibility and discomfort and noise does not usually interfere with the speech of others. Threshold elevation (1) may prevent audibility of the speech of others and, in extreme cases, of self-generated speech. Because of feedback problems in personal hearing aids, it is often difficult to provide full audibility of the speech of others, and a reduced dynamic range (2) may be insufficient to encompass both self-generated speech and the speech of others unless peak-clipping or amplitude compression are used. To make matters worse, discrimination loss (3) reduces the clarity of the amplified speech and increases the interfering effects of noise (4).

formance. No matter what we do with the amplified speech signal, it must ultimately be processed by a damaged sensorineural mechanism.

In the meantime, there is a proven technique that can go a long way toward addressing issues of severe threshold elevation, dynamic range reduction, and increased noise susceptibility. This technique involves nothing more complicated than locating a microphone close to the mouth of the talker (see, for example, Ross 1978; Bess, Freeman, and Sinclair 1981; Hawkins 1984; Boothroyd 1991). By this simple expedient, one accomplishes several things. First, there is an increase in the level of the signal. This reduces gain requirements, and makes it possible to provide full audibility of speech to subjects with losses well in excess of 90 dB. Second, the changes of speech level with talker distance are eliminated, making it easier to keep the output signal within the dynamic range of the wearer. And third, there is a dramatic improvement of signal-to-noise ratio because the input level of speech is increased while the input level of environmental noise remains un-changed. These benefits are illustrated in figure 2. The only issue not addressed by the remote microphone is the wearer's discrimination loss.

A major problem with the remote microphone is the need for a cable to connect it to the rest of the hearing aid, but a practical solution was developed many years ago in the form of wireless microphones (Ross and Giolas 1971; Ross 1987). These microphones transmit the speech signal to a receiver worn by the hearing-impaired person. The signal is then amplified in the normal manner, as illustrated in figure 3.

Many options exist for wireless transmission in this application; the one that has emerged as the most popular is Frequency Modulation (or FM). The purpose of this chapter is to summarize the nature of FM wireless transmission and to discuss some of the ways in which its characteristics affect the performance of complete FM amplification systems.

WIRELESS TRANSMISSION

Wireless transmission capitalizes on our ability to generate and detect electromagnetic waves. These waves consist of rapid fluctuations of

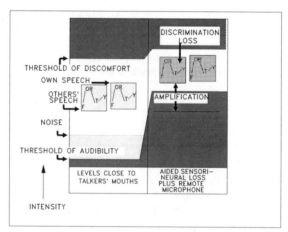

Figure 2. A remote microphone, placed close to the talker's mouth, accomplishes several things. First, the input to the remote microphone is more intense, reducing the need for amplification; second, the difference between "others' speech" and "own speech" is eliminated, making it possible for both to fit within the dynamic range of hearing; and, third, the intensity of the remote speech is well above that of the background noise, thus eliminating problems of increased noise susceptibility. Unfortunately, the problem of discrimination loss remains but, at least, this problem is not exacerbated by inadequate amplification, excessive range of input intensity, and poor signal-to-noise ratio.

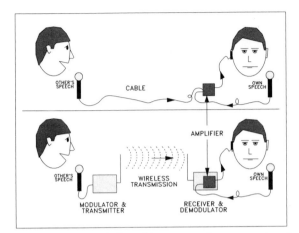

Figure 3.   The inconvenience of a cable, connecting a remote microphone to the hearing aid amplifier, is eliminated by the use of a wireless link. This link consists of a modulator and transmitter at one end and a receiver and demodulator at the other. The demodulated signal is then amplified in the normal manner.

electric and magnetic field strength and they travel through space at enormous speeds, taking only about five seconds to travel a million miles. We are most familiar with electromagnetic waves in the form of visible light. There are, however, many other kinds—for example: x-rays, ultraviolet light, infrared waves, microwaves, and radio waves.

What distinguishes these different varieties of electromagnetic waves is the frequency of the vibrations. In light waves, the electric and magnetic fields fluctuate at the rate of over a million million times a second. In microwaves, the frequencies are more like a thousand million times a second (see figure 4). The radio waves used in FM amplification systems vibrate at the rate of around 75 million times per second (or 75 MHz).

The process of radio transmission is illustrated in figure 5. First, an electronic circuit sets up rapid fluctuations of voltage. These voltage fluctuations are then passed to a transmitting antenna. The voltage fluctuations in the antenna generate a fluctuating electric field, which generates a fluctuating magnetic field, which generates a fluctuating electric field, and so on. The resulting waves travel away from the antenna in all directions, becoming weaker as they travel. A receiving antenna picks up the fluctuating electric field and passes the resulting voltage fluctuations to an amplifier where they are amplified. Because there are many radio waves in the space around us, a filter is required to select the frequency of interest from the other signals to which the antenna responds. In this way, the original vibrations, that were created in the electronic circuit of the transmitter, are reproduced in the

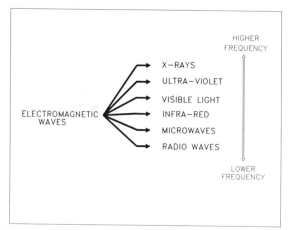

Figure 4.   There are many varieties of electromagnetic waves. The only way in which they differ is in the frequency at which the electric and magnetic fields vibrate.

receiver (Peebles 1976). Moreover, they are reproduced at a distance and without the use of an intervening wire, hence the term *wireless*. The radio signal is, essentially, an invisible cable.

MODULATION

The radio wave, by itself, is not audible. (The human ear can only hear vibrations with frequencies up to about 20,000 per second, and these must be physical vibrations of air molecules, not electromagnetic vibrations of the space between them.) The radio wave can, however, be used to "carry" the vibration patterns of sound. These vibrations are imposed on the radio wave by a process called *modulation*. After the radio wave has been received and amplified, the carrier wave is removed, leaving behind the vibration pattern that it has carried. This reverse process is called *demodulation*. Further amplification and connection to an earphone or loudspeaker recreates the original sound— once again, at a distance, and without the use of an intervening wire (see figure 4). In essence, the sound has been carried along the invisible cable provided by the radio wave.

There are two basic ways in which the patterns of sound vibration can be imposed on the radio wave (Peebles 1976). In the first, known as "amplitude modulation" (or AM), the strength of the radio wave fluctuates in step with the sound vibrations, as illustrated in the upper portion of figure 6. In the second, known as "frequency modulation" (or FM), the frequency of the radio wave fluctuates in step with the sound vibrations, as illustrated in the lower portion of figure 6. Both tech-

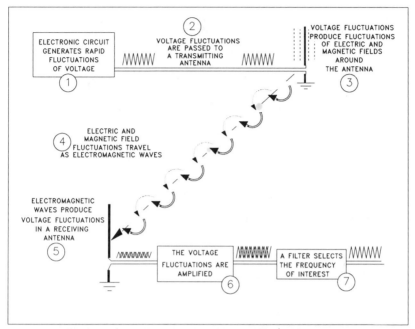

Figure 5.   Wireless transmission involves the generation of very rapid voltage fluctuations in an antenna. The resulting electric and magnetic fields are transmitted through space as electromagnetic (or radio) waves. These waves produce weak voltage fluctuations in a remote receiving antenna. Amplification of these fluctuations, followed by filtering to remove unwanted signals, restores the original signal. This signal is, by itself, inaudible, but it can be used to carry speech and other sounds over considerable distances without the use of an intervening cable, hence the term *wireless*.

niques are widely used for broadcasting and have been applied in wireless group hearing aids. Frequency modulation, however, has advantages in terms of sound quality and resistance to interference. For this reason, it has emerged as the technique of choice for high fidelity broadcasting, and for educational amplification.

ADVANTAGES OF FM

The Capture Effect

It will be recalled that one component of a radio receiver is a filter that selects the frequency of interest from among the many frequencies that are always present in the space around us. But what happens if there are two signals at the same frequency? A particular advantage of FM is

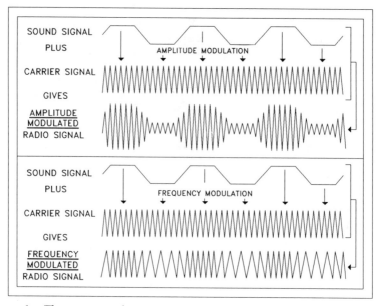

Figure 6.   There are two basic ways in which low frequency speech sounds can be carried on a high frequency radio wave. In amplitude modulation (AM) the amplitude of the radio signal varies according to the instantaneous value of sound pressure but the frequency of the radio signal remains constant. In frequency modulation (FM) the frequency of the radio signal varies according to the instantaneous value of sound pressure, but the amplitude of the radio signal remains constant.

its ability to deal with this situation. When there are two amplitude modulated signals at the same frequency, an AM receiver must respond to both and the user will hear the interfering message as well as the one he is supposed to listen to. With frequency modulated signals, however, the FM receiver responds only to the stronger of the two and the interfering signal can be completely suppressed. This convenient aspect of FM, which is illustrated in figure 7, is known as the capture effect. Essentially, the stronger signal "captures" the attention of the receiver and the weaker signal is excluded. The capture effect is a direct result of the fact that intensity differences in the speech signal are coded as frequency differences in the radio signal (Peebles 1976).

Fidelity and Bandwidth

A second advantage of FM is that, by modulating the frequency over a wide enough range, the signal can be kept well above the levels of noise generated in the transmitting and receiving equipment. It is this

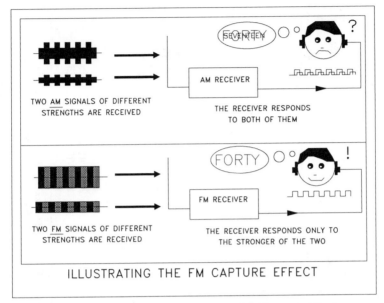

ILLUSTRATING THE FM CAPTURE EFFECT

Figure 7. When an AM receiver receives two signals carried by the same radio frequency, it responds to both of them, resulting in interference. An FM receiver, however, responds only to the stronger of the two signals and interference is suppressed. This second phenomenon is known as the FM capture effect.

ability to transmit a high quality signal that has led to the popularity of FM transmission for commercial high fidelity broadcasting. There is, however, a price to pay for quality. The FCC allocates only a limited range of frequencies to this application. In order to provide professional users with several different frequencies, the manufacturer must divide the allocated band into a limited number of channels. If these channels are made very wide, in the interests of quality, then there can only be a few of them. If, on the other hand, the manufacturer decides to make many channels available, then each must be narrow and quality will suffer. As a reasonable compromise, most current FM amplification systems divide the available band into 32 channels, each 50,000 Hz wide, as illustrated in table I, which shows The Federal Communication Commission's allocation of frequency bands to educational FM transmission, together with the frequency ranges for each of the 32 channels currently used by manufacturers of FM amplification equipment. (Note that each narrow-band channel is 0.05 MHz [or 50000 Hz] wide. Each wide-band channel is 0.20 MHz [or 200000 Hz] wide.) With this arrangement, manufacturers can transmit signals that are approximately 45 dB above the level of noise generated in the transmitter and

Table I.

Channel Letter Color	No.	From (MHz)	To (MHz)
A (Red):			
Red/Gry[a]	1	72.00	72.05
Brn[b]/Gry	2	72.05	72.10
Red/Brn	3	72.10	72.15
Brn/Red	4	72.15	72.20
B (Brown):			
Ong[c]/Gry	5	72.20	72.25
Brn/Ong	6	72.25	72.30
Ong/Brn	7	72.30	72.35
Brn/Ylw[d]	8	72.35	72.40
C (White):			
Ylw/Gry	9	72.40	72.45
Brn/Grn	10	72.45	72.50
Ylw/Pink[e]	11	72.50	72.55
Brn/Blu[f]	12	72.55	72.60
D (Violet):			
Ylw/Wht[g]	13	72.60	72.65
Brn/Pnk	14	72.65	72.70
Grn[h]/Gry	15	72.70	72.75
Brn/Wht	16	72.75	72.80
E (Yellow):			
Grn/Brn	17	72.80	72.85
Blk[i]/Gry	18	72.85	72.90
Grn/Red	19	72.90	72.95
Blk/Brn	20	72.95	73.00

Lower Band — 72 to 73 MHz

Channel Letter Color	No.	From (MHz)	To (MHz)
F (Green):			
Blk/Ong	21	75.40	75.45
Grn/Ylw	22	75.45	75.50
Blk/Ylw	23	75.50	75.55
Grn/Blu	24	75.55	75.60
G (Black):			
Blk/Grn	25	75.60	75.65
Grn/Pnk	26	75.65	75.70
Blk/Blu	27	75.70	75.75
Grn/Blk	28	75.75	75.80
H (Blue):			
Blk/Pnk	29	75.80	75.85
Pnk/Gry	30	75.85	75.90
Blk/Wht	31	75.90	75.95
Pnk/Ylw	32	75.95	76.00

Upper Band — 75.4 to 76 MHz

Notes: Capital letters refer to wide band channels (e.g., Wide band channel A goes from 72.0 to 72.2 MHz). Narrow band colors refer to Phonic Ear codes (Source: Phonic Ear). Wide band colors refer to ComTek codes. Numbers refer to Telex, Earmark, and ComTek codes. Proposed new channels are in the range 74.6 to 74.8 MHz and 75.2 to 75.4 MHz.

[a]Gry = Gray. [b]Brn = Brown. [c]Ong = Orange. [d]Ylw = Yellow. [e]Pnk = Pink. [f]Blu = Blue. [g]Wht = White. [h]Grn = Green. [i]Blk = Black.

receiver. The option exists to improve quality and signal-to-noise ratio by expanding the channel bandwidth to 200000 Hz, but this step reduces the number of available channels to eight (Hammond 1991). Although most manufacturers have opted for the larger number of channels, at least one, at the time of writing, provides the option for the higher quality wide band operation.

CAUTIONS

Remote microphones with FM wireless links have much to offer as we seek ways of dealing with the consequences of sensorineural hearing loss. It is important, however, to recognize that these systems leave some problems unsolved. Moreover, they can introduce problems of their own, especially if they are misused. Some words of caution are, therefore, in order.

Multiple Inputs

An inherent limitation of FM amplification systems is that they do not provide the opportunity for high quality amplification from multiple sources. There are many potential sound sources that are of importance to the developing child and, in the best of all possible worlds, each would be heard with the same benefits of high input level and high signal-to-noise ratio that are made possible by an FM wireless microphone (Boothroyd 1981). In theory, this could be accomplished by providing every possible talker with an FM microphone transmitter, but each transmitter would have to have its own frequency and its own receiver. This solution is impractical. A compromise approach, suitable for a classroom setting, is to have each student's receiver function as a temporary transmitter whenever that student is talking. A single receiver worn by the teacher can then retransmit that student's speech to the rest of the class. Such a system was developed by Siemens several years ago. It used two FM channels per classroom and required students to switch manually from "receive" to "transmit" whenever they wanted to speak. Another compromise approach that can be used in a small group or at a conference table, is to pass the teacher microphone from talker to talker. Neither of these approaches is ideal, however, because they are suitable only for certain environments and, even in those environments, they place quite high demands on the users. In most situations, it is only a single talker who wears the microphone transmitter.

There are, of course, one or more microphones built into the student receiver. These are usually labeled "environmental" microphones and are expected to serve as pickups for sounds other than those transmitted by the FM microphone. Unfortunately, if the sensitivity of the built-in microphones is increased to the point at which distant speech becomes audible, the accompanying noise eliminates a principal benefit of the wireless microphone. Judicious use of automatic gain control can serve to counteract this effect but can also introduce disturbing distortions as the automatic gain control continually responds to changes of input level. At the time of writing, good solutions to the problem of multiple inputs are not readily available.

While on the subject of multiple inputs, it is important to recognize that an input of major importance is that of the student's own speech (Ling and Milne 1981; Boothroyd 1985, 1988). Amplification for subjects with sensorineural hearing loss is intended not only to provide access to the speech of others but also to provide a means for auditory monitoring and control of self-generated speech, as acknowledged in figures 1, 2, and 3. In fact, the principal purpose of the microphones built into the FM receiver/amplifier is to permit the student to hear himself or herself. Audibility of environmental sounds is a secondary purpose. For this reason, it is inappropriate that these microphones have directional qualities that discriminate against self-generated speech. It is also important for children to wear their receivers in locations that place their microphones within a few inches of the mouth. It is *not* appropriate to wear the receiver on a waist band or in a trouser pocket, unless an external tie-clip or ear-level student microphone is used.

Interference

Unfortunately, the capture effect (the ability of an FM receiver to respond only to the stronger of two signals) is of no advantage when the interfering signal is stronger than that coming from the wireless microphone. This was often the case in the early days of FM amplification, when FM systems shared the air waves with the educational portion of the regular FM broadcast band. To deal with this problem, schools had to find spaces in the broadcast band between the frequencies used by the local radio stations.

In the 1970s, the Federal Communications Commission (1987), which oversees the use of radio waves and issues licenses to users, allocated to educational amplification the special bands, in the range 72 to 76 mHz, that are in use today (see table I). These bands had previously been protected from use because of the risk of interference with an airplane navigation beacon at 75 MHz, but technical improvements made it possible to open them up to use by low level transmitters such as those used in FM microphones. This step was taken in response to pressure from the manufacturers of FM amplification equipment.

There were a few other users of this band, but their signals were usually weak enough to be suppressed by the capture effect.

Unfortunately, at the time of writing, the issue of interference is again becoming serious. The problem is that the Federal Communication Commission has permitted a variety of users to transmit in the FM amplification bands. Examples are beeper services, mobile police transmitters, and road emergency transmitters. In addition, there are unlicensed users such as radio-controlled model enthusiasts. There are also potential problems from airport navigation beacons and TV stations that are located at nearby frequencies. The consequence is that the FM amplification band is rapidly becoming crowded with signals that may be stronger than those coming from the wireless microphones. To make matters worse, current regulations state that FM amplification systems, because they are unlicensed, must tolerate interference from licensed users of the same bands. Moreover, if the FM microphones interfere with those licensed users, the FM microphones must be turned off. The use of FM amplification systems for educational purposes is rapidly being compromised, especially in large urban areas. On a more positive note, the protection bands for the 75 MHz aircraft navigation beacon were narrowed further on January 1, 1991, creating the possibility of another 8 narrow-band channels for FM amplification. The FCC is proposing to allow FM amplification systems to operate in these channels. Because of their proximity to the aircraft beacon, any other users of these bands will be limited in terms of signal strength and the likelihood of interference is, therefore, reduced (Federal Communications Commission 1991).

An additional interference problem exists in school settings where there are many classrooms. Sometimes it is not possible to give each classroom its own frequency. There is then a danger that one class will interfere with another. Adequate separation of classrooms sharing the same frequency can usually take care of this problem, but teachers should note that, if the local microphone is switched off, the student receivers may begin responding to the other transmitter.

This last point is important and deserves a little more attention. The capture effect does not guarantee against the reception of unwanted signals. It only guarantees that the student receiver will respond to the strongest signal that is being transmitted on the frequency to which it is tuned. Usually, because of proximity, this is the transmission from the teacher's microphone. If, however, the teacher microphone is turned off, then the student receiver will, essentially, look for the next strongest transmission and respond to that. This might come from a teacher down the hall or a police car in the neighborhood. Two options exist for preventing this undesirable state of affairs. The first is that students are instructed to switch off the FM portion of their receivers, leaving only the student microphones active. The drawback, here, is that the students must be instructed to turn their receivers back on before they can begin receiving the teacher transmission. A better alternative is to have the teacher switch off the microphone input to the transmitter but to leave the FM signal switched on. This can be accomplished in some systems by switching the teacher transmitter to an "audio-only" condition but with no audio input connected. The student receivers are then "captured" by the silence being broadcast from the teacher microphone. This second option may not be available on all transmitters, but its addition is technically simple.

A final cautionary note on interference relates to the simultaneous use of broad band and narrow band FM systems. Because they share the same frequencies, these systems are likely to cause mutual interference. Moreover, a single broad band transmitter will interfere with as many as four narrow band receivers (see table I). Great caution must be exercised if broad band and narrow band systems are to be mixed within a single school.

Microphone Compression

Professional users of this equipment should note that the FM wireless microphone is equipped with a compression circuit. Because frequency modulation codes amplitude as frequency, a signal that becomes louder and louder occupies an increasing range of frequencies. But each channel is restricted to a specific range of frequencies. The signal cannot, therefore, be allowed to become so wide that it spills over into neighboring channels. For this reason, the manufacturer must limit the amplitude of the microphone signal passed to the transmitter. The practical implication of this amplitude limitation (or compression) is that there is no point in shouting into the microphone. The extra loudness will not be passed on to the receiver, and the only effect will be to distort the microphone signal either by overloading or by introducing the noise of air flow from the lips. With the microphone a few inches from the mouth and a normal vocal effort, the speech signal to the wearer will already be as loud as it can be. If this is not loud enough, then the gain and/or maximum output level of the receiver should be adjusted rather than the speech level into the microphone.

It should also be noted that the "knee" of the microphone compressor—that is, the dB level at which it begins to limit the teacher's signal level—is fixed by the manufacturer. If this level is too low, then, when the teacher is not talking, microphone sensitivity will rise and the background noise in the room may be amplified to levels that interfere with the student's reception of his or her own speech, thus eliminating one of the intended benefits of an FM system. Professional users of FM amplification should consult manufacturers and suppliers about this issue. In my opinion, based on the results of ongoing research on the effects of microphone position on input speech level, the appropriate level for the knee of the teacher microphone compressor is approximately 95 dB SPL when measured with pure tones at around 1000 Hz. This value translates into 85 dB SPL for the rms average level of open vowels. With the compressor knee set to this level, and the microphone on the chest, the speech of a talker with lower-than-average speech levels should be transmitted without compression while the louder vowels in the speech of an average talker would be reduced by, perhaps, 5 dB in relation to the other sounds.

Monitoring and Maintenance

Although manufacturers do all they can to make FM amplification systems durable within practical limitations of cost, it is important for professional users to realize that these are complex systems, with small and sensitive components, that are often subjected to a lot of heavy use and rough treatment. A rigorous program of monitoring and maintenance is mandatory if the systems are to be used effectively. This comment, of course, also applies to hearing aids, but the addition of a wireless receiver and transmitter makes the need even more acute for FM amplification systems.

Roving Ear

Professional users of FM wireless microphones should be sensitive to the fact that they are, effectively, in control of the child's ear. They control where it is and what goes into it. Although the benefits of this arrangement for the reception of remote speech are considerable, it is important to avoid indiscriminate use. A developing child who is playing alone, for example, should be hearing the sounds of his or her own activities, speech or otherwise, in order to develop auditory-motor associations and general auditory perceptual skills (Boothroyd 1988). If the child is bombarded by input from a remote source that is not of immediate relevance, auditory and speech development are likely to be impeded rather than facilitated. Such misuse can occur in the classroom when a teacher engages in one-to-one conversation with a student or another teacher, while the remaining members of the class are working independently. The increasing use of FM systems as primary amplification for preschool children introduces further opportunities for misuse, as illustrated in figure 8.

Figure 8.   The microphone essentially constitutes a "roving ear" whose location and input are under the control of another person. This arrangement offers many benefits when correctly used (upper illustration), but also introduces the possibility of misuse (lower illustration). In the example of misuse shown here, a hearing-impaired child is bombarded with intense speech that is not only irrelevant to his immediate activities but may well be interfering with the development of auditory perceptual skills and attentional behaviors.

FM Is Not Magic

Finally, it is important for teachers and parents to understand that the only purpose of FM amplification is to permit the use of a remote microphone without the need for an intervening cable. The benefits that are observed with the use of FM systems come from the simple fact that a microphone can be placed close to the mouth of a talker, thereby increasing input level and signal-to-noise ratio. There is nothing magic about the FM signal. It is not processed in any way to make it superior to other signals. The quality of the signal is only as high as that of the microphone in the FM transmitter. The FM signal is not inherently stronger, louder, or better than other signals. Exactly the same effect can be obtained by speaking close to the microphones built into the student's receiver or by connecting a remote microphone with a cable. Once again, it must be stressed that the FM link serves only as an invisible cable, making possible the use of remote microphones in situations where a cable would be impractical or inconvenient.

Note, also, that the student's receiver contains both an FM receiver and a hearing aid. The fact that an FM wireless link is being used in no way eliminates the need for the characteristics of that hearing aid to be selected and adjusted to the auditory characteristics of the wearer (see Chapter 4). It is disturbing to hear manufacturers report that approximately 50% of the student FM receivers returned for maintenance carry the same settings with which they left the factory—indicating that they have not been adjusted to the needs of the individuals wearing them. Perhaps it is unfortunate that the term *FM amplification* has become so widely accepted. What this equipment really consists of is hearing aids with added FM wireless links to remote microphones. This fact is most obvious, of course, in the personal FM system, in which the output of the FM receiver is fed to the wearer's personal hearing aid (see Chapter 3).

In short, it is erroneous, and potentially dangerous, to assume that an FM signal possesses some unique quality capable of overcoming the discrimination loss imposed by sensorineural damage. The use of a remote microphone, however, does allow one to provide the wearer's hearing aid with an acoustic input signal of the highest possible quality. Assuming that the hearing aid is optimally adjusted, this arrangement permits the wearer to make full use of whatever discrimination capacity is available.

SUMMARY

Sensorineural hearing damage causes increased threshold, reduced dynamic range, decreased discrimination, and increased noise susceptibility. Personal hearing aids deal with problems of threshold elevation, but performance is limited by acoustic feedback, variations of speech input level, and the low signal level and signal-to-noise ratio for remote speech. Remote microphones solve these problems by increasing input levels and signal-to-noise ratio for remote speech, thus permitting the hearing-impaired person to perceive remote speech up to the limits imposed by the discrimination loss. FM wireless links remove the inconvenience of a cable while preserving fidelity and resisting interference. Professional users should be aware of the need for multiple inputs, the risk of interference from strong FM sources, the need for monitoring and maintenance, the consequences of microphone compression, and the many possibilities for misuse. They should also have a clear understanding of what FM systems do and do not offer in the management of sensorineural hearing loss. In particular they should be aware that, when the student's receiver functions as both an FM receiver and a hearing aid, the latter must be adjusted to the needs and capabilities of the wearer with the same skill and care called for in personal hearing aids.

REFERENCES

Bess, F. H., Freeman, B. A., and Sinclair, J. S. 1981. (Eds.) *Amplification in Education*. Washington, DC: Alexander Graham Bell Association for the Deaf.

Boothroyd, A. 1978. Speech perception and sensorineural hearing loss. In *Auditory Management of the Hearing Impaired Child*, eds. M. Ross and G. Giolas. Baltimore, MD: University Park Press.

Boothroyd, A. 1981. Group hearing aids. In *Amplification in Education*, eds. F. H. Bess, B. A. Freeman, and J. S. Sinclair. Washington, DC: Alexander Graham Bell Association for the Deaf.

Boothroyd, A. 1984. Auditory perception of speech contrasts by subjects with sensorineural hearing loss. *Journal of Speech and Hearing Research* 27:134–44.

Boothroyd, A. 1985. Auditory capacity and the generalization of speech skills. In *Speech Planning and Production in Normal and Hearing-Impaired Children*, ed. J. Lauter. ASHA Reports #15, 8–14.

Boothroyd, A. 1988. *Hearing Impairments in Young Children*. Washington, DC: Alexander Graham Bell Association for the Deaf. (Originally published by Prentice-Hall, Englewood Cliffs, NJ, 1982).

Boothroyd, A. 1992. Speech perception, sensorineural hearing loss, and hearing aids. In *Acoustical Factors Affecting Hearing Aid Performance*, eds. G. Studebaker and I. Hochberg. Austin, TX: Pro-Ed.

Boothroyd, A., Springer, N., Smith, L., and Schulman, J. 1988. Compression amplification and profound hearing loss. *Journal of Speech and Hearing Research* 33:362–76.

Braida, L. D., Durlach, N. I., DeGennaro, S. V., Peterson, P. M., and Bustamante, D. K. 1982. Review of recent research on multi-band amplitude compression. In *The Vanderbilt Hearing Aid Report*, eds. G. A. Studebaker and F. H. Bess. Upper Darby, PA: Contemporary Monographs in Audiology.

Davis, H., and Silverman, R. 1978. *Hearing and Deafness*. New York: Holt, Reinhart, and Winston.

Dirks, D. D., Morgan, D. E., and Dubno, J. R. 1982. A procedure for quantifying the effects of noise on speech recognition. *Journal of Speech and Hearing Disorders* 47:114–22.

Egolf, D. P. 1982. Review of the acoustic feedback literature from a control system point of view. In *The Vanderbilt Hearing Aid Report*, eds. G. A. Studebaker and F. H. Bess. Upper Darby, PA: Contemporary Monographs in Audiology.

Engebretsen, A. M., Morley, R. E., and Popelka, G. R. 1987. Development of an ear-level digital aid and computer-assisted fitting procedure: An interim report. *Journal of Rehabilitation Research and Development* 24:55–64.

Erber, N. P., and Alencewicz, C. M. 1976. Audiologic evaluation of deaf children. *Journal of Speech and Hearing Disorders* 41:256–67.

Federal Communications Commission. 1987. *Assistive Devices for the Hearing-Impaired: Frequencies Available in the 72 to 75 mHz Band*. Part 15, sub-part G, Paragraph 15.351 of the FCC Code of Federal Regulations: Telecommunications, Parts 0 to 19. Washington, DC: Office of the Federal Register, National Archives, and Records Administration. Revised 1987.

Federal Communications Commission. 1991. Notice of proposed rule making (91–167), ET Docket 91–150: Additional frequencies for Audition Assistance Devices for Hearing Impaired, May 30, 1991.

Gordon-Salant, S. 1987. Effects of acoustic modification on consonant recognition by elderly hearing-impaired subjects. *Journal of the Acoustical Society of America* 81:1199–1202.

Graupe, D., Grosspietsch, J. K., and Basseas, S. P. 1987. A single-microphone-

based self-adaptive filter of noise from speech and its performance evaluation. *Journal of Rehabilitation Research and Development* 24:119–26.
Grover, B. C., and Martin, M. C. 1974. On the practical gain limit for post aural hearing aids. *British Journal of Audiology* 8:121–24.
Guelke, R. W. 1987. Consonant burst enhancement: A possible means to improve intelligibility for the hard-of-hearing. *Journal of Rehabilitation Research and Development* 24:217–20.
Hammond, L. B. 1991. *FM Auditory Trainers.* Minneapolis, MN: Gopher State Litho.
Hawkins, D. 1984. Comparison of speech recognition in noise by mildly-to-moderately hearing-impaired children using hearing aids and FM systems. *Journal of Speech and Hearing Disorders* 49:409–418.
Kamm, C., Dirks, D. D., and Mickey, M. R. 1978. Effect of sensorineural hearing loss on loudness discomfort level and most comfortable loudness judgments. *Journal of Speech and Hearing Research* 21:668–81.
Levitt, H. 1987. Digital hearing aids: A tutorial review. *Journal of Rehabilitation Research and Development* 24:7–20.
Levitt, H., Sullivan, J. A., Neuman, A. C., and Rubin-Spitz, J. A. 1987. Experiments with a programmable master hearing aid. *Journal of Rehabilitation Research and Development* 24:29–54.
Ling, D., and Milne, M. 1981. The development of speech in hearing-impaired children. In *Amplification in Education*, eds. F. H. Bess, B. A. Freeman, and J. S. Sinclair. Washington, DC: Alexander Graham Bell Association for the Deaf.
Peebles, P. Z. 1976. *Communication System Principles.* Reading, MA: Addison Wesley.
Revoile, S. G., Holden-Pitt, L., Edward, D., Pickett, J. M., and Brandt, F. 1987. Speech cue enhancement for the hearing impaired: Amplification of burst/murmur cues for improved perception of final stop voicing. *Journal of Rehabilitation Research and Development* 24:207–216.
Ross, M. 1978. Classroom acoustics and speech intelligibility. In *Handbook of Clinical Audiology*, (2nd Edition), ed. J. Katz. Baltimore, MD: Williams & Wilkins.
Ross, M. 1987. FM auditory training systems as an educational tool. *Rehabilitation Quarterly* 12:4–6.
Ross, M., and Giolas, T. G. 1971. The effects of three classroom listening conditions on speech intelligibility. *American Annals of the Deaf* 116:580–84.
Ross, M., Brackett, D., and Maxon, A. 1982. *Hard of Hearing Children in Regular Schools.* Englewood Cliffs, NJ: Prentice Hall.
Skinner, M. W. 1988. *Hearing Aid Evaluation.* Englewood Cliffs, NJ: Prentice Hall.
Stelmachowicz, P. G., Jestaedt, W., Gorga, M. P., and Mott, J. 1985. Speech perception ability and psychophysical tuning curves in hearing-impaired listeners. *Journal of the Acoustical Society of America* 77:620–27.
Studebaker, G. A., and Bess, F. H. 1982. (Eds.). *The Vanderbilt Hearing Aid Report.* Upper Darby, PA: Contemporary Monographs in Audiology.
Studebaker, G. A., Bess, F. H., and Beck, L. B. 1991. (Eds.). *The Vanderbilt Hearing Aid Report II.* Parkton, MD: York Press.
Studebaker, G. A., Sherbecoe, R. L., and Matesich, J. S. 1987. Spectrum shaping with a hardware digital filter. *Journal of Rehabilitation Research and Development* 24:21–28.
Weiss, M. 1987. Use of an adaptive noise canceler as an input preprocessor for a hearing aid. *Journal of Rehabilitation Research and Development* 24:93–102.

Chapter • 2

Room Acoustics and Speech Perception

Mark Ross

If all conversations with hearing-impaired people occurred in quiet, nonreverberant rooms at distances no greater than three feet, FM Auditory Training systems would not be necessary. There would then be no need to locate a microphone close to a speaker's lips in order to reduce the impact of existing acoustical conditions. Because, however, noise is a ubiquitous and ever increasing presence in our society, and distance from the speaker cannot always be controlled, FM systems *are* going to be necessary in many situations. Given the present state of the art, there is no better way to improve speech perception than by increasing the signal-to-noise (S/N) ratio. (Really an index, rather than a ratio, but conventional usage defines the intensity relationship between the speech and noise levels as a ratio.) This concept, described in Chapter 1 by Boothroyd, represents the most basic and fundamental contribution of FM systems and it is a theme that permeates this book.

This chapter describes the concept and the conditions of noise and reverberation existing in classrooms, and indicates their effect upon speech perception for both hearing-impaired and normally hearing people. The relevance of S/N is described in terms of its impact on both of these topics.

NOISE

Noise is defined as any undesired sound. What I label as *noise* will differ from what most teenagers call noise; the bottom line for all of us, however, is the *effect* of the noise upon *speech perception*. (Noise has psychological and physiological effects as well, but in this chapter only the relevance of noise to speech perception is considered.) In this respect, it does not matter how noise is created or whence it emanates, only that it exists in the listening environment of hearing-impaired persons. (It is important, of course, to locate the source of the noise when attempting to eliminate or reduce its presence.)

Measuring Noise

Much confusion in respect to noise measurements can be circumvented if readers understand the basic function of a *sound level meter* (SLM). Many of these devices are on the market, and it is possible to obtain different kinds of noise measurements for different purposes. For our purposes, it suffices to describe two of the most common and useful types of noise measurements.

The first measurement is dB(A). When a sound-level meter is switched to the dB(A) position, it activates a set of acoustical filters that closely follow the normal *sound pressure level* (SPL) sensitivity curve of the human ear. The normal ear is less sensitive to very low frequency sounds than to higher frequencies. (On an audiogram each of these SPL thresholds is designated as 0 dB hearing threshold level.) In a sense, a sound level meter turned to the dB(A) weighting network "sees" the sound level in the same way as a normal ear does. When the potential hazards of noise upon hearing thresholds are discussed, it is the dB(A) measurements that are usually invoked.

The second measurement employs the dB(C) weighting network. Basically, this SLM network responds equally to all sound frequencies regardless of their relationship to normal human ear sensitivity. Some SLMs also provide a linear scale dB(LIN), but in practical terms this is indistinguishable from the dB(C) scale. When the same noise is measured with dB(A) and dB(C), the amount of low frequency sounds determine the different readings. In the presence of low frequency sounds, dB(C) will exceed dB(A). The difference between the two measures is an approximate estimate of the intensity of the low frequencies. When both readings are about the same, this indicates that the predominant energy in the noise is located above about 600 Hz.

Noise Levels in Classrooms

Over the years, a number of investigators have measured sound pressure levels in different types of classrooms. The results shown in table I are fairly representative of these measurements (Finitzo-Hieber 1981). All classrooms are noisy places, more so when they are occupied, uncarpeted, and not specifically designated for hearing-impaired chil-

Table I. Noise Measurements in Decibels for Activities Occurring in Representative Classrooms in the Dallas and Chicago Areas

Type of Environment	Range of Measurements dB Scale	
	A	C
Traditional Classrooms		
Unoccupied (morning, with traffic noise)	42–44	55–58
With 25 students, 1 teacher	58–60	62–65
Open-Plan Classrooms		
Unoccupied (morning)	42–47	63–64
With 100 students, 10 teachers	66–73	69–74
Classes for Hearing-Impaired Children in Mainstream Environment		
1. Carpeted Classroom		
Unoccupied (morning)	36–39	52–55
With 15 students, 2 teachers	55–62	63–65
2. Uncarpeted Classroom		
Unoccupied	42–44	56–58
With 5 students, 1 teacher	60–67	68–72
Self-Contained School for Hearing-Impaired Children (Carpeted)		
1. Unoccupied (morning)	35–38	50–55
2. With 5 students, 1 teacher	40–45	53–56
Gymnasiums		
Occupied	82–86	85–88
Cafeterias		
Occupied	75–80	79–81
Computer Terminal	73–79	80–87

Finitzo-Heiber, T., Classroom Acoustics in *Auditory Disorders in School Children;*
R. Roeser and M. Downs (Eds.). New York, 1981, Thieme Medical Publishers, Inc. Reprinted
by permission.

dren. Only the levels obtained in the occupied rooms are really relevant; if there are no children in the classroom, clearly none of them is
going to be affected by the noise. No one who has spent much time in a
school building would be surprised at the high noise levels found in
gymnasiums, cafeterias, and other general purpose rooms. It is often
impossible for *normally hearing people* to communicate effectively in
these situations. Not surprisingly, classrooms for children in lower
grades are noisier than those for older children.

(S/N) Ratio

The results in table I can best be interpreted in conjunction with the
speech levels existing in the same classroom. In a classroom, the SPL of

a teacher's speech is about 65 to 70 dB at a distance of three feet from the speaker. If we estimate that the SPL of the noise is about 60 to 65 dB(C) throughout the classroom, then the S/N ratio would be approximately plus 5 dB; i.e., the speech level exceeds the noise level by 5 dB. The same S/N figures apply if the teacher's speech and the ambient noise levels are expressed in hearing level (HL) terms, but the relative values in this instance would be 45 to 50 dB HL for the speech and 40 to 45 dB HL for the noise (i.e., SPL and HL are different reference levels for expressing the intensity of sounds in the same way that both meters and feet can be used to express length). If speech and noise levels are equal, as they sometimes are, then the S/N would be zero. If, as also happens frequently (Markides 1986), the *noise* level exceeds the speech level, say by 5 dB, then the S/N is −5 dB. An example of the relationship between speech and noise levels can be seen in figure 1.

The horizontal axis in figure 1 represents distance from the source (the person talking). The SPL of the sound (noise or speech) is plotted on the vertical axis. The horizontal line midway up the figure indicates that the ambient noise level throughout the room is a constant 60 dB SPL. The vertical bars delineate the SPL of the speech signal at different distances from the source. At the three foot distance, the speech signal exceeds the noise level by 6 dB, which means at that position the S/N is +6 dB.

In most rooms, at distances of six feet or less, the *inverse square law* of sound propagation applies. What this means is that for every halving or doubling of distance, the SPL is increased or decreased by 6 dB. If the S/N at three feet is +6 dB, it would be 0 dB at the six foot distance because the speech energy would have decreased by 6 dB. Conversely, at the 18 inch distance, the speech level would be increased 6 dB, to 72 dB, and the resulting S/N would be +12 dB. At the nine inch distance, the S/N is +18 dB and at 4½ inches, the resulting S/N is 24 dB. In other words, a significant increase in the S/N ratio occurs simply by locating the microphone (or listener) closer to the sound. This is exactly what the FM microphone does; it permits detection of a speaker's voice at a significantly higher level than background sounds. The inverse-square law does not apply in most rooms at distances greater than about six feet because of the presence of sound reflections (as discussed below).

Household Noises

Classrooms are not the only places in which FM systems are, or should be, used. Increasingly, they are being employed by preschool children, sometimes as the first amplification device to be fitted on a child (Madell this volume). Because the most important years in children's linguistic development occur *before* they enter school, it is particularly important that the S/N ratio be maximized for as much of this time as is

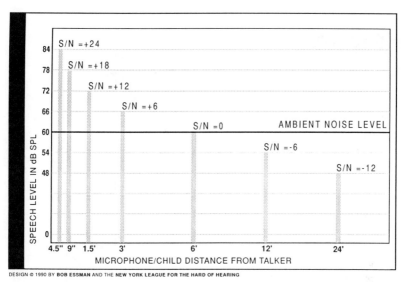

DESIGN © 1990 BY BOB ESSMAN AND THE NEW YORK LEAGUE FOR THE HARD OF HEARING

Figure 1.   Speech-to-noise ratio as a function of distance in a room with an ambient noise level of 60 dB SPL.

possible or practicable. The SPLs of common household appliances range from an average of 65 dB to over 83 dB (ASHA 1990) with levels as high as 94 dB recorded. Blenders and vacuum cleaners are particularly notorious culprits, but these are relatively uncommon sounds (we don't vacuum more than once a week in my house). In most households, it is the TV set that is never turned off, or a noisy fan or air conditioner, the clattering of flatware and dishes during dinner (and the ever-present cross-conversations), and the rambunctious play of other children that are responsible for the almost continuous presence of high noise levels. True, it is easier for the speaker to get closer to the hearing-impaired person in a house than in a classroom, but because noise has a relatively minor effect upon a normal-hearing person, the interfering effects of household noise upon a hearing-impaired person are easily overlooked. A good general rule is that in any noisy (or reverberant) environment, acoustical conditions that are only mildly or moderately annoying for normal-hearing people will severely reduce or eliminate auditory speech perception for hearing-impaired individuals (Humes 1991).

REVERBERATION

Sound Propagation in Rooms

Figure 2 illustrates some common properties of sound propagation in a room. As sound leaves its source (either a person or a loudspeaker), it

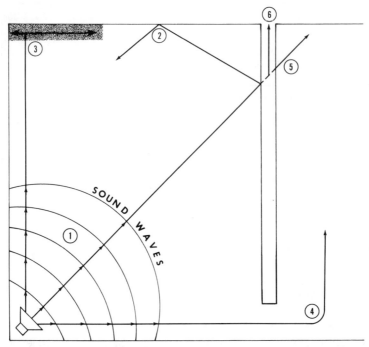

Figure 2. Behavior of sound in an enclosed space: (1) incident or direct sound, (2) reflected sound, (3) sound absorbed by surface treatment, (4) sound bending (diffracted) around structure to adjacent room, (5) sound transmitted through structure to adjacent room, (6) sound conducted within structure.

travels outward in a series of spherical waves that soon impinge upon all surfaces and fill the room. *Direct* sound is that portion of sound that occurs before it encounters a surface (#1 in the figure). After direct sound collides with a surface, it is converted into *reflected* sound. Several reflections are shown in figure 2. *Reverberation* is defined as a continuing series of sound reflections in a room after the source has ceased to produce sound waves.

Each time sound impinges upon a surface, some of its energy is absorbed; the amount of absorption depends upon the nature of the sound treatment. In #3, most of the direct sound energy is shown being absorbed by the surface. Low frequency components of sound tend to bend around or under obstacles and drift into adjoining rooms (via partitions that do not quite meet the ceiling, open doors, large spaces under doors, etc.). This is illustrated in #4. Sound can also pass though a surface or through vents or other openings into adjacent rooms (#5 and #6). Not shown in the figure is how concave, convex, or irregular surfaces or room shapes can diffuse or focus sound energy. In a room with average dimensions and no significant variation in shape, reflected energy builds up and is soon distributed fairly equally throughout the room. The eventual level of this reflected energy depends upon the sound-treatment in the room: less sound treatment means a higher level of reflected sound energy.

Precedence Effect

For a normally hearing person, the reception of speech sounds in a room seems straightforward. The acoustic energy of a talker's speech travels through the room to the ears of the listener, and from there to the brain where the spoken message is decoded. Even with his or her eyes closed, a normal-hearing person has no difficulty in localizing the speech source as the talker moves around the room. This ability requires no conscious effort or thought on the part of the listener. It is something that is simply taken for granted. It is only when one analyzes the behavior of actual speech waves in a room that the marvelous capacities of the normal auditory system can be appreciated. This can be observed in figures 3 and 4.

In figure 3, the speech signal leading from a speaker to a listener is depicted as it would occur in an anechoic chamber or an open (free) field. As in figure 2, straight lines represent a simplified view of a section of the speech wave. As the waves reach a surface in an anechoic chamber, they are completely absorbed. In an open or free field the

Figure 3. Simplified diagram of sound propagation and absorption in an anechoic room.

Figure 4. Simplified diagram of sound propagation and reflection in a conventional hard-surfaced room. Sequentially thinner lines for direct sound, 1st, 2nd, 3rd, and 4th reflections indicate some absorption of sound by surfaces and dissipation of sound energy in space. (Olsen 1988, used with permission.) (Originally adapted from Dale 1962.)

sound waves would follow the inverse-square law and continue until their energy is completely dissipated. There is only one source of sound, and localizing it does not present much of a challenge to the normal auditory system.

The actual acoustical situation in a room, however, looks much more like figure 4 than figure 3. In this figure, in addition to direct sound waves reaching the listener's ears, numerous reflections of the same sound wave reach the person's ears from every direction in the room. Each reflection of direct sound is *not only another source of sound*, but a source that arrives at the person's ear from a different direction than the direct sound. Somehow, a normal-hearing person is able to focus on the direct sound waves and suppress later reflections of the same sound waves arriving from different room surfaces. This ability, termed the *precedence effect*, depends upon the relative time of arrival and the spectral content of the speech waves as they arrive at the two ears. (Yes, binaural listening *does* have advantages.) For the normal-hearing listener, reflected sounds arriving at his or her ears within 20 to 30 milliseconds of direct sound are integrated into the total perception and give speech signals a feeling of "liveness." Hearing-impaired people ordinarily do not possess this capacity; for them, reflections are separate sound sources that interfere with perception of direct sounds.

Reverberation as a Speech Self-Masker

Reverberation is a particularly deceptive and detrimental masker of speech in a room. When speech is the sound source, reflections of previously occurring speech sounds overlap and mask subsequent speech elements. For example, consider a syllabic sequence of strong vowel sounds and somewhat weaker consonant sounds; as they are prolonged in time, the energy in reflected vowels arrives at a listener's ears at the same time as direct path consonants. Reverberation is particularly detrimental because this self-masking of speech by a series of speech reflections compounds the usual difficulty hearing-impaired people have in perceiving consonants (Nabelek in press). Reverberation is deceptive: in a quiet room with no one talking, the room may seem to be perfectly suitable. If, however, the room is poorly sound-treated, the self-masking of speech occurs as soon as someone talks.

A visual display of the blurring effect of reverberation can be seen in figure 5. The top panel shows a spectrogram of an utterance with no reverberation and the bottom panel shows the same utterance as it appears when recorded in 0.5 second reverberation time (defined below). This loss of visual clarity in the speech signal can be translated into increased speech perception difficulty for a hearing-impaired person. Not so for a normal-hearing person, who has no difficulty comprehending the stimulus sentence under this condition of reverberation.

A more realistic visual display showing the effect of room acoustics upon a speech signal can be seen in figure 6. In this figure, the utterance was recorded in a reverberation time of 0.8 second and a S/N ratio of +6 dB. It should be noted that both of these values are realistic estimates of conditions existing in many classrooms. The original signal is barely discernible in the bottom panel. A normal-hearing listener receiving this utterance under these acoustical conditions would have little difficulty understanding it. For many hearing-impaired people listening to this signal with conventional hearing aids, about all that could be perceived auditorily would be an occasional syllable.

Critical Distance

Critical distance ties together the phenomena of direct and reflected sounds. This is shown in figure 7. Direct sound (curve a) follows the inverse-square law until it reaches the energy level of reverberant sounds (curve b). The point where the energy level of direct and reverberant sounds is equal is defined as critical distance (point D). Curve c is the summation of direct sound energy and reverberant sounds. The difference between curves c and b reflects additional sound energy created in the room by the series of reflections. The more a room is reverberant, the shorter the critical distance and the higher the level of re-

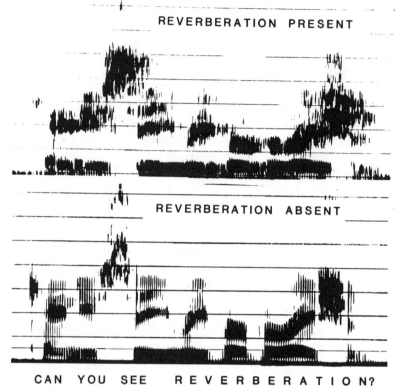

Figure 5. A sound spectrogram of the sentence "Can you see reverberation" spoken in a sound booth and a room with a reverberation time of .5 second. (Hawkins 1988, used with permission.)

verberant sound energy. For optimal reception of speech in a room, listeners should be located in the direct sound-field, that is within the critical distance (Johnson, Nabelek, and Asp 1990). In a highly reverberant room, with a short critical distance, this is not a realistic alternative. The microphone of an FM system, however, because it is located only about six inches from the mouth of a talker, is almost always within the critical distance.

The difference in intensity between direct and reflected sound-fields can be conceptualized as a S/N ratio difference. This ratio is greatest not only when sound is picked up closest to a talker's lips (thus increasing the signal component), but when the level of the reverberant sound field is less (reducing the noise component). Therefore, while an FM system is crucial in detecting a more intense speech signal before it has been contaminated by noise and reverberation, this does

QUIET

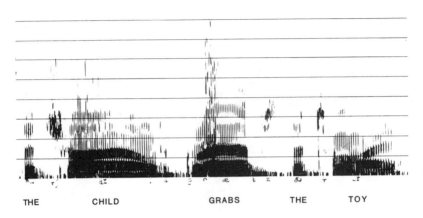

| THE | CHILD | GRABS | THE | TOY |

NOISE and REVERBERATION

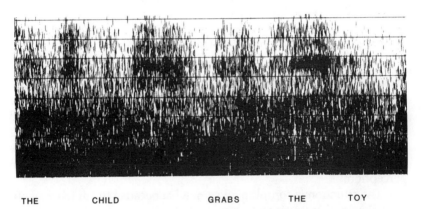

| THE | CHILD | GRABS | THE | TOY |

Figure 6.   Spectrogram of the sentence "the child grabs the toy" in quiet (upper panel) and in noise and reverberation (lower panel). The S/N ratio was +6 dB and the reverberation time was 0.8 second. (From Bess, F. H., and Tharpe, A. M. An introduction to unilateral sensorineural hearing loss in children. *Ear and Hearing* 7(1). © 1986, The Williams & Wilkins Co., Baltimore. Used with permission.)

not negate the necessity for reducing the other half of the ratio—the level of noise.

Reverberation Time

As mentioned above, each time a sound wave impinges upon a room surface, the sound loses some of its energy. Reflections and absorptions, therefore, are reciprocal qualities: the more absorption that oc-

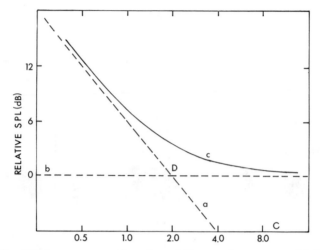

Figure 7. SPL in a room as a function of distance from source: (a) direct, (b) reverberant and (c) total. Intersection of curves a and b (point D) defines the critical distance. (From Nabelak, A. K., and Nabelak, I. V. Room acoustics and speech perception. In *Handbook of Clinical Audiology, 3rd edition*, ed. J. Katz. © 1985, The Williams & Wilkins Co., Baltimore. Used with permission.)

curs, the fewer reflections, and conversely, the less absorption, the more energy that is reflected. The time it takes for the intensity level of the original sound to weaken by 60 dB after cessation of the sound source is termed *reverberation time*. Reverberation time is a widely used metric for judging acoustical conditions of a room. Generally, the shorter the reverberation time, the more suitable the room is for speech perception.

The situation is complicated somewhat because the amount of energy absorbed by different room surfaces is a frequency dependent function. Therefore, reverberation time also will differ across frequency. The usual practice is to average the reverberation times at 500, 1000, and 2000 Hz to arrive at a single number for noting reverberation time. Normally hearing people can tolerate reverberation times up to 1.2 seconds before speech comprehension is degraded (Nabelek 1980). As seen below, however, this capacity is an age-related function. The optimal reverberation time for hearing-impaired people is much lower: the optimal reverberation time for speech perception is zero. For hearing-impaired people, even at minimal reverberation times of 0.3 to 0.4 second, speech perception scores are poorer than would be obtained if no reverberation at all were present (as in listening through earphones). This is essentially what an FM system will do: by locating the microphone close to a talker's lips, in the direct sound-field, the impact of reverberation is eliminated.

Effect of Reverberation, Time, and Distance upon Sound Pulses

An insightful way to demonstrate visually the effect of distance and reverberation time is shown in figure 8 (Niemoeller 1981). This figure shows how a room with different reverberation times processes sound pulses at three different distances. The sound pulses were 125 msec long separated by a 75 msec silent interval. Only the beginning of the second pulse is shown for each condition. Much important speech information is transmitted by short sound pulses (plosives, for example), and the effect of room characteristics upon such pulses is applicable to speech perception in the room. The pertinent information in figure 8 is indicated by the differences between dotted lines, which show "pure" pulses unaffected by room reverberation, and solid lines, which reflect the acoustical effects of the room.

As can be noted, at one meter distance and reverberation time of 0.25 seconds the effect of the room is minimal. Very little reflected sound fills the gap between the two pulses, and there is little difference between direct (dotted lines) and reflected pulses (solid lines). As distance is increased at 0.25 second, the intensity drops, as would be expected, but at the same time the differences between dotted and solid

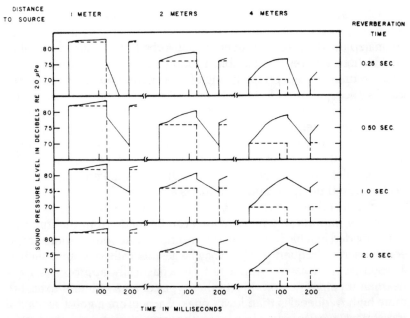

Figure 8. Onset and decay of the envelope of sound in rooms when excited by two 125 msec sound bursts separated by a 75 msec silent interval. The envelope of the direct sound is indicated by dashed lines; the reflected sound envelope is indicated by the solid lines. (Niemoeller 1981, used with permission.)

lines increase. As reverberation time increases at the shortest distance, reflected sounds almost fill in the gap between the two pulses. This visually demonstrates the persistence of reflected sound energy, which then masks subsequently produced sounds. As both distance and reverberation times increase, not only do gaps disappear, but the configuration of pulses is completely obscured. In speech terms, this indicates a severe masking effect of reflected speech energy upon direct speech sounds. The acoustical characteristics of the room, in other words, severely deform the integrity of the original signal.

This concept, termed the modulation transfer function (MTF), was used by Houtgast and Steeneken (1985) to predict speech intelligibility in a room. Basically, this method compares a direct sound with the totality of its reflections plus ambient room noise; the more reflected sound differs from direct sound, the poorer the room for perception of speech. The concept has recently been refined and termed RASTI (Rapid Speech Transmission Index). In Chapter 9 of this volume Flexer describes the use of RASTI as it applies to recommendations and use of FM sound-field classroom systems.

Absorbing Sound Reflections

As noted above, each time a sound impinges upon a room surface some of its energy is absorbed (converted to heat in the interstices of the material). The more sound energy absorbed, the fewer the number of reflections and resulting ambient sound energy, the lower the reverberation time and internal masking of speech, and the greater the critical distance. All these factors are interrelated. The ratio of absorption to reflections is termed the *absorption coefficient*. If, at a particular frequency, one material absorbs 75% of the incident energy, the absorption coefficient would be 0.75 (and the amount of reflected energy 0.25); if another type of material absorbs only 1% of the energy, the absorption coefficient would be 0.01 (with 99% of the energy being reflected each time the sound encounters a surface). The absorption coefficients of common materials can be found in table II.

A few important generalizations can be made from the information provided in table II. Hard surfaces reflect more sound, more or less equally, across frequency. What may be aesthetically pleasing, such as a wood-paneled room, would not be acoustically appropriate for a hearing-impaired person. Most other types of material tend to absorb more high frequencies than lower ones. Carpets are a good acoustical investment, particularly when pads (the more inexpensive, the better) are placed under them. Acoustical tiles are also very effective, especially when they are suspended a bit from the ceiling because this significantly increases the absorption coefficient at low frequencies. Good

Table II. Average Sound Absorption Coefficients of Common Materials and Room Surfaces

Room Surface	125	250	500	1000	2000	4000
			Frequency in Hz			
Floor Finishes						
Concrete, stone, etc.	0.01	0.01	0.02	0.02	0.02	0.03
Resilient tile on concrete	0.03	0.03	0.04	0.05	0.05	0.05
Carpet without pad	0.07	0.12	0.20	0.35	0.50	0.65
Carpet (unbacked) on pad	0.10	0.25	0.55	0.70	0.70	0.75
Wall Finishes						
Brick (painted)	0.02	0.02	0.02	0.03	0.03	0.03
Plaster on lath	0.05	0.05	0.05	0.05	0.05	0.05
Thin wood paneling (½″)	0.28	0.24	0.17	0.09	0.09	0.10
Normal window glass	0.25	0.15	0.10	0.07	0.05	0.03
Ceiling Finishes						
Plaster on solid	0.02	0.02	0.03	0.04	0.04	0.05
¾″ acoustical tile on solid	0.10	0.25	0.80	0.95	0.80	0.65
¾″ acoustical tile suspended	0.60	0.60	0.70	0.95	0.85	0.65
Sound-Absorbing Treatments						
1″ glass fiber on solid	0.15	0.30	0.60	0.80	0.80	0.80
3″ glass fiber on solid	0.30	0.75	0.85	0.90	0.90	0.90
4″ glass fiber on solid	0.40	0.85	0.90	0.95	0.95	0.95

Finitzo-Heiber, T., Classroom Acoustics in *Auditory Disorders in School Children;* R. Roeser and M. Downs (Eds.). New York, 1981, Thieme Medical Publishers, Inc. Reprinted by permission.

sound treatment will reduce the amount of energy reaching the environmental microphones and, thus, preserve the favorable S/N ratio existing at the teacher microphone (Hawkins 1984).

SPEECH PERCEPTION IN NOISE AND REVERBERATION

Introduction

Superficially, a hearing loss simply means that sounds must be more intense in order to be perceived. The louder the sounds have to be in order to be heard, the greater the hearing loss. This is obviously true, but it is not the complete story. Hearing losses, particularly those that are severe-to-profound and of sensorineural origin, manifest psychoacoustic abnormalities, such as problems in temporal and frequency resolution, in addition to the loss itself (Dubno and Dirks 1989; Lamore, Verweij, and Brocaar 1985; Irwin and McAuley 1987; Turner and Henn 1989). These problems cause hearing-impaired people to have difficulty in resolving a simultaneous, complex speech signal into its various frequency components, and to experience internal speech masking effects. Consequences of these psychoacoustic abnormalities include difficulty in distinguishing two adjacent formants, thus obscuring the identification of vowels; and an upward spread of masking from intense low frequency sound vowel elements to higher frequency consonants. Temporal abnormalities would be reflected in increased difficulty in identifying phonemes that depend upon making fine time distinctions (voiced and voiceless cognate sounds, for example).

The overall impact of these psychoacoustic abnormalities is demonstrated by a greater sensitivity to noise and reverberation (or any kind of acoustical distortion for that matter, such as heavy foreign accents, strong regional dialects, children's speech, etc.). This is the basis for the perennial complaint hearing-impaired people make about their difficulty understanding speech in the presence of poor (for them) acoustical conditions. It is possible to compensate to some extent for the effect of these psychoacoustic abnormalities and poor acoustical conditions by providing a higher S/N ratio. As already noted, this is precisely what an FM system is designed to do.

Noise

The classic study documenting interfering effects of noise and reverberation upon speech reception of hard-of-hearing children was written by Finitzo-Hieber and Tillman (1978). In table III, taken from their study, the top row shows the effects of noise with no reverberation present. There is a clear-cut difference between the normal and hearing-impaired groups. Not only is the best speech perception score of the hard-of-hearing group less than that of the normal-hearing group, but the effects of increasing noise have a disproportionately greater effect on them (from 83% to 39%) than the normal-hearing children (95% to 60%). As is also apparent, and will be discussed below, when reverberation is added to the noise, the cumulative effect is greater than either noise or reverberation by itself.

Table III. Speech Perception Scores of a Group of Normal-Hearing Children and Hard-of-Hearing Children Using Hearing Aids Under Different Reverberation Times and Speech-to-Noise Ratios

R Time	Normal				Hearing-Impaired			
	Quiet	+12	+6	0	Quiet	+12	+6	0
0	95	89	80	60	83	70	60	39
0.4	93	83	71	48	74	60	52	28
1.2	77	69	54	30	45	41	27	11

Adapted from Finitzo-Hieber and Tillman (1978).

Another way of reporting the increased sensitivity of hearing-impaired people to the interfering effects of noise is shown in figure 9, adapted from a study by Dirks, Morgan, and Dubno (1982). In all conditions, the speech level remained 72 dB SPL; noise was varied above and below this level to give varying S/N conditions. In a conventional analysis, the difference between speech discrimination scores of the normal-hearing group and the hearing-impaired subject is of interest. The normal-hearing group obtained about a 90% score at +6 dB S/N and close to a 100% at +12 dB S/N. For the same conditions, a typical moderately hearing-impaired listener obtained scores of about 30% and 50%. The differences, obviously, are great.

It is also useful, however, to plot the S/N ratio difference between the normal-hearing group and the hearing-impaired subject at the same speech perception score. If, for example, we examine the S/N difference between the two curves where they intersect the 50% speech perception score, we see that it is about 15 dB. This indicates that the hearing-impaired person needed a S/N ratio 15 dB more favorable than the normal-hearing group in order to obtain a 50% score. In other words, the score the hearing-impaired subject obtained at +10 dB S/N could be attained by a normal-hearing person at −5 dB S/N. It is as if the impaired auditory system contributes an additional 15 dB of subjective noise to the objective noise conditions existing in a room.

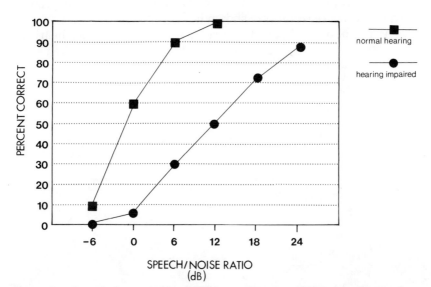

Figure 9.   Speech discrimination scores as a function of S/N ratio. The performance of one hard-of-hearing subject as compared to the average results of a group of normal-hearing people. (Adapted from Dirks, Morgan, and Dubno 1982.)

The subjects in the Dirks, Morgan, and Dubno (1982) study display a mild-to-moderate high-frequency sensorineural hearing loss. Recently, Smith and Boothroyd (1990) extended these findings to cover severely and profoundly hearing-impaired children. The results of their study showed a S/N difference between them and a normal-hearing group of 19 dB. In addition, they report that vowel height (intensity) was basically the only speech feature the hearing-impaired group could perceive at a S/N ratio of 0. Under the same conditions, the normal-hearing group could perceive at a better-than-chance level all speech features tested (such as place of articulation, the most difficult of all speech features to perceive).

Reverberation

Hawkins and Yacullo (1984) investigated the effect of binaural and directional hearing aids under different levels of reverberation. For our purpose in this review, it is necessary to compare only the relative effects of varying reverberation times upon speech perception scores of normal-hearing and hearing-impaired children. (But it is worth noting that higher scores were obtained with binaural and directional hearing aids than with monaural and omnidirectional microphone hearing aids.) As did Dirks, Morgan, and Dubno (1982), Hawkins and Yacullo noted the S/N differences needed to obtain a 50% score by both groups of children. These results are shown in figure 10.

At the best condition, 0.3 second reverberation time, hearing-

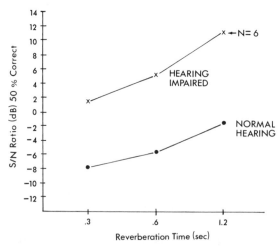

Figure 10.   Mean S/N ratios yielding 50% correct performance at the three reverberation times for a normal-hearing and a hearing-impaired group of children. (Hawkins and Yacullo 1984, used with permission.)

impaired children required an increase in the S/N of about 9 dB compared to the normal-hearing group in order to achieve a 50% score. Similar results can be seen at the 0.6 second time. At 1.2 second reverberation time, the difference is much greater. Because only 6 of the 11 hearing-impaired children could achieve a 50% score at the 1.2 second condition, these results underestimate the difference between the two groups.

The effects of reverberation upon speech perception in children also were tested in the now classic study by Finitzo-Hieber and Tillman (1978). These results can be seen in table III by looking down the columns. For each S/N condition, for both the normal-hearing and hearing-impaired groups, the speech perception scores diminish as reverberation times increases. The *relative* effect of reverberation conditions is poorer for the hearing-impaired group. When one considers the *combined* effects of noise *and* reverberation, the reduction in speech perception scores is truly massive. These effects apply to both groups, but are more pronounced for the hearing-impaired children. At the poorest condition—a S/N of 0 and a reverberation time of 1.2 seconds—the hearing-impaired children achieved an average score of 11%.

It is worth noting that the 30% score achieved by the normal-hearing group under this same condition will undoubtedly make learning very difficult for them. The rationale behind the FM sound-field classroom system (Flexer, Chapter 9, this volume) is based on just this type of research. While hearing-impaired children suffer disproportionately from poor acoustical conditions, normal-hearing children are not immune from their effects.

The combined effects of reverberation and noise also were investigated by Harris and Swenson (1990). They used three groups of adult subjects: those with normal hearing, mild sensorineural hearing loss, and moderate-to-severe sensorineural hearing loss. They tested under three conditions of reverberation (none, 0.54 reverberation time, and 1.55 reverberation time) and two levels of noise (none, and a +10 dB S/N ratio). As reverberation time increased, so did score differences between the groups, with the detrimental effect of reverberation increasing for the more severe hearing-loss group. They also found, as did Finitzo-Heiber and Tillman (1978), that speech perception effects were compounded with the simultaneous presence of reverberation and noise.

Speech Perception Scores in Reverberation as a Function of Age

Neuman and Hochberg (1983) investigated the effect of variations in reverberation time upon speech perception of normal-hearing children *as a function of age.* For the most part, this particular factor has been overlooked. Young children do not have the same capacity to deal with acoustical distortions as do adults and older children. Acoustical conditions that may be perfectly suitable in high school may not be appropriate at the elementary level (which is ironic, considering that there is usually more noise in lower grade classrooms than in upper grades). The Neuman and Hochberg results can be seen in figure 11.

No effect of age could be noted at 0 reverberation time. As reverberation times increased to 0.4 and 0.6 second, there was a marked effect of age. The children's speech perception scores did not stabilize until they reached 13 years of age. If these are the effects upon normal-hearing children, the results can only be exacerbated for children with hearing losses. Such results give further support to the recommendations made by Flexer (Chapter 9, this volume) for more FM sound-field classroom systems in regular use.

Listening Effort

It is insufficient to express the difficulties experienced by hearing-impaired children listening in noise and/or reverberation only in terms of speech perception scores. It is possible for some hearing-impaired

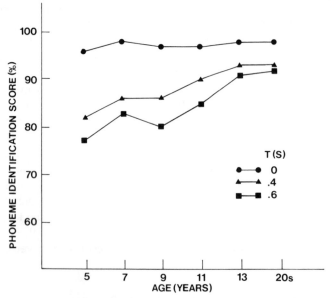

Figure 11.   Phoneme identification scores of normal-hearing subjects as a function of age and reverberation time. (Reprinted, by permission, from Neuman, A. C., and Hochberg, I. 1983. Children's perception of speech in reverberation. *Journal of the Acoustical Society of America* 73:2145–2149.)

people to attain fairly high speech perception scores under poor acoustical conditions, but only with the expenditure of a great deal of effort and more processing time (Downs 1982). Several studies have shown that the presence of noise not only increases learning effort but reduces the energy available for performing other cognitive operations (Rabbitt 1966; Downs and Crum 1978). As a personal observation, I can attest to the fatigue caused by prolonged intensive listening in noise through hearing aids (such as in the corridors at an ASHA Convention!).

The behavior of hard-of-hearing children listening to speech through FM systems and hearing aids is relevent to this observation. When taking orally dictated tests while using FM systems, children keep their eyes on the paper and make the required responses. When listening with hearing aids, they observe the teacher, and at the *conclusion* of the utterance they look down to mark the paper. Apparently children unconsciously take in as much information as they need to comprehend messages. If they can get it all auditorily with the FM, then visual cues are not used. If, however, listening through hearing aids *does not* provide them with all the required verbal information, they then employ vision as a supplementary channel.

Some Concluding Remarks

There has been a great deal of research on the topic covered in this section (for a comprehensive review, see Nabelek in press). Only a few representative studies have been reviewed and discussed here, just enough to make some valid generalizations. The effect of noise and reverberation on speech perception capacities of hearing-impaired children is severe, more so in combination than separately, and worse for younger than older children. What has not been discussed is the consequence upon classroom learning and auditory language development of these speech perception difficulties (Ross, Brackett, and Maxon 1991). It takes no great leap of imagination to realize that if the acoustic signal that hearing-impaired children receive is unnecessarily obscured, then there must be consequences for learning and development of language coded by the acoustic signal.

An FM system, therefore, by bridging the distance between the source and the listener, not only improves speech perception and reduces listening effort, but increases the likelihood that language and academic learning can be maximized. As one confronts the technical complexity of modern FM systems, this overriding purpose has to be kept in mind. An FM system is not just *another* therapeutic tool; rather, it is a clear and enhanced auditory avenue to the brain, whence all learning takes place. Whatever it takes to keep the FM systems operating optimally (Evans, Chapter 6, this volume) is worth the effort.

REFERENCES

American Speech-Language-Hearing Association. 1990. Let's talk. No. 23. *Asha* 32:83.
Bess, F. M., and Tharpe, A. M. 1986. An introduction to unilateral sensorineural hearing loss in children. *Ear and Hearing* 7(1):3–13.
Dale, D. C. M. 1962. *Applied Audiology for Children.* Springfield, IL: Charles C Thomas.
Dirks, D. D., Morgan, D. E., and Dubno, J. R. 1982. A procedure for quantifying the effects of noise on speech recognition. *Journal of Speech and Hearing Disorders* 47:114–22.
Downs, D. W. 1982. Effect of hearing aid use on speech discrimination and listening effort. *Journal of Speech and Hearing Disorders* 47:189–93.
Downs, D. W., and Crum, M. A. 1978. Processing demands during auditory learning under degraded listening conditions. *Journal of Speech and Hearing Research* 21:702–714.
Dubno, J. R., and Dirks, D. D. 1989. Auditory filter characteristics and consonant recognition for hearing-impaired listeners. *Journal of the Acoustical Society of America* 85:1666–1675.
Finitzo-Hieber, T. 1981. Classroom acoustics. In *Auditory Disorders in School Children*, eds. R. Roeser and M. Downs. New York: Thieme-Stratton, Inc.
Finitzo-Hieber, T., and Tillman, T. W. 1978. Room acoustics effects on monosyllabic word discrimination ability for normal and hearing-impaired children. *Journal of Speech and Hearing Research* 21:440–58.
Harris, R. W., and Swenson, D. W. 1990. Effects of reverberation and noise on speech recognition by adults with various amounts of sensorineural hearing impairment. *Audiology* 29:314–21.
Hawkins, D. B. 1984. Comparison of speech recognition in noise by mildly-to-moderately hearing-impaired children using hearing aids and FM systems. *Journal of Speech and Hearing Disorders* 49:409–18.
Hawkins, D. B., and Yacullo, W. S. 1984. Signal-to-noise advantage of binaural hearing aids and directional microphones under different levels of reverberation. *Journal of Speech and Hearing Disorders* 49:278–86.
Hawkins, D. B. 1988. Options in classroom amplification systems. In *Hearing Impairment in Children*, ed. F. H. Bess. Parkton, MD: York Press.
Houtgast, T., and Steeneken, H. J. M. 1985. A review of the MTF concept in room acoustics and its use for estimating speech intelligibility in auditoria. *Journal of the Acoustical Society of America* 77(3):1069–1077.
Humes, L. E. 1991. Understanding the speech-understanding problems of the hearing impaired. *Journal of the American Academy of Audiology* 2:59–69.
Irwin, R. J., and McAuley, S. F. 1987. Relations among temporal acuity, hearing loss, and speech distorted by noise and reverberation. *Journal of the Acoustical Society of America* 81:1557–1565.
Johnson, C. E., Nabelek, A. K., and Asp, C. W. 1990. Effect of distance on normal-hearing and hearing-impaired listeners' phoneme recognition. Paper presented to the Annual Convention of the American Speech-Language-Hearing Association, November 1990, Seattle, WA.
Lemore, P. J. J., Verweij, C., and Brocaar, M. P. 1985. Investigations of the residual hearing capacity of severely hearing-impaired and profoundly deaf subjects. *Audiology* 24:343–61.
Markides, A. 1986. Speech levels and speech-to-noise ratios. *British Journal of Audiology* 20:84–90.

Nabelek, A. 1980. Effect of room acoustics on speech perception through hearing aids. In *Binaural Hearing and Amplification*, ed. R. Libby. Chicago: Zenetron.

Nabelek, A. In press. Communication in noisy and reverberant environments. In *Acoustical Factors Affecting Hearing Aid Performance*, eds. G. Studebaker and I. Hochberg. Austin, TX: Pro-Ed.

Nabelek, A. K., and Nabelek, I. V. 1985. Room acoustics and speech perception. In *Handbook of Clinical Audiology*, 3rd edition, ed. J. Katz. Baltimore: Williams & Wilkins, Inc.

Neuman, A. C., and Hochberg, I. 1983. Children's perception of speech in reverberation. *Journal of the Acoustical Society of America* 73:2145–2149.

Niemoeller, A. F. 1981. Physical concepts of speech communication in classrooms for the deaf. In *Amplification in Education*, eds. F. H. Bess, F. A. Freeman, and J. S. Sinclair,. Washington, DC: A. G. Bell Association.

Olsen, W. 1988. Classroom acoustics for hearing-impaired children. In *Hearing Impairment in Children*, ed. F. H. Bess. Parkton, MD: York Press.

Rabbitt, P. M. 1966. Recognition: Memory for whole words correctly heard in noise. *Psychonomic Science* 6:383–84.

Ross, M., Brackett, D., and Maxon, A. 1991. *Assessment and Management of Mainstreamed Hearing-Impaired Children: Principles and Practices*. Austin, TX: Pro-Ed, Inc.

Smith, L. Z., and Boothroyd, A. 1990. Speech perception in noise for severely and profoundly hearing impaired children. Paper presented at the Annual Convention of the American Speech-Language-Hearing Association, November 1990, Seattle.

Turner, C. W., and Henn, C. C. 1989. The relation between vowel recognition and measures of frequency resolution. *Journal of Speech and Hearing Research* 32:49–58.

Chapter • 3

Physical Components and Features Of FM Transmission Systems

Linda M. Thibodeau

FM transmission allows for an improved signal-to-noise ratio and as much as 32% improvement in speech recognition (Hawkins 1984). Despite this significant advantage, the selection and use of FM systems in the classroom has become increasingly complex because of the variety of options available today. The purpose of this chapter is to review the physical components and features of the variety of systems that are available.

A basic FM system, shown in figure 1, consists of two units, a transmitter and a receiver. There is a microphone to pick up sound in the acoustic environment and convert it to an electrical signal. The transmitter uses the electrical signal to modulate the frequency of a high frequency carrier signal, which is then broadcast via an antenna. This frequency-modulated signal is demodulated by the receiver, amplified, and delivered to the user. FM systems may be grouped into two classes according to how the signal is delivered to the user. With the basic FM system, the signal is delivered via a button earphone. This has also been called a self-contained system or auditory trainer. The personal FM system is similar to the basic FM system except that it requires the use of one's personal hearing aid to deliver the signal.

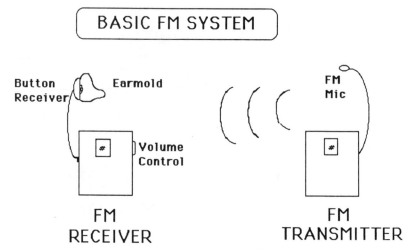

Figure 1.   Schematic of a basic FM system.

TRANSMITTER OPTIONS

The options associated with the transmitter unit may be grouped into four areas: microphones, transmitter frequencies, alternate signal inputs, and transmitter controls. These options are summarized in schematic form in Appendix A.

Microphones

In the early FM systems, the microphone and the transmitter were one unit, as shown in figure 2. These units with built-in microphones are still available today. One characteristic of units with an internal microphone is that there is always a dangling antenna.

Probably the most common microphone in current use is the lapel microphone shown in figure 3. It is clipped onto clothing at a distance 6 to 8 inches from the mouth. The antenna is in the microphone cord. Lapel microphones may be one of two types, *omnidirectional* or *unidirectional*. A unidirectional microphone is also called a directional microphone. It is distinguished by openings around the sides, which allow for a reduction in amplification of sounds impinging on the sides relative to sounds impinging on the top. Therefore, the signal may be enhanced relative to environmental sounds provided that the directional microphone is pointed toward the speaker's mouth.

To determine spectral differences between these two lapel microphones, measurements were performed of the average level of running speech by a female speaker through each of the microphones when

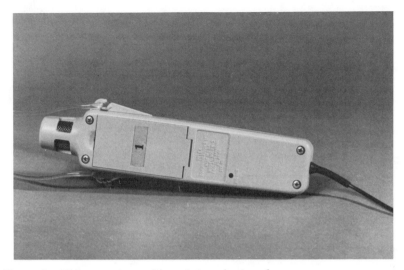

Figure 2.   FM transmitter with an internal microphone.

connected to a Phonic Ear® 461 transmitter. The output of a Phonic Ear 461 receiver was delivered to a Zwislocki coupler and measured via a portable probe microphone system and B & K dynamic signal analyzer. A sound-level meter was used by the speaker to maintain constant vocal intensity across the comparisons. Figure 4 is a comparison of the

Figure 3.   Omnidirectional (left) and unidirectional (right) lapel microphones to be used with an FM transmitter. The arrow points to the openings around the side of the unidirectional microphone.

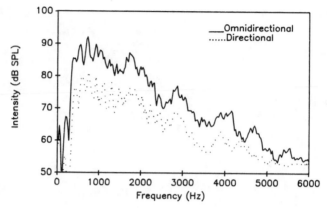

Figure 4. Averaged spectrum of running speech through omnidirectional (solid line) and unidirectional (dotted line) lapel microphones when worn in the proper position.

omni- versus the unidirectional microphone when each was worn in the normal upright position. The output of the unidirectional microphone is approximately 15 dB lower than the output of the omnidirectional one. The difference in the outputs shown in figure 4 is about 7 to 10 dB greater than that reported by the manufacturer. (It is possible that this particular unidirectional microphone may have varied from the norm. Thibodeau and Saucedo [1991] evaluated several FM microphones and reported that all microphones are not individually tested by the manufacturer. If a subset meets specifications, a whole batch of microphones is considered acceptable. Therefore, it is possible for disparities to exist between microphones.)

Figure 5a illustrates the changes that occur when the omnidirectional microphone is pointed to the left shoulder, as might happen if it is carelessly attached to the wearer's clothing. There is actually not much difference from the curve observed when the microphone is worn properly. However, when that error is made with a unidirectional microphone there is a significant reduction in output across the frequency range, as shown in figure 5b.

A microphone that is not subject to variations with head movement is the boom microphone shown in figure 6. It is worn with a headband or clipped to one's eyeglasses so that the microphone is approximately two inches from the lips and moves with the head. Given its proximity to the lips, it allows for increased amplification of the signal relative to the environmental noise. Some boom microphones, referred to as noise-cancelling, are unidirectional, so that they are more sensitive to sounds produced by the speaker than to environmental noise in front of the speaker. Proper placement of the boom micro-

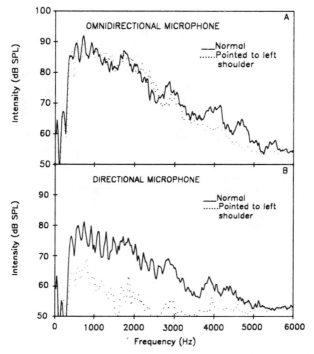

Figure 5. Averaged spectrum of running speech through (a) omnidirectional and (b) unidirectional lapel microphones when worn properly (solid line) and when pointed to the left shoulder (dotted line).

phone so that it provides minimal obstruction of lipreading cues is also important.

In group conference situations, when it is desirable to pick up voices from around the table, a conference microphone may be used, which is also shown in figure 6. The conical shape at the bottom of the case directs sounds from sources around the table to the microphone at the apex. The transmitter is plugged in under a wood-grained cover. The metal base serves as the antenna.

Another alternative for group situations is a pass-around microphone. This microphone is plugged into the transmitter along with the lapel or boom microphone. The main speaker uses the lapel or boom microphone while members of the group pass the alternate microphone from one speaker to another.

Transmitting Frequencies

Another variation on the transmitter is the frequency of the carrier wave for transmission. Most transmitters operate on one of 32 available

Figure 6.   Boom (left) and conference (right) microphones to be used with an FM transmitter. The conference microphone is laying on its side so that the conical shape at the base may be seen. The arrows point to the microphone ports.

narrow frequency bands between 72 and 76 mHz that are identified by a color code or a number (see Chapter 1). In some instances it may be desirable to have a variable frequency transmitter. For example, when a fixed frequency transmitter is in need of repair, a variable frequency transmitter may be easily substituted. One way that the transmitting frequencies may be varied is by having a removable oscillator. Another way is to dial in the desired transmitting frequency by rotating numbered dials on the transmitter as shown in figure 7.

Alternate Signal Inputs

Some FM transmitters have an option for auxiliary input. To maintain an optimum signal-to-noise ratio when the source is electronic, the signal can be delivered directly into the transmitter rather than through the transmitter microphone which may pick up unwanted ambient sounds. An important feature on the transmitter is the option to have the microphone active while there is auxiliary input, allowing a teacher to add information to a tape that is being played. A transmitter may have a switch, such as mic + audio, which allows the teacher's voice to be transmitted along with the auxiliary audio source.

Figure 7. A variable frequency transmitter in which the transmitting frequency is selected by dialing the appropriate numbers.

Transmitter Controls

Other transmitter features include an automatic gain control adjustment to vary the kneepoint, i.e., the intensity level of the input signal at which the reduction in gain begins. The higher the kneepoint, the greater the dynamic range of the speech signal. Another feature on most transmitters is a Low Battery light. Unfortunately, lack of illumination of this light does not mean an adequate battery, because it is not illuminated when the battery is completely exhausted. On some transmitters there is also a NO FM light, which means that the microphone has not been plugged in correctly or there is a problem with the microphone cord.

RECEIVER OPTIONS

The receiver options may be reviewed in five areas: microphones, receiver frequencies, input/output connections, receiver controls, and coupling methods. These options are summarized in schematic form in Appendix A.

Microphones

The microphone options are summarized in figure 8. For persons with mild or unilateral hearing losses or in situations where resources are limited, a receiver with one omnidirectional microphone may be selected. However, dual microphones are preferable for binaural losses. These may be unidirectional or omnidirectional. The unidirectional microphones have ports on the front and on the side so that sounds impinging on the front are amplified to a lesser degree than those impinging on the side. This is based on the notion that the user wants to hear persons on either side. An even closer approximation of binaural hearing is achieved by housing the microphones in behind-the-ear cases. When these microphones are used, the environmental microphones on the receiver case must be deactivated. Another option is to use a pass-around microphone plugged into an audio-input jack on the receiver. A final possibility is that some receivers designed to be used with personal hearing aids may not have environmental microphones because it is expected that the microphone on the personal hearing aid will be used.

Receiver Frequencies

The variables regarding receiver frequencies are shown in figure 9. The interchangeable oscillators that designate the frequency are coded by colors, letters, or numbers. Some receivers are capable of receiving only one frequency, while others can receive one of two different frequencies. As shown in figure 9a, there may be a switch on the oscillator to allow receipt of the coded frequency or a general frequency that is included in every dual-channel oscillator. On some receivers the frequency is selected by a switch on the case, as shown in figure 9b. In these units the general frequency is internal and the class or specific frequency is removable. The general frequency is an advantage when two classes join together to view a film or all students in a school attend an assembly.

Input/Output Connections

Input/output variables on the receiver include the output jacks to deliver the signal to the user, which are 1, 2, 3, or 6 pin connectors. There may also be an output jack to another audio source such as a tape recorder. This allows the hearing-impaired student to make a tape with a good S/N ratio. This is ideal for the college student who wants to tape-record a lecture for later review. It is also possible to deliver the receiver signal to a cochlear implant, which allows the user to benefit from the improved S/N ratio.

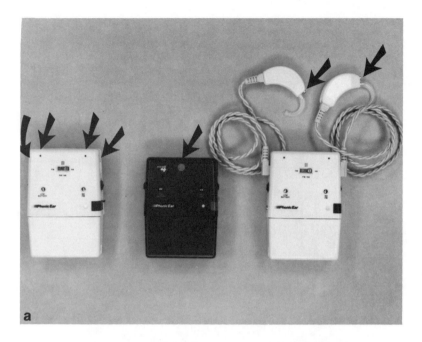

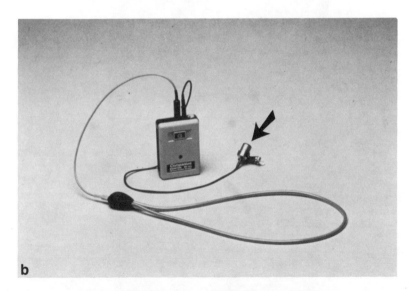

Figure 8. Summary of microphone options for FM receivers: (a) unidirectional with two ports on the front and one on each side (left), monaural with port in the center (center), and behind-the-ear with ports by the earhooks (right), and (b) pass-around shown with a neckloop arrangement. The arrows point to the microphone ports.

Figure 9.   Dual-channel oscillators that are (a) removable or (b) housed within the FM receiver. The arrows point to the switches for selecting the general or specific frequency.

Receiver Controls

The controls on the FM receiver include switches to activate the environmental microphone. This may be accomplished by two switch settings on the side, a single switch on the front, or a single switch on the side of the case, as shown in figure 10.

There is always a control for volume on the receiver and often saturation sound pressure level (SSPL) and tone controls as well. In receivers with two separate amplifiers, these controls are set independently for each channel as shown in figure 11. For monaural receivers, which do not have two independent amplifiers, it may be possible to set the relative gain for the two ears. The output channels may be set to provide equivalent gain in the case of a symmetrical loss or up to 24 dB more gain for the poorer ear. The control for FM ratio allows the FM signal to be boosted up to 10 dB above the environmental microphone signal.

The final control options on the receiver are the indicator lights. The Low Battery light is similar to the one on the transmitter in that it will not come on if the battery is completely exhausted. The NO FM light is lit when the FM transmitter is not set to the "ON" position. Unfortunately, it does not indicate improper connection of the lapel microphone to the transmitter.

Coupling Methods

The methods for coupling the signal to the user's ear are summarized in figure 12. For persons with auditory processing problems but normal thresholds, a stetoclip or headset may be used. Button earphones may be used for persons with more severe losses. These allow for the greatest power with the least chance of feedback. When behind-the-ear microphones are used, the signal may be delivered to the user via receivers in the case, much like a personal hearing aid. In fact, these microphone/receivers are often mistaken for personal hearing aids. The difference between the behind-the-ear microphone/receiver and the personal hearing aid is that the amplifier and power supply are housed in the FM receiver. However, recently an FM receiver became available that has all the components (microphone, amplifier, receiver, battery, and non-interchangeable oscillator) entirely contained within a behind-the-ear case. For persons with atresia or draining ears, a bone vibrator may be used to deliver the signal.

For the coupling arrangements discussed thus far, the child must remove the personal hearing aid in order to wear the FM system. There was concern that a hearing-impaired child would not receive a consistent signal when wearing two amplification devices during the day. As a result, three types of Personal FM systems were developed, as shown

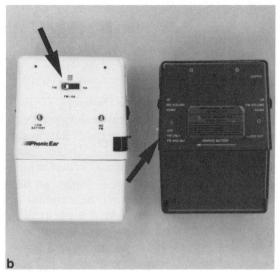

Figure 10. Options for signal selection on FM receivers: (a) separate on/off switches for environmental microphone and FM signal on the side of the receiver (top left), and (b) three-selection switch on the front of a receiver with environmental microphones (bottom left) and two-selection switch on the side of a receiver (bottom right).

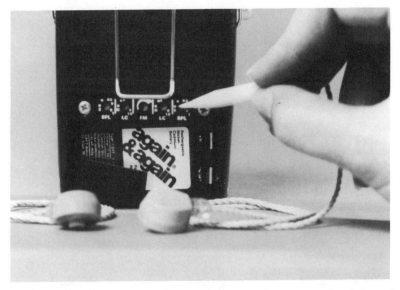

Figure 11. FM receiver controls for setting maximum output and tone for right and left channels separately. The center control is for adjustment of the FM ratio (see text).

in figure 13. For each of these arrangements the signal is delivered through the personal hearing aid.

In the case of the neckloop arrangement, shown in figure 13a, the electrical signal from the FM receiver is delivered to a neckloop that creates an electromagnetic signal. This signal is picked up by the T-coil of the hearing aid and amplified. Concerns regarding the use of neckloops include increase in the overall internal noise, reduction in the low frequency amplification, and variation in signal strength as the head is turned (Thibodeau, McCaffrey, and Abrahamson 1988; Thibodeau and Saucedo 1991). The silhouette arrangement, shown in figure 13b, also requires a hearing aid with a T-coil and operates on a principle similar to the neckloop except that the electromagnetic field is created in a wafer-shaped piece worn between the head and the hearing aid. Signal variation is minimized because the position of the silhouette relative to the hearing aid remains constant with head movement.

In the case of direct-input, shown in figure 13c, the electrical signal from the FM receiver is led directly into the hearing aid via a boot or audio-shoe connection. Despite this direct connection, there may still be some signal alteration when the aid is coupled to the FM receiver (Thibodeau 1990). There is a variety of shapes of boots, as shown in figure 14. Some fit rather tightly into a slight notch on the hearing aid. Others merely slip over the battery compartment and have no firm at-

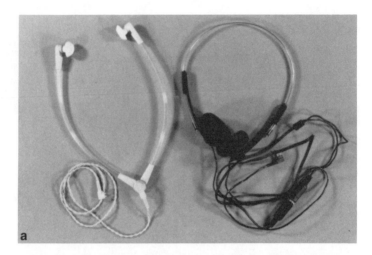

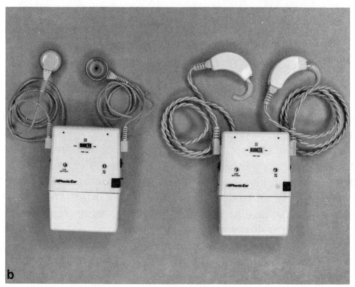

continued

Figure 12.   Summary of FM receiver coupling options: (a) stetoclip (left) or lightweight headset (right), (b) button earphones (left) or behind-the-ear receivers (right), and (c) bone conduction transducer.

tachment; slight movement can displace the contact and disrupt the signal. Some have prongs that insert into the aid. Still another variation on some boots is a *trim pot* that allows for matching the output signal level from the receiver to the input signal level of the hearing aid. This matching may also be done in the cord. Some boots have switches that

Figure 12. *continued*

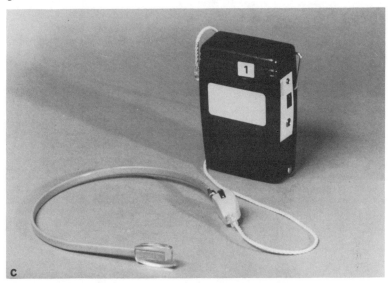

c

allow for receipt of the FM signal only or the FM + environmental (ENV) signal.

Appropriate boot and cords are obtained from the hearing aid manufacturer. From some manufacturers a cord may be ordered with attenuation that results in 5 dB attenuation of the signal from the hearing aid microphone; this provides a better signal-to-noise ratio when receiving the FM + ENV signals. As shown in figure 15, some boot and cord arrangements are contained within one component, with the cord attached to the boot; many others have two components, which adds to the complexity of having the correct cord for a boot. There has been an attempt to standardize direct-input cord connections by the development of a smooth gray cord called the Europlug cord. Some manufacturers state that an aid has a standard Europlug connection, which means it uses this standard 3-pin gray cord.

The direct-input feature is standard on some aids. Others require adjustments that allow them to function in a direct-input mode. For example, with some aids the case may have to be opened and a small contact plate put in place. Other aids simply require removal of a small circular plate on the outside of the case and placement of a circular contact plate.

The availability of hearing aids that could be used in personal FM arrangements was investigated by Thibodeau, O'Neal, and Richards (1989). Based on the belief that it is important for a child who may use an FM system to be fitted with a hearing aid with optimal features for

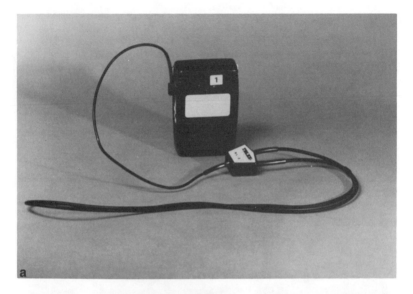

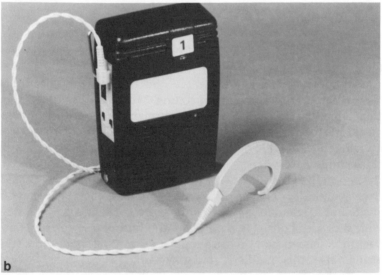

continued

Figure 13.   Summary of options for personal FM systems: (a) neckloop, (b) silhouette, and (c) direct-input.

use in a direct-input or neckloop arrangement, they compiled a list of aids and their features. In response to questionnaires mailed to 33 hearing aid manufacturers, 65 behind-the-ear hearing aids with direct-

Figure 13.   *continued*

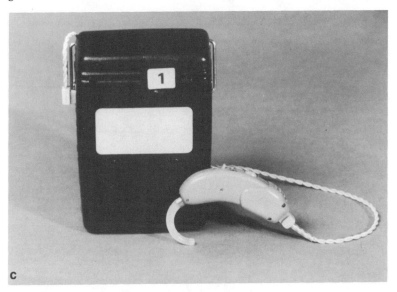

c

input and T-coil capability were identified. An important part of the
survey was the availability of signal options. In the neckloop mode, all
aids allowed for receipt of the FM signal only, i.e., all had T switches.
Yet less than 25% had MT switches or the ability to receive FM + ENV
signals. In the direct-input mode, just over half allowed for FM only
and nearly 80% allowed for FM + ENV. However, less than one-fourth
allowed both signal options on the same hearing aid. In some cases the
signal option could be specially ordered, but it is important to check
with the manufacturer when doing this because it may result in the
loss of other signal options. For example, Unitron aids are manufactured with a T switch that allows receipt of only the FM signal when
used with a neckloop or silhouette. An MT switch may be specially
ordered to allow receipt of the FM and environmental signals; however, this replaces the T switch or the off switch.

Evaluation of other desirable features revealed that few aids had
directional microphones on these aids or two-year warranties, but just
over half had compression and direct-input as standard features. It
was recommended that hearing aid dispensers consider this information when preselecting hearing aids for hearing aid evaluations, so that
children are fitted with aids that are optimally compatible with FM systems. The information regarding aids with direct-input and neckloop
options was recently updated and is provided in Appendix B. With the

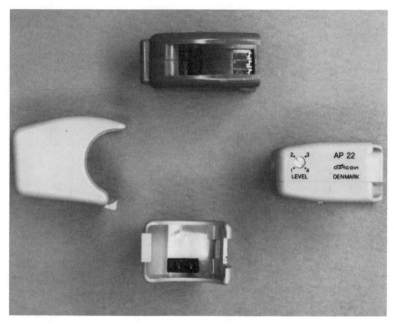

Figure 14. Examples of boot configurations include metal contacts that slip over the aid (top), metal contacts held on more tightly by molded notch at edge (left), metal pins that insert into the aid when boot is attached (bottom), and impedance adjustment trim pot (right).

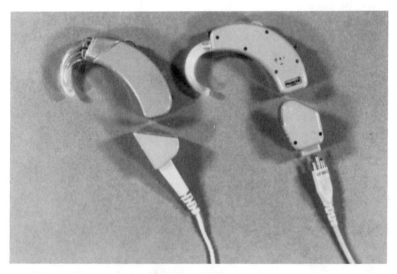

Figure 15. Examples of boot and cord configurations include single component (left) and two components (right).

addition of 34 aids, there has been a slight increase in the availability of MT switches, and of both FM and FM + ENV signal options in direct-input mode.

BATTERY OPTIONS

There are two main issues involving batteries for FM systems: the battery types and the charging units. These options are summarized in Appendix A.

Battery Types

One battery type is the rechargeable nicad battery pack, shown in figure 16a. These packs may stay on the transmitter or receiver during charging or can be removed and charged separately. The charge lasts 18 to 25 hours. Another option on some units is to use a 9-volt rechargeable battery, as shown in figure 16b. These batteries remain in the units during charging and the charge lasts 7 to 14 hours. A final option is to use 9-volt or two 1.5-volt alkaline batteries which last approximately 15 to 20 hours.

Charging Units

The styles of chargers include a case charger with spaces for 12 units, as shown in figure 17a. Charging time is approximately 8 to 12 hours, but chargers may be left on longer without the possibility of overcharging. A two-pocket charger is used for a transmitter and receiver pair. A modular charger, shown in figure 17b, can be expanded by adding on sections to charge up to 12 units. The final style is a wall charger, shown in figure 17c, which charges a transmitter/receiver pair. The plugs are connected to the units and the charging unit is plugged into a standard wall socket.

When working with FM systems, it is important to check the various components frequently. In some cases, the NO FM and Low Battery lights on the transmitters and receivers may be used to evaluate the components. Some systems may be evaluated by a test unit, shown in figure 18, that has connections for certain cords, oscillators, and batteries.

CONCLUSIONS

An array of options available for the transmitter, receiver, and battery components of FM systems has been reviewed. Although a variety of

Figure 16.   Summary of battery options: (a) rechargeable nicad battery pack, and (b) rechargeable nine-volt battery.

factors influences the decision for an optimal arrangement for a child, an estimation of ideal features can be made. The ideal transmitter would have variable channel capability for maximum flexibility and have the audio-input with talkover option. The optimal microphone would be the boom microphone that allows for a consistent signal as

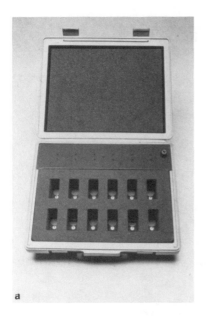

Figure 17. Summary of charging options: (a) case charger, (b) modular charger, and (c) wall charger.

the head turns. Low Battery and NO FM lights would be helpful on the transmitter as well as the receiver. The optimal receiver would have dual-channel oscillators and audio-input and output jacks. Depending on the coupling arrangement, the receiver or personal hearing aid should allow all three signal options: FM only, ENV only, or FM + ENV, so that the student may receive the best possible signal-to-noise ratio relative to the instructional task. Although the method of delivering the signal to the ear is determined largely by the degree of hearing loss, the personal FM arrangement is optimal when possible because

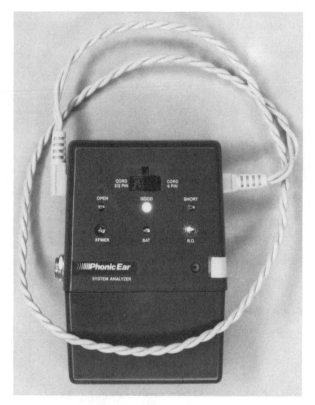

Figure 18.   FM test unit showing a cord that is working properly.

the child may wear his or her hearing aid all day. Of the three personal
FM arrangements, direct-input coupling is preferable because internal
noise is lowest and the signal is most consistent. The transmitter and
receiver would function ideally on either nicad or alkaline batteries so
that the user is not dependent on electrical sources for chargers. However, when charging is convenient, one has the option to benefit from
the cost-effectiveness of the nicad battery and the longer period of
operation.

The number of available features on FM transmitters and receivers
creates a complex set of factors to consider when fitting hearing-
impaired persons. The selection of options must be determined relative to the age of the child, type of hearing aid, degree of hearing loss,
instructional arrangement, availability of support personnel to monitor systems, financial resources, and student preference. Therefore,
although the various options may be complex, variety is necessary in
order that optimal decisions are made to fulfill amplification requirements of an individual within inevitable budgetary constraints.

ACKNOWLEDGMENTS

Photographs of equipment were provided by Telex Communications, Inc.; Phonic Ear, Inc.; Comtek, Inc.; and the author. Technical information was provided by Linda Hammond of Telex, Bob Mendoza of Phonic Ear, and EllaVee Yuzon of Audio Enhancement.

REFERENCES

Hawkins, D. 1984. Comparisons of speech recognition in noise by mildly-to-moderately hearing-impaired children using hearing aids and FM systems. *Journal of Speech and Hearing Disorders* 49:409–18.

Thibodeau, L. 1990. Electroacoustic performance of twenty direct-input hearing aids with two FM amplification systems. *Language, Speech, and Hearing Services in the Schools* 21:49–56.

Thibodeau, L., McCaffrey, H., and Abrahamson, J. 1988. Effects of coupling hearing aids to FM systems via neckloops. *Journal of the Academy of Rehabilitative Audiology* 21:49–56.

Thibodeau, L., O'Neal, J., and Richards, N. 1989. A review of desirable features of children's hearing aids. *Journal of the Academy of Rehabilitative Audiology* 22:74–81.

Thibodeau, L., and Saucedo, K. 1991. Consistency of electroacoustic characteristics of FM systems. *Journal of Speech and Hearing Research* 34:628–35.

Phonic Ear is the registered trademark of Phonic Ear, Inc.

APPENDIX A   SUMMARY OF OPTIONS AVAILABLE FOR FM SYSTEMS

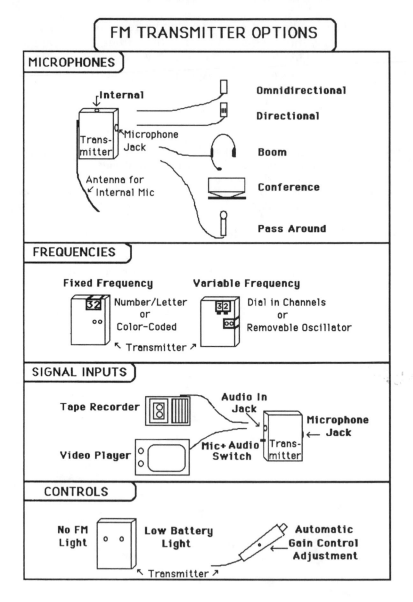

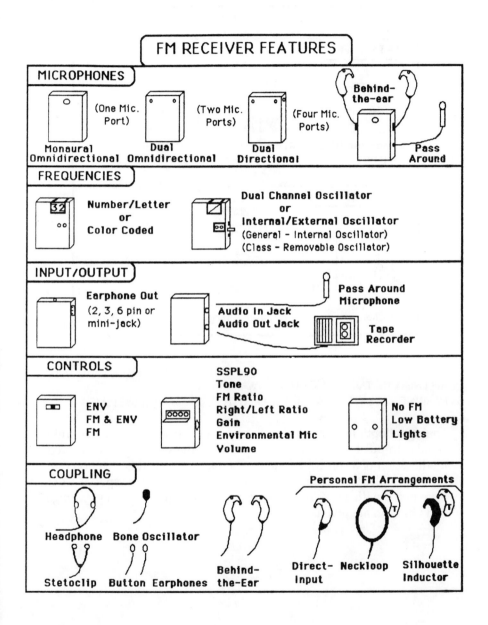

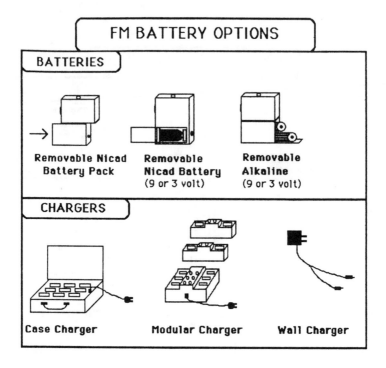

APPENDIX B   TABLE OF OPTIONS AVAILABLE FOR
HEARING AIDS THAT CAN BE USED WITH PERSONAL FM SYSTEMS

The signal options were credited as present if an elementary-age child could manipulate the necessary switches. If the signal option required modification of a control by the teacher/audiologist, this was noted in the table with a " + ." Signal options that were available by special order were noted with a "*." T-coil Sensitivity and High Frequency Average Full On Gain are given in dB SPL.

Model	Direct Input FM Only	Signal Fm & Env.	Options Both	Neckloop FM only	Signal FM & Env.	Options Both	Directional	Compression	Direct-Input	T-Coil	T-Coil Sensitivity	HFA FOG	Warranty (years)
AUDIOTONE													
A72	•	✓	•	✓	•	•			•	✓	93	59	1
A63	•	✓	•	✓	•	•		✓	✓	✓	118	61	1
A65	•	✓	•	✓	•	•		✓	✓	✓	111	61	1
A2000	•	✓	•	✓	•	•		✓	✓	✓	121	70	1
A61	•	✓	•	✓	•	•		✓	✓	✓	126	71	1
BELTONE													
Prima		✓		✓	✓	✓			✓	✓	115	64	1
Suprimo		✓		✓	✓	✓	•	✓	✓	✓	125	68	1
Avanti		✓		✓	✓	✓	•	✓	✓	✓	121	71	1
DAHLBERG													
HV	•	✓	•	✓	•	•		✓	✓	✓	120	69	2
SP	•	✓	•	✓	•	•		•	•	✓	88	59	2
DANAVOX													
143AGCI	✓	✓	✓	✓	•	•	•	✓	✓	✓	90	47	2
133AGCI	✓	✓	✓	✓	•	•	•	✓	✓	✓	90	47	2
143V	✓	✓	✓	✓	•	•	•	✓	✓	✓	98	47	2
143 ASP	✓	✓	✓	✓	•	•		✓	✓	✓	98	47	2
133VT	✓	✓	✓	✓	•	•	•	✓	✓	✓	97	52	2
143PPAGCI	✓	✓	✓	✓	•	•	•	✓	✓	✓	103	58	2
133PPAGCO	✓	✓	✓	✓	•	•	•	✓	✓	✓	103	58	2
133PPAGCI	✓	✓	✓	✓	•	•	•	✓	✓	✓	103	59	2
133PP	✓	✓	✓	✓	•	•	•	✓	✓	✓	106	61	2
125PPAGCI	✓	✓	✓	✓	•	•		✓	✓	✓	110	64	2
135PPAGCI	✓	✓	✓	✓	✓	✓	•	✓	•	✓	108	70	2
OTICON													
E35F	✓	✓	✓	✓	•	•		✓	✓	✓	100	47	1
E40	•	✓	•	✓	•	•		✓	•	✓	103	47	1
E37F	✓	✓	✓	✓	•	•		✓	✓	✓	100	49	1
E44	•	✓	•	✓	•	•	✓	✓	•	✓	110	49	1
E30V	•	✓	•	✓	•	•		✓	•	✓	111	52	1
E31V	•	✓	•	✓	•	•	✓	✓	•	✓	111	54	1
E42P	•	✓	•	✓	•	•		✓	•	✓	112	60	1
E30P	•	✓	•	✓	•	•		✓	•	✓	115	61	1
E25P	•	✓	•	✓	•	•		✓	•	✓	120	62	1
E27P	•	✓	•	✓	•	•	✓	✓	•	✓	120	65	1
E39PL	✓	✓	✓	✓	✓	✓		✓	✓	✓	123	66	1
E38P	•	✓	•	✓	✓	✓		✓	✓	✓	125	70	1
E28P	•	✓	•	✓	✓	✓		✓	•	✓	125	71	1
E34	✓	✓	✓	✓	✓	✓		✓	✓	✓	132	75	1

Model	Direct Input FM Only	Signal Fm & Env.	Options Both	Neckloop FM only	Signal FM & Env.	Options Both	Directional	Compression	Direct-Input	T-Coil	T-Coil Sensitivity	HFA FOG	Warranty (years)
PHONAK													
Pico CST	•	√	•	√	•				√	√	89	43	1
Audinet CHD	√	+	+	√	•		√		√	√	89	46	1
Pico SC	•	+	•	√	•			√	√	√	94	46	1
Pico SCD	•	√	•	√	•		√	√	√	√	94	46	1
Pico CS HT	•	√	•	√	•				√	√	91	47	1
Pico SCH	•	√	•	√	•			√	√	√	95	48	1
Varionet CD2	√	+	+	√	•		√		√	√	100	50	1
Audinet CD	√	+	+	√	•		√		√	√	98	51	1
Pico Forte C	•	√	•	√	•	√	√	√	√	√	102	52	1
Varionet SCD2	√	+	+	√	•		√		√	√	100	52	1
Audinet PPCH	√	+	•	√	•			√	√	√	107	63	1
Pico Forte PPSC	•	√	•	√	√	√	•	√	√	√	115	63	1
Pico Forte PPC	•	√	•	√	√	√			√	√	115	64	1
Pico Forte PPCL	•	√	•	√	√	√			√	√	114	66	1
SuperFront PPC2D	√	+	+	√	•		√		√	√	127	66	1
Audinet PPC	√	+	•	√	•				√	√	119	67	1
SuperFront PPSCL	√	+	•	√	√	√	•	√	√	√	120	67	1
Audinet PPCL	√	+	•	√	•				√	√	117	68	1
SuperFront PPSC	√	+	•	√	√	√	•	√	√	√	124	69	1
SuperFront PPCL4	√	+	•	√	√	√	• •		√	√	126	69	1
SuperFront PPC4	√	+	•	√	•		• •		√	√	126	70	1
Super Front PPC2	√	+	+	√	•				√	√	126	70	1
Audinet PPCP	√	+	+	√	•				√	√	115	72	1
Pico Forte PPCP	•	√	•	√	√	√			√	√	115	73	1
REXTON													
Mini Primo Plus PP0HC	√			√				√	√	√	92	48	2
Mini Primo Plus PPIHC	√			√				√	√	√	92	48	2
Mini Primo Plus ASP	√			√				√	√	√	100	54	2
Mini Primo Plus PPIGC	√			√				√	√	√	98	55	2
Mini Primo Plus PP0GC	√			√				√	√	√	98	55	2
Selectra PP6DM	√	√	√	√	√		√	√	√	√	115	63	2
PP-142	√	√	√	√	•	√		√	√	√	118	68	2
PP-142L	√	√	√	√	•			√	√	√	124	70	2
Selectra PP6	√	√	√	√	√	√		√	√	√	118	71	2
TELEX													
353CAI	√	√		√	√			√	√	√	107	53	1
363CAI	√	√		√	√			√	√	√	117	63	1
366	√	√		√	√			√	√	√	128	66	1
372LAI	√	√		√	√				√	√	120	72	1
350PC	√	√		√	√				√	√	120	70	1

Model	Direct Input FM Only	Signal Fm & Env.	Options Both	Neckloop FM only	Signal FM & Env.	Options Both	Directional	Compression	Direct-Input	T-Coil	T-Coil Sensitivity	HFA FOG	Warranty (years)
UNITRON													
UM60D	✓	✓	✓	✓				✓	•	✓	97	42	2
UM60H	✓	✓	✓	✓			✓	✓	•	✓	97	44	2
UE8	✓	✓	✓	✓				✓		✓	105	47	2
UM60UH	✓	✓	✓	✓				✓	•	✓	93	48	2
UM60	✓	✓	✓	✓					•	✓	102	50	2
UM60AGC	✓	✓	✓	✓	•			✓	•	✓	100	50	2
UE7D	✓	✓	✓	✓			✓		•	✓	105	51	2
UE10H	✓	✓	✓	✓	•			✓	•	✓	105	52	2
UE7	✓	✓	✓	✓	•				•	✓	105	54	2
UM60 PP	✓	✓	✓	✓	•			✓	•	✓	110	60	2
UE10	✓	✓	✓	✓	•				•	✓	117	62	2
EIP	✓	✓	✓	✓	•				•	✓	120	69	2
EIPL	✓	✓	✓	✓	•				•	✓	120	69	2
UE12PP	✓	✓	✓	✓	•				•	✓	120	69	2
UE12PPL	✓	✓	✓	✓	•				•	✓	120	69	2
US80PPL	✓	✓	✓	✓	•			✓	•	✓	125	72	2
US80PP	✓	✓	✓	✓	•			✓	•	✓	125	75	2
WIDEX													
ES10T(ASP)		✓		✓	✓	✓		✓	•	✓	90	41	1
ES8T		✓		✓	✓	✓		✓	•	✓	93	44	1
ES9T		✓		✓	✓	✓	✓	✓	•	✓	92	48	1
Q8				✓	✓	✓		✓	•	✓	97	48	1
ESIT		✓		✓	✓	✓	✓	✓	•	✓	100	49	1
Q9				✓	✓	✓		✓	•	✓	94	50	1
ES6T		✓		✓	✓	✓		✓	•	✓	101	53	1
Q16		✓		✓	✓	✓		✓	•	✓	103	55	1
ES2T		✓		✓	✓	✓		✓	•	✓	109	61	1
TOTAL 99	60	80	41	99	28	28	14	61	64	99			

73

Chapter • 4

Electroacoustic Considerations

Richard C. Seewald and K. Shane Moodie

The primary purpose in fitting FM systems is to provide the listener with greater access to speech signals in generally unfavorable listening environments. This is accomplished by locating the FM system's remote microphone in close proximity to the signal of primary importance. This relatively simple signal enhancement strategy results in a more favorable relationship between the level of the signal relative to the level of environmental noise (i.e., signal-to-noise ratio) at a listener's ear.

To realize the potential this technology offers, however, a number of conditions must be established. First, the basic electroacoustic performance of an FM system must be ensured. Second, the real-ear electroacoustic performance characteristics of an FM system should be compatible with the child's residual hearing characteristics. Finally, a system must provide the child with a reasonably consistent amplified speech signal over time. This chapter presents the rationale and describes a number of specific procedures for ensuring that these conditions are established for children who use FM systems.

BEGINNING WITH THE END PRODUCT

The working premise we have applied in fitting amplification with children is that a consistent amplified speech signal should be provided to a child regardless of the means employed to deliver it. If a certain range of amplified speech levels is required across frequencies to optimize auditory learning, a child should be provided with these levels, consistently, across all listening conditions (Byrne and Christen 1981; Ross 1981; Hawkins and Schum 1985; Seewald and Ross 1988). Similarly, maximum levels of amplified sound that are delivered to an ear should be the same for all modes of amplification employed since, as Byrne and Christen (1981) observed, the requirement for an appropriate signal that is consistent with comfort and safety does not change. Unfortunately, consistency is not easily accomplished when more than one amplification system is used by the same child. The following case example is presented to illustrate this point.

The monaural air conduction thresholds for the child under consideration are shown in figure 1. The same air conduction thresholds, converted to dB SPL, have been plotted in figure 2. The child's loudness discomfort levels (LDLs) also have been plotted in this figure. Additionally, long-term average levels associated with conversational speech (Cox and Moore 1988) are shown along with an intensity range of approximately 30 dB, around the mean levels, across frequencies. It should be noted that all variables presented in figure 2 have been defined in dB SPL in situ (i.e., level of sound within the child's ear canal). It should also be noted that the greatest proportion of the unamplified spectrum of conversational speech is projected to fall well below this child's unaided hearing threshold levels.

Information presented in figure 3 illustrates the theoretical end result of hearing aid selection and fitting with this child. It can be seen

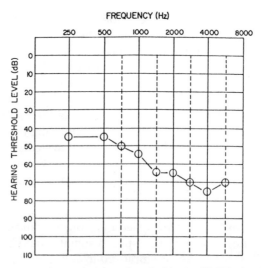

Figure 1.   Pure tone air conduction thresholds, in dB HL, for the right ear of the case example.

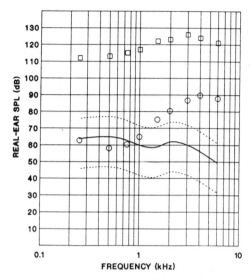

Figure 2. Pure tone air conduction thresholds (○) and loudness discomfort levels (□) in dB SPL in situ. Also shown are the one-third octave band levels for average conversational speech (— [Cox and Moore 1988]), transformed to the eardrum (Shaw 1974), with an associated intensity range of 30 dB (– – –) across frequencies.

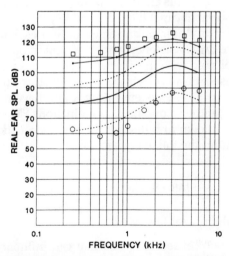

Figure 3. Electroacoustic end result of the hearing aid selection and fitting process. Auditory variables include thresholds (○) and loudness discomfort levels (□) in dB SPL as a function of frequency. Electroacoustic variables include the output limiting characteristic of the child's hearing aid (■—■) and amplified long-term average speech levels (—) with the associated intensity range of approximately 30 dB (– – –) from 250 to 6000 Hz.

that levels associated with the long-term average spectrum of speech have been amplified to levels that fall well within this child's auditory area across frequencies. Also, the maximum hearing aid output has been limited to levels below the child's LDLs. Information presented in this figure, then, represents the electroacoustic end product (i.e., amplified spectrum of speech) within the child's ear canal, under an optimal listening condition with a hearing aid.

The amplified speech signal that this child receives from an FM system should approximate the electroacoustic end product provided by the hearing aid if a reasonable degree of consistency is to be ensured across listening conditions. As a result, the child will benefit from signal enhancement provided by the FM system and, simultaneously, receive amplified speech at sensation levels that are appropriate for a child with this degree of hearing loss.

The final figure in this series illustrates an undesirable result in FM system fitting. Specifically, figure 4 displays the electroacoustic end product, in terms of the average amplified speech spectrum, delivered to the child from an FM system coupled to the child's hearing aid. It can be observed that long-term average levels of amplified speech have been modified relative to the hearing aid-alone condition (see figure 3). Most notably, a substantial reduction in sensation levels of amplified speech is observed at frequencies above approximately 1500 Hz. It is unlikely therefore, that this child will be able to take full advantage of the signal enhancement capability of the FM system.

A comparison of findings presented in figures 3 and 4 indicates that the objective for consistency across amplification conditions has not been accomplished with this particular child. In some way, the FM system has imposed its own electroacoustic signature on the end product. This unsuccessful FM system fitting might have resulted from a variety of factors, either alone or in combination. FM system-related variables that are known to influence the electroacoustic end product are described within the following section.

ELECTROACOUSTIC VARIABLES

Sources of Variability: An Overview

A list of FM system-related variables that can influence the electroacoustic end product delivered to the child is provided in the following outline. While this list is not exhaustive, it should serve to illustrate the relatively large number of factors, from the talker to the child's ear canal, that can influence the nature of the amplified signal ultimately delivered to the child. These sources of variability in FM system performance can be identified at all locations along the signal transmission

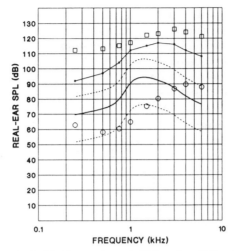

Figure 4. An undesirable electroacoustic FM system fitting for the case example. The projected output within the child's ear canal is shown (—) for a speech spectrum input to the FM system microphone having an overall level of 84 dB SPL (Hawkins 1987).

pathway including: (1) the source (e.g., a talker or audio-visual device), (2) the FM system's remote microphone, (3) the FM transmitter, (4) the environment in which the system is to be used, (5) the FM system's receiver, and (6) the coupling apparatus.

The effects these variables may have, either alone or in combination, will depend on the specific system configuration employed with a given child as well as conditions under which the system is used. At a minimum, anyone who is responsible for selection, fitting, and monitoring of FM systems should be aware that the variables identified in outline below can influence the signal that a child receives from an FM system.

I. Talker Variables
   A. Average Speech Level of the Talker
   B. Gender and Age Factors (e.g., fundamental frequency)
   C. Vocal Effort as a Function of the Environment
II. FM System Remote Microphone Variables
   A. Microphone Position
      1. lapel
      2. boom
   B. Microphone Type
      1. omnidirectional
      2. unidirectional
   C. Microphone Frequency Response

III. FM System Transmitter Variables
    A. Frequency Response Characteristics
    B. Compression Limiting Characteristics
        1. compression threshold
        2. compression ratio
    C. Output Impedance for Auxiliary Input

IV. Environmental Variables
    A. Electromagnetic Radiation
    B. Radio-Frequency Interference
    C. Reverberation Characteristics
    D. Acoustic Noise Factors
        1. temporal characteristics
        2. spectrum
        3. overall level

V. FM System Receiver Variables
    A. Volume Control Taper Characteristics
    B. Compression Limiting Characteristics
        1. compression threshold
        2. compression ratio
    C. Frequency Response Shaping
    D. Output Limiting Characteristics
    E. Environmental Microphone Characteristics
        1. microphone location
            a. in the unit
            b. at ear level
        2. physical isolation/location of microphones
        3. FM/environmental microphone ratio control
        4. microphone type
            a. omnidirectional
            b. unidirectional

VI. Coupling Variables
    A. Self-Contained (SC) Units
        1. receiver frequency response
        2. receiver output characteristics
        3. earmold acoustics
    B. Direct-Input (DI)
        1. impedance matching
        2. T/M/TM switching effects
    C. Neck-Loop (NL)
        1. loop electromagnetic strength
        2. position/distance re. hearing aid
        3. hearing aid telecoil sensitivity
        4. hearing aid telecoil orientation re. loop

      5.   hearing aid telecoil frequency response
      6.   T/M/TM switching effects
  D.   Silhouette Inductor (SI)
      1.   silhouette movement effects
      2.   hearing aid telecoil sensitivity
      3.   hearing aid telecoil orientation re. silhouette
      4.   hearing aid telecoil frequency response
      5.   T/M/TM switching effects

Electroacoustic Variability Within and Between Systems

There is very little that can be assumed with respect to the electroacoustic performance of FM systems. Perhaps the only assumption that can be made in the application of these systems is that if any system component or system control is modified, the electroacoustic performance of that system will be altered in some way. Findings of relevant studies reviewed within this section tend to support the need for this cautious orientation to the application of FM systems with children.

Ideally, the electroacoustic end product of FM system amplification should be essentially the same regardless of how a system is coupled to a child's hearing aid (e.g., direct input, neck loop). As seen in the outline above, however, there are a relatively large number of variables associated with coupling an FM system to a hearing aid. The literature suggests that the effects of these variables are, unfortunately, quite unpredictable. Thus, equivalence among different coupling methods for the same hearing aid cannot be assumed.

As part of a larger study, Hawkins and Schum (1985) measured frequency responses obtained from the same hearing aid and FM system under four different conditions: (1) a hearing aid-alone, and the same hearing aid coupled to an FM system via (2) direct input (DI), (3) neck loop (NL), and (4) silhouette inductor (SI). The findings obtained with one FM system-hearing aid combination are shown in figure 5. For this analysis, responses obtained under each coupling method condition were matched to the hearing aid alone response at 1000 Hz.

As can be observed in figure 5, regardless of the coupling method employed, the high frequency response obtained with the FM system conditions fell below that obtained with the hearing aid alone. In contrast, no such pattern is seen for the results at frequencies below approximately 1000 Hz. For this particular FM system-hearing aid combination, the lowest output, across frequencies, was obtained in the SI coupling condition. This finding, however, was not consistent across the other FM system-hearing aid combinations included in the study.

Hawkins and Schum (1985) observed that only one result was con-

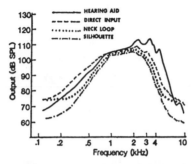

Figure 5. Frequency response curves obtained with a hearing aid alone and with the same hearing aid connected to an FM receiver via direct input, neck loop, and silhouette inductor coupling. (From Hawkins and Schum 1985. *Journal of Speech and Hearing Disorders* 50:132–41. Used with permission.)

sistent across the FM systems, hearing aids, and coupling methods they considered: when hearing aids were coupled to FM systems, the high frequency response was reduced relative to that obtained with the hearing aid alone. For certain FM system-hearing aid combinations, the magnitude of this reduction was as much as 25 dB.

In another experiment, Hawkins and Schum (1985) studied volume control taper characteristics of two FM receivers connected to the same hearing aid via DI, NL, and SI coupling. The results of these measurements are presented in figure 6. As can be seen, a substantial degree of variability in volume control taper characteristics was measured both as a function of the FM receiver and coupling method employed. For the six FM system-hearing aid conditions studied, the most undesirable volume control taper characteristic was measured for the Phonic Ear receiver-SI coupling combination. As can be seen, virtually all of the available range in gain control was achieved within the first 10 to 25% of the volume control wheel rotation. Interestingly, the volume control taper characteristics for the same FM system, but with different coupling (i.e., DI, NL), were found to be the most desirable of the six measured. On the basis of their findings, Hawkins and Schum advised that adjustment of an FM receiver volume control wheel be approached with special care. As their findings illustrate, only minor adjustments (i.e., < 5 mm) of the volume control wheel resulted, in some cases, in changes of up to 15 to 20 dB in output. Hawkins and Schum concluded that volume control taper characteristics of each FM system receiver be evaluated and that volume control wheels of both the FM receiver and hearing aid (for personal FM systems) be set appropriately before the unit is used by the child. Finally, the findings of this experiment serve to illustrate how different FM system-related variables can interact with each other, producing electroacoustic results that are generally unpredictable from one condition to another.

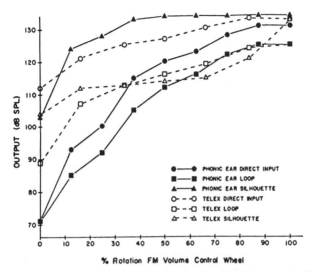

% Rotation FM Volume Control Wheel

Figure 6. Volume control wheel taper curves obtained from a single hearing aid connected to two different FM receivers via direct input, neck loop, and silhouette inductor coupling. (From Hawkins and Schum 1985. *Journal of Speech and Hearing Disorders* 50:132–41. Used with permission.)

The volume control taper findings reported by Hawkins and Schum (1985) have some additional implications with regard to quality of the signal delivered to the child. This particular issue has been discussed in some detail in a recent publication by Lewis et al. (1991). Figure 7 presents a family of frequency response curves that Lewis et al. obtained from a single FM system. Curves were obtained at seven different volume control wheel settings (#2–8) using a 75 dB SPL pure tone signal. As can be seen, nearly all of the effect of the volume control wheel on output occurred below the #3 setting, particulary for the 250 to 4000 Hz frequency range. Apparently, at any volume control setting above #3, this particular FM system was driven well above its linear operating range by a 75 dB SPL input signal. This result is not unlike some of the volume control taper characteristics described in the earlier report by Hawkins and Schum (1985).

Lewis et al. (1991) performed a second set of measurements with this particular FM system. Specifically, in addition to frequency response measures, they obtained measurements of harmonic distortion at each of the seven volume control wheel settings. Results of these measurements are shown in figure 8 with harmonic distortion, in percent, presented as a function of frequency (500 and 1000 Hz) and volume control setting (#2–8). As can be seen, the volume control setting of #2 was the only position of the seven evaluated at which less than 10% distortion was measured for both frequencies. These findings il-

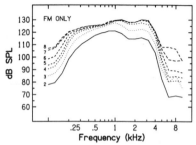

Figure 7. Family of frequency response curves obtained from an FM system. Output from the FM receiver, in dB SPL, is shown as a function of frequency and volume control setting (#2–8). (From Lewis et al. 1991. *Ear and Hearing* 12. Used with permission.)

lustrate the importance of assessing the distortion levels produced by each instrument before a particular volume control setting is recommended for a child. Thorough assessment of FM system nonlinearities is strongly supported by the results of studies reported by Hawkins and Van Tasell (1982) and Hawkins and Schum (1985).

It may be recalled that one of the conditions we wish to maintain in FM system use is related to provision of a consistent amplified speech signal over time. The results of some recent studies on different coupling methods suggest that even when the FM system, coupling method, and hearing aid are held constant, consistent electroacoustic performance cannot be assumed. For example, Lewis et al. (1991) recently provided an example of how output from an FM system can vary as a function of slight changes in position of a SI. Figure 9 shows that a reasonably good match was accomplished between the frequency re-

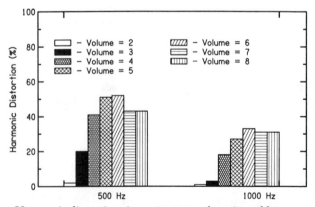

Figure 8. Harmonic distortion, in percent, as a function of frequency and volume control wheel setting obtained from measurements with an FM system. (From Lewis et al. 1991. *Ear and Hearing* 12. Used with permission.)

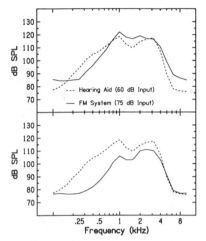

Figure 9. Effect resulting from slight movement of a silhouette inductor on the frequency response of an FM system-hearing aid combination. The upper panel presents the match in output obtained between the FM system response and the hearing aid-alone response as a function of frequency. The lower panel presents the effect, on the FM system's output, of repositioning the silhouette inductor. (From Lewis et al. 1991. *Ear and Hearing* 12. Used with permission.)

sponse obtained from a hearing aid alone (60 dB SPL input) and the frequency response obtained from the same hearing aid, in the telecoil mode, when connected to an FM receiver via SI coupling (75 dB SPL input). The lower panel of this figure shows results obtained under the same conditions with the exception that the SI was moved approximately one-eighth inch from the original position. Because such relatively large changes in output can result from only slight changes in position of the SI, Lewis et al. (1991) concluded that the SI coupling method would appear to be inappropriate for very young or multiply handicapped children. Assuming that consistency in the amplified speech signal is an important condition to maintain, and that the findings reported by Lewis et al. (1991) can be replicated with other hearing aid-SI coupling configurations, it is difficult to see how the SI coupling method could be considered as a viable option for children who use FM systems.

Along somewhat similar lines, Thibodeau, McCaffrey, and Abrahamson (1988) reported results of a study in which the effects of head orientation were examined when a NL coupling method was employed. Specifically, three frequency response curves were obtained from the same hearing aid (telecoil mode) when coupled to two different FM systems via an NL arrangement. Three frequency response curves measured for each system were obtained with the hearing aid positioned on the left ear of KEMAR with the manikin's head positioned straight ahead and at 90° to left and right. Findings of this experiment are presented in the two panels of figure 10.

As can be observed in figure 10, some effect of head orientation on hearing aid output can be observed for both FM receiver-NL systems employed. The effects, however, appear to have been greater, overall, for neck loop system #2 (lower panel). Although the effect of head orientation appears to have been less for neck loop system #1, the magnitude of differences that were measured between head right and head left positions are potentially significant to a child using this system; overall, differences appear to be approximately 10 dB across most frequencies. For some children who use FM systems, a difference of 10 dB in output can mean the difference between audibility and inaudibility of amplified speech. Furthermore, the magnitude of differences in output that resulted from changes in head orientation for neckloop system #2 are simply incompatible with the requirement for consistency over time. Similar findings with NL coupling systems were also reported in an earlier publication by Hawkins and Van Tasell (1982).

Collectively, research findings to date provide support for the earlier observation that little can be assumed regarding electroacoustic performance of FM systems. Certainly, if any modification is made to a system, however slight, the electroacoustic performance must be reevaluated and monitored carefully over time.

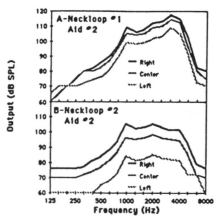

Figure 10. Variations in frequency responses of two FM systems with neck loop coupling as a function of frequency and head orientation. (From Thibodeau, McCaffrey, and Abrahamson 1988. *Journal of the Academy of Rehabilitative Audiology* 21:49–56. Used with permission.)

CHARACTERIZING ELECTROACOUSTIC PERFORMANCE

There are two purposes for characterizing the electroacoustic performance of FM systems. The first is to verify that the FM system performs in accordance with the manufacturer's specifications at the time of the initial fitting and that this performance is maintained over time. The second purpose is to ensure that overall electroacoustic performance of the FM system is compatible with the amplification requirements of the child.

Basic Electroacoustic Analyses

Basic electroacoustic measurements should be performed at the time of the initial fitting and at regular intervals for as long as the instrument is in use. Lieberth (1986) has identified three purposes for performing this set of electroacoustic measures: (1) affirming that a new FM system functions in accordance with specifications provided by the manufacturer, (2) establishing a performance baseline against which results of all subsequent measurements can be compared, and (3) periodically monitoring electroacoustic performance of the FM system. Electroacoustic measurement procedures applied at this stage, as well as interpretation of test findings, are both relatively straightforward. This is due primarily to the fact that criteria against which adequacy of the instrument's performance characteristics will be evaluated (i.e., manufacturer's published specifications) should be clearly defined.

Although there is not presently an ANSI standard for electroacoustic evaluation of FM systems, several authors have described procedures for applying the ANSI S3.22 hearing aid standard in evaluating FM systems (Lybarger 1981; Sinclair, Freeman, and Riggs 1981; Lieberth 1986). As these authors suggest, a basic electroacoustic measurement protocol should include assessment of the system's full-on-gain, reference test gain, SSPL90, harmonic distortion, equivalent noise input level, and the volume control taper characteristic. Furthermore, if both FM microphone and environmental microphone (EM) modes of operation are to be employed, each mode should be subjected to a complete electroacoustic analysis since performance characteristics in one mode cannot be predicted from the other (Freeman, Sinclair, and Riggs 1980; Bess, Sinclair, and Riggs 1984).

Finally, a great deal of clinical time and effort can be lost in performing real-ear measurement procedures with a poorly functioning FM system. It is advisable, therefore, that clinicians perform a careful visual inspection of the FM system and basic electroacoustic analysis prior to implementing real-ear fitting and/or evaluation procedures.

Thus, whenever performance difficulties have been identified through basic electroacoustic analyses, all testing procedures with the child should be deferred until the unit's electroacoustic functioning can be confidently ensured.

Electroacoustic Fitting Procedures

Under no circumstance should a child be provided with an FM system before a careful electroacoustic fitting has been performed. The second purpose for characterizing electroacoustic performance of FM systems is, therefore, to ensure that the system's electroacoustic characteristics are compatible with the child's unique amplification requirements.

Results of several studies provide reason to question the validity of FM system fitting practices that have been applied in the past (Bess, Sinclair, and Riggs 1984; Lieberth 1986). For example, Bess, Sinclair, and Riggs (1984) reported the results of a field study in which electroacoustic analyses were performed on 78 FM receivers. For the units evaluated, the median high frequency average 2-cm³ coupler gain measured at the as-worn volume control settings was 44.7 dB with a range of 2 to 66 dB. These data were subjected to further analyses to determine the relationship between the amount of gain with which the children were provided and their pure tone average hearing levels. Remarkably, the results of this analysis revealed absolutely no relationship between degree of hearing loss and amount of gain provided by the FM systems for this sample of children. As noted by Bess, Sinclair, and Riggs, " . . . it seems ironic that a child may be repeatedly evaluated for a precise fitting of a personal hearing aid, but experience a more casual assignment of the amplification device worn at school" (p. 144).

In recent years, several FM system electroacoustic fitting protocols have been described in the literature (Turner and Holte 1985; Lieberth 1986; Hawkins 1987; Lewis et al. 1991). Despite certain procedural differences among these protocols, an attempt has been made with each to account for variables that are uniquely associated with FM selection and fitting.

Electroacoustic fitting of an FM system differs in several important ways from fitting a hearing aid. First, as discussed in a previous section, there are a greater number of electroacoustic variables that need to be accounted for in fitting an FM system. For this reason, the as-worn performance of any FM system cannot be assumed from published specifications and, therefore, must be quantified on an individual-by-individual basis. Second, any protocol that is designed for FM system fitting needs to account for differences between average speech input levels to the microphone of the FM system's transmitter as compared to average speech input levels we assume in fitting personal hearing aids (Lybarger 1981; Turner and Holte 1985; Hawkins 1987).

In the hearing aid selection approach we currently employ with children (Seewald and Ross 1988; Seewald et al. 1991), an average over-all input level to the microphone of the hearing aid of 70 dB SPL is as-sumed. In contrast, it has been estimated that the average input level of speech that is delivered to the microphone of an FM transmitter under normal classroom conditions is approximately 80 to 85 dB SPL (Cor-nelisse, Gagné, and Seewald 1991; Hawkins 1987, 1988). These differ-ences in assumed input levels result primarily from relative differences in distance between the source of the speech signal and the micro-phones of these two different devices.

The one-third octave band levels of the long-term average speech spectra that have been proposed for both hearing aid selection and FM system selection are shown in figure 11. Specifically, the lower curve in this figure shows the long-term average one-third octave band levels of conversational speech which have been proposed by Cox and Moore (1988) for hearing aid selection purposes. In contrast, the upper curve in figure 11 shows the long-term average one-third octave band levels of speech proposed by Hawkins (1987) for FM system electroacoustic se-lection and fitting. While the overall difference in level between these two average spectra is 14 dB, frequency specific level differences range from 7 to 22 dB.

These differences between average speech input levels to hearing aids and the microphone of the FM transmitter have important implica-tions in amplification selection and fitting. Specifically, the output from an amplification device (e.g., hearing aid/FM system) will be the prod-

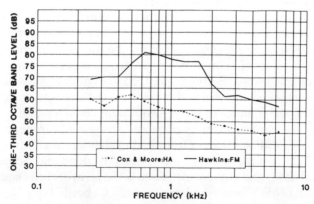

Figure 11. The one-third octave band levels, as a function of frequency, of long-term average spectra of speech recommended for the purpose of hearing aid selection by Cox and Moore (1988) and for the purpose of FM system fitting proposed by Hawkins (1987).

uct of input signal level plus gain provided by the device. Thus, if a child is provided with an equal amount of gain in both the hearing aid alone and FM system conditions, a higher in situ output from the FM system would be expected, on average, due to higher speech input levels delivered to the microphone of the FM system transmitter. In the final analysis, the child would be provided with a different amplified signal depending on which system was being worn. If, however, the objective in electroacoustic fitting is to provide a reasonably consistent amplified speech signal, regardless of the system employed to deliver it, then overall gain provided by the FM system will need to be reduced, relative to that provided by the personal hearing aid, to account for higher input signal levels we assume for the FM system condition.

A major complicating factor in the electroacoustic fitting of FM systems relates to input-output (I/O) performance characteristics that are typically associated with these systems. Most commercially available systems currently employ some form of input compression circuitry within the FM transmitter. A set of findings reported by Hawkins and Schum (1985) clearly illustrates the effect of the input compression circuitry used in one commercially available FM system.

Hawkins and Schum (1985) measured the I/O functions for a hearing aid alone and for the same hearing aid coupled to an FM system via DI for a 30 dB range in input level. The results of these measurements are shown in figure 12. It can be observed that the 30 dB range in input level was linearly amplified by the hearing aid, resulting in a 30 dB range in output. In the FM-DI condition, however, the 30 dB range in input level was compressed, resulting in only a 5 dB range in measured output levels (i.e., 6:1 compression ratio).

There are at least two important implications of these findings for FM system fitting. First, as Hawkins and Schum (1985) observed, these findings illustrate that one cannot assume that I/O characteristics of an FM system-hearing aid combination will be the same as those for the hearing aid by itself. Thus, the electroacoustic performance of each must be characterized. Secondly, any FM system fitting protocol must incorporate procedures that will provide a valid characterization of the unique I/O performance of the system under consideration.

As noted earlier, a variety of procedures have been described for the purposes of FM system fitting and evaluation in children. These include 2-cm³ coupler based procedures (Hawkins and Schum 1985; Lewis et al. 1991) and real-ear measures in the form of either sound field aided thresholds (Turner and Holte 1985; Lieberth 1986; Van Tasell, Mallinger, and Crump 1986) or probe-tube microphone measures (Hawkins 1987; Lewis et al. 1991). An excellent review of these procedures has been provided in a recent publication by Lewis et al. (1991).

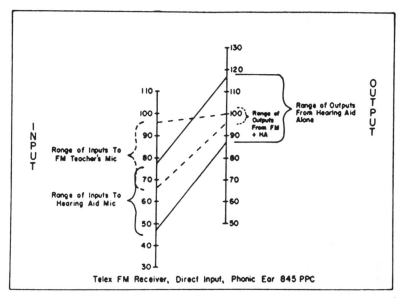

Figure 12.   The input-output relationships for a hearing aid alone (——) and for the same hearing aid coupled to an FM system via DI (– – –). (From Hawkins and Schum 1985. *Journal of Speech and Hearing Disorders* 50:132–41. Used with permission.)

Therefore, only a brief presentation of these measurement options has been included herein.

Before considering various measurement options that have been proposed for FM system electroacoustic fitting and evaluation, however, there is need to address a more fundamental issue. Each of the available measurement options, whether 2-cm³ coupler or real-ear based, will tell us something about how the system performs under very specific measurement conditions. Regardless of which procedures have been employed, results of such measurements will be of only limited value, however, unless the clinician has carefully formulated a set of electroacoustic performance criteria against which results of these measurements can be compared. In other words, the clinician must first decide, on some theoretical basis, what will be required from the FM system in terms of its electroacoustic performance. Once this has been determined, the clinician can then proceed to measure the actual performance of the system and assess the extent to which the measured performance meets with the predetermined requirements for the individual child.

An additional advantage of this general approach to fitting relates to selection of specific measurement procedures. There should be a logical relationship between how FM system performance criteria have been defined and the selection of procedures employed to verify the extent to which the criteria have been met. If on some basis, for example, the clinician has determined that output from the FM system should not exceed a certain level within the child's ear canal, this will require implementation of a specific measurement procedure to verify that this particular performance criterion has been met. With this general orientation to the problem in mind, the following provides a brief overview of various measurement options that have been proposed for purposes of FM system electroacoustic fitting in children.

Sound Field Aided Threshold Procedures. Prior to the availability of probe-tube microphone systems, sound field aided audiograms provided the primary means for assessing real-ear performance of hearing aids in children. Over the years, a number of sound field aided threshold procedures have been proposed for evaluating the real-ear performance of FM systems (Turner and Holte 1985; Lieberth 1986; Van Tasell, Mallinger, and Crump 1986). Sound field thresholds obtained with an FM system in place have been used in a variety of ways. For example, Van Tasell, Mallinger, and Crump (1986) proposed that functional gain measures could be used to compare relative amounts of real-ear gain provided by different FM systems and/or different coupling methods with the same system. Others have suggested the use of sound field aided threshold data for comparing relative real-ear performance differences between hearing aid only and FM system conditions (Lieberth 1986). Additionally, some have proposed the use of sound field threshold data for estimating sensation levels at which speech will be received under the FM condition (Turner and Holte 1985).

The usefulness of sound field aided thresholds will depend upon the nature of the clinical question that is being asked, as well as the validity of the measurement procedure itself. If the primary reason for measuring real-ear performance with an FM system is to determine the lowest level of sound that can be detected by a child, then measurement of sound field aided thresholds would be the procedure of choice. For any other purpose, however, the value of sound field aided threshold data is relatively limited.

A major limitation of these measures relates to the fact that aided thresholds are obtained using relatively low level input signals that are not representative of real-world input signal levels at which these systems must operate. Recall that the input signal level delivered to the microphone of an FM system transmitter will be approximately 80 to 85 dB SPL on average. Recall also that most FM systems employ some form of input compression within the FM transmitter's circuitry. Unfortunately, due to the interaction of these two factors, it is simply not possible to predict the amount of gain that the system will provide under typical classroom conditions on the basis of sound field aided threshold data (Stelmachowicz and Lewis 1988; Lewis et al. 1991). In the final analysis, for the majority of FM systems, sound field aided threshold data obtained with an FM system will generally overestimate gain that the system will provide under normal operating conditions. Consequently, these data will also tend to overestimate sensation levels at which amplified speech will be received via the FM system (Seewald et al. 1989). For these, as well as several other reasons to be outlined below, we advocate application of alternative measurement procedures primarily for the purposes of FM system electroacoustic fitting in children.

Probe-Tube Microphone Measurement Procedures. Probe-tube microphone systems lend themselves readily to the process of FM system fitting and offer several important advantages over more traditional sound field aided threshold procedures. First, probe-tube microphone systems provide the means to characterize a variety of electroacoustic dimensions. Measurement possibilities include: insertion gain, in situ gain, in situ frequency response, output limiting characteristics, I/O functions, and harmonic distortion measures, among others. Second, probe-tube microphone measures allow for characterization of FM system electroacoustic performance in response to signals that better approximate input signals that will be delivered to the system during actual use.

Recently, Hawkins (1987) and Lewis et al. (1991) have described how probe-tube microphone measurements can be applied in the electroacoustic fitting of FM systems. Physical arrangements for these measurements, as proposed by Hawkins (1987), are illustrated in figure 13. Note that the microphone of the FM transmitter is located adjacent to the monitoring microphone of the probe-tube microphone system. This arrangement ensures that the input signal to the microphone of the FM transmitter is maintained at a constant and known level.

Sample results that Hawkins (1987) obtained from probe-tube microphone measurements are presented in figure 14. The three response curves presented in this figure were obtained with a hearing aid alone and with an FM system coupled to the hearing aid via DI and NL arrangements. It can be seen that each system produced a somewhat different output within the ear canal across frequencies. Additionally, findings presented in this figure illustrate an additional advantage of probe-tube microphone systems in FM system fitting. If the sound field aided threshold approach had been employed to compare performance under these three conditions, data would be available at several audiometric frequencies only. In contrast, the probe-tube microphone system provided Hawkins with data across all frequencies between 125 and 8000 Hz. This allowed for a precise definition of all real-ear response irregularities within this frequency range.

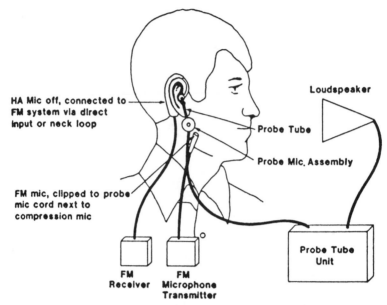

Figure 13.   Physical arrangement of apparatus proposed by Hawkins (1987) for probe-tube microphone measurements of FM system electroacoustic performance. (From Hawkins 1987. *Ear and Hearing* 8:301–303. Used with permission.)

2-cm³ Coupler Based Procedures.   Either alone, or in combination with measurements obtained using a probe-tube microphone system, 2-cm³ coupler based measures can facilitate the process of FM system fitting in children. One practical advantage of this general approach is that the amount of time required for direct electroacoustic measurements with a child can be greatly reduced. This is particularly helpful in our work with many preschool children who do not appear to be impressed by the importance of probe-tube microphone measurement procedures.

There are two basic assumptions that underlie our use of 2-cm³ coupler measurements in FM system fitting. First, we enter the FM system fitting process with an assumption that the child's personal hearing aids have been fitted appropriately. The specific criteria we use to assess adequacy of the hearing aid fitting are derived from the Desired Sensation Level (DSL) approach to electroacoustic selection for children (Seewald and Ross 1988; Stelmachowicz and Seewald 1991; Seewald et al. 1991). Certainly, any one of a number of contemporary electroacoustic selection strategies can be used for this purpose (e.g., Skinner et al. 1982; Cox 1988).

The second assumption we make in applying 2-cm³ coupler measurements is that any relative differences that are observed between

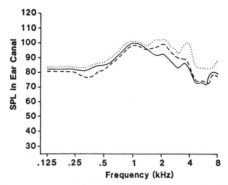

Figure 14.   In situ output, as a function of frequency, for three different systems measured with a probe-tube microphone system. The dotted line is output measured for the hearing aid alone. The dashed line is output measured with the hearing aid coupled to an FM system via NL arrangement. The solid line is output measured with the same hearing aid coupled to an FM system via DI. (From Hawkins 1987. *Ear and Hearing* 8:301–303. Used with permission.)

hearing aid performance and FM system performance when measured in a 2-cm^3 coupler will hold constant in the real ear, regardless of absolute levels of sound produced within these two different cavities. Specific details of the 2-cm^3 coupler based measurements we currently employ in FM system fitting with children are described below.

An Approach to FM System Electroacoustic Fitting

The general approach we employ in electroacoustic fitting of FM systems is to equate output of the FM system, within the child's ear canal, to that provided by the child's hearing aids. This approach is consistent with the FM system fitting principles outlined by Hawkins and Schum (1985), Hawkins (1987, 1988) and Lewis et al. (1991).

Two factors need to be accounted for in developing a clinical protocol that implements this theoretical orientation to FM system electroacoustic fitting. First, input signal levels that provide a reasonable approximation to those that will be encountered, on average, within the field should be used in the output matching procedure. Second, the protocol must account for unique I/O performance characteristics of the device to be fitted.

The data presented in figure 15 illustrate results of the output matching procedure we currently employ in FM system fitting. The solid curve is the I/O function obtained with a child's hearing aid with all controls adjusted to user settings. The input signal applied in this measurement was a speech-weighted composite noise (Frye 1986) that ranged in level from 50 to 90 dB SPL. Note that output of this hearing

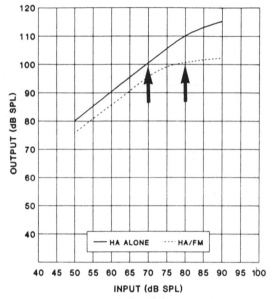

Figure 15.   Input-output (I/O) functions for two different amplification systems obtained in response to a speech-weighted composite noise signal (Frye 1986). The solid line is the I/O function for a hearing aid alone. The dashed line is the I/O function for the same hearing aid coupled to an FM system via DI. The two arrows show that output of the FM/HA combination (80 dB SPL input) has been matched to output of the hearing aid alone (70 dB SPL input).

aid was approximately 100 dB SPL with an input of 70 dB SPL. The dashed line is the I/O function for an FM system after the output matching procedure has been accomplished. It should be noted that the general shape of these two I/O functions is not the same. As can be seen, the FM system provides linear amplification in response to input levels up to approximately 75 dB SPL. Above this level however, the output from the FM system reflects activation of the input compression circuitry.

Presently, the operational definition of average conversational speech level that we use for the purposes of hearing aid selection is 70 dB SPL. In contrast, our operational definition of average speech input level to the microphone of the FM transmitter is 80 dB SPL (Cornelisse, Gagné, and Seewald 1991). Therefore, our objective in electroacoustic fitting is to match output from the FM system, using an 80 dB input, to output from the hearing aid alone in response to a 70 dB input. As can be seen in figure 15, an adequate match in output from these two different devices was accomplished for this child. Thus, we anticipate that this child will receive an equivalent output in the ear canal for amplified speech delivered by either the hearing aid alone or by the FM system. It should be noted that this output matching procedure can be accomplished through the use of either 2-cm³ coupler based measures or probe-tube microphone measures or real-ear electroacoustic performance.

The following provides a step-by-step description of the strategy we currently employ for purposes of FM fitting in children. The use of 2-cm³ coupler or probe-tube microphone measures will depend, primarily, upon three factors: (1) the type of electroacoustic analysis instrumentation that is available, (2) the FM system-hearing aid configuration to be employed (e.g., SC, NL, DI) and (3) the child's ability to cooperate for probe-tube microphone measurement procedures.

An FM System Electroacoustic Fitting Protocol

I. Shaping the 2-cm³ coupler response characteristics:
    A. Ensure that the child's hearing aid is adjusted to the preferred user settings.
    B. Place the hearing aid with earmold coupling (attached to an HA-1 coupler) in the test chamber and obtain a frequency response curve using a 70 dB SPL speech-weighted composite noise signal.
    C. Obtain an SSPL curve using a 90 dB SPL pure tone sweep.
    D. Place the microphone of the FM system transmitter in the test box and re-level the system.
    E. Connect the output from the FM system (FM system/hearing aid combination) to the HA-1 coupler. The coupler should be located outside of the test chamber. In the case of a personal FM system, the hearing aid microphone should be deactivated or, if this is not possible, the microphone should be isolated from environmental noise. If a NL arrangement is to be employed, the NL should be placed around the child's neck with the hearing aid in place at the child's ear. The output from the hearing aid should then be attached to the 2-cm³ coupler that is held in place at the child's ear during the measurement process (see Lewis et al. [1991] for further details concerning this procedure).
    F. Deliver an 80 dB SPL speech-weighted composite noise signal to the microphone of the FM system.
    G. Adjust the volume control of the FM receiver until output of the FM system matches output level obtained with the hearing aid alone.
    H. Obtain a frequency response curve using the 80 dB SPL speech-weighted composite noise signal.
    I. Obtain an SSPL curve using a 90 dB SPL pure tone sweep.
    J. Compare the output produced by the FM system to that of

the hearing aid alone. Frequency response and SSPL curves should match closely across frequencies.

II. Real-ear verification procedures

    A. Measure the in situ output (i.e., real ear aided response [REAR]) of the hearing aid employing a 70 dB SPL speech-weighted composite noise input signal.

    B. Measure in situ output of the hearing aid employing a 90 dB SPL pure tone sweep.

    C. Connect the FM system to the child, using the physical arrangement described by Hawkins (1987) (see figure 13).

    D. Measure in situ output (REAR) from the FM system employing an 80 dB SPL speech-weighted composite noise signal.

    E. Measure in situ output of the FM system employing a 90 dB SPL pure tone sweep.

    F. Compare curves obtained in this fashion for adequacy of a match.

    G. Make any fine-tuning adjustments to the FM system that might be required.

Results of this electroacoustic matching procedure, as performed in a 2-cm³ coupler, are presented in figure 16. The solid line in this figure is the frequency response of the child's hearing aid that was measured in response to a 70 dB SPL speech-weighted composite noise signal. The dashed line is the frequency response of the FM system obtained in response to an 80 dB signal after volume control of the FM receiver had

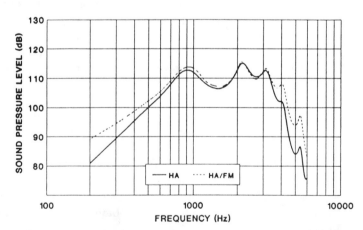

Figure 16.   2-cm³ coupler frequency response curves for two amplification systems obtained in response to a speech-weighted composite noise signal (Frye 1986). The solid line is the frequency response of the hearing aid alone (70 dB SPL input). The dashed line is the frequency response of the HA/FM combination (80 dB SPL input).

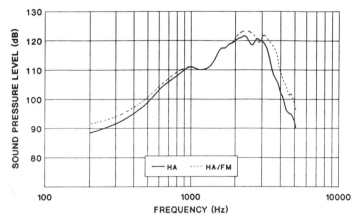

Figure 17.   Real Ear Aided Responses (REARs) for two amplification systems obtained with a speech-weighted composite noise signal (Frye 1986). The solid line is the REAR of the hearing aid alone (70 dB SPL input). The dashed line is the REAR of the HA/FM combination (80 dB SPL input.)

been adjusted to provide a match in output to the hearing aid-alone response curve.

Results of the real ear verification procedure with the same hearing aid and FM system are presented in figure 17. Despite the predictable differences in the absolute levels between the responses obtained in the coupler and those measured within the child's ear canal, the relative differences between the two curves are slight regardless of the cavity in which the measurements had been obtained (i.e., 2-cm³ coupler or real ear).

On the basis of these measurements, we have ensured that electroacoustic characteristics of the FM system are generally compatible with this child's requirements for amplification. Furthermore, we expect that this child will be able to take full advantage of the signal enhancement capability of the FM system. We view these conditions as a necessary prerequisite to intervention strategies that will be employed with all hearing-impaired children who use FM systems.

REFERENCES

Bess, F. H., Sinclair, J. S., and Riggs, D. E. 1984. Group amplification in schools for the hearing impaired. *Ear and Hearing* 5:138–44.
Byrne, D., and Christen, R. 1981. Providing an optimal signal with varied communication systems. In *Amplification in Education*, eds. F. H. Bess, B. A. Freeman, and J. S. Sinclair. Washington, DC: A.G. Bell Association.
Cornelisse, L. E., Gagné, J. -P., and Seewald, R. C. 1991. Long-term average

spectrum of speech at the chest-level microphone location. *Journal of Speech-Language Pathology and Audiology* 15:7–12.

Cox, R. M. 1988. The MSU hearing instrument prescription procedure. *Hearing Instruments* 39:6,8,10.

Cox, R. M., and Moore, J. N. 1988. Composite speech spectrum for hearing aid gain prescriptions. *Journal of Speech and Hearing Research* 31:102–107.

Freeman, B., Sinclair, J. S., and Riggs, D. 1980. Electroacoustic performance characteristics of FM trainers. *Journal of Speech and Hearing Disorders* 45:16–26.

Frye, G. J. 1986. High-speech real-time hearing aid analysis. *Hearing Journal* 39:21–26.

Hawkins, D. B. 1987. Assessment of FM systems with an ear canal probe-tube microphone system. *Ear and Hearing* 8:301–303.

Hawkins, D. B. 1988. Options in classroom amplification. In *Hearing Impairment in Children*, ed. F. H. Bess. Parkton, MD: York Press.

Hawkins, D. B., and Schum, D. 1985. Some effects of FM-system coupling on hearing aid characteristics. *Journal of Speech and Hearing Disorders* 50:132–41.

Hawkins, D. B., and Van Tasell, D. J. 1982. Electroacoustic characteristics of personal FM systems. *Journal of Speech and Hearing Disorders* 47:355–62.

Lewis, D. E., Feigan, J. A., Karasek, A. E., and Stelmachowicz, P. G. 1991. Evaluation and assessment of FM systems. *Ear and Hearing* 12:268–80.

Lieberth, A. K. 1986. FM evaluation: A protocol. *Journal of the Academy of Rehabilitative Audiology* 21:136–42.

Lybarger, S. F. 1981. Standard acoustical measurements on auditory training devices. In *Amplification in Education*, eds. F. H. Bess, B. A. Freeman, and J. S. Sinclair. Washington, DC: A.G. Bell Association.

Ross, M. 1981. Personal versus group amplification: The consistency versus inconsistency debate. In *Amplification in Education*, eds. F. H. Bess, B. A. Freeman, and J. S. Sinclair. Washington, DC: A.G. Bell Association.

Seewald, R. C., and Ross, M. 1988. Amplification for young hearing-impaired children. In *Amplification for the Hearing-Impaired*, ed. M. C. Pollack. Orlando, FL: Grune and Stratton.

Seewald, R. C., Hudson, S. P., Gagné, J. -P., and Cornelisse, L. E. 1989. Comparing two methods for estimating the sensation level of amplified speech. Paper read at the annual convention of the American Speech-Language-Hearing Association, November 1989, St. Louis.

Seewald, R. C., Zelisko, D. L., Ramji, K., and Jamieson, D. G. 1991. Computer-assisted implementation of the desired sensation level approach: Version 3.0. Poster presented at the annual convention of the American Academy of Audiology, April 1991, Denver.

Shaw, E. A. 1974. Transformation of sound pressure level from the free field to the eardrum in the horizontal plane. *Journal of the Acoustical Society of America* 56:1848–1861.

Sinclair, J. S., Freeman, B., and Riggs, D. 1981. The use of the hearing-aid test box to assess the performance of FM auditory training units. In *Amplification in Education*, eds. F. H. Bess, B. A. Freeman, and J. S. Sinclair. Washington, DC: A.G. Bell Association.

Skinner, M. W., Pascoe, D. P., Miller, J. D., and Popelka, G. R. 1982. Measurements to determine the optimal placement of speech energy within a listener's auditory area: A basis for selecting amplification characteristics. In *The Vanderbilt Hearing Aid Report*, eds. G. A. Studebaker and F. H. Bess. Upper Darby, PA: Monographs in Contemporary Audiology.

Stelmachowicz, P. G., and Lewis, D. E. 1988. Some theoretical considerations concerning the relation between functional gain and insertion gain. *Journal of Speech and Hearing Research* 31:491–96.

Stelmachowicz, P. G., and Seewald, R. C. 1991. Probe-tube microphone measures in children. *Seminars in Hearing* 12:62–72.

Thibodeau, L. M., McCaffrey, H., and Abrahamson, J. 1988. Effects of coupling hearing aids to FM systems via neck loops. *Journal of the Academy of Rehabilitative Audiology* 21:49–56.

Turner, C. W., and Holte, L. A. 1985. Evaluation of FM amplification systems. *Hearing Instruments* 36:6–12.

Van Tasell, D. J., Mallinger, C. A., and Crump, E. S. 1986. Functional gain and speech recognition with two types of FM amplification. *Language, Speech, and Hearing Services in the Schools* 17:28–37.

Chapter • 5

FM Selection and Use for School-Age Children

Antonia Brancia Maxon

The information presented in this chapter is based on the underlying assumption that all school-age children with hearing losses are candidates for FM systems. Regardless of age or grade, degree, configuration, or symmetry of the hearing loss, educational setting, primary mode of communication, or type of personal amplification, a child can benefit from the improved signal-to-noise ratio (S/N) afforded by using an FM system in the classroom.

FM USER DESCRIPTIONS

Wireless FM systems have been in use in regular and special education classrooms since the mid-1970s. Although initially recommended only for children in programs for the hearing impaired, use became more widespread as the benefits were acknowledged. In order to ascertain which children were using FM systems in various school settings, data were collected in three separate time periods. Between 1976 and 1980 a representative sample of FM users in regular education settings in Connecticut was described. Table I displays these data collected as part of the UConn Mainstream Project. In spite of the fact that FM systems were relatively new to the public schools, a wide range of hearing losses was represented. Further, the majority of the children in the sample were in fully or partially mainstreamed settings and were

Table I. Children Who Use FM Systems: UConn Mainstream Project* 1976–80, (N = 98)

Age:	
Range	4–17 years
Majority	7–13 years (75%)
Grade:	
Range	Pre K–12th, Regular Education
Majority	1st–2nd (21%) and 5th–7th (44%)
	Special Education Classification (24%)
Hearing Loss:	
Range	Mild–Profound
Majority	Severe–Profound (81%)
Full-time FM Users	100%
Traditional Models	100% (13%, Waist-mounted)
Adaptive Coupling	0%
Ear Level Hearing Aids	92%
Communication Mode:	
Oral/Aural	30%
O/A + Speechreading	62%
Cued Speech	0%
Total Communication	8%
Educational Placement:	
Full Mainstream	73%
Partial/Social Mainstream	19%
Self-Contained	8%

*The UConn Mainstream Project was housed in the Communication Sciences Department at the University of Connecticut and funded by the U.S. Department of Education, Office of Special Education and Research. Principal Investigator–Mark Ross; Project Co-Directors–Antonia Brancia Maxon and Diane Brackett.

Of the 213 children on the UConn Mainstream Project between September 1976 and June 1980, 98 (46%) had wireless FM systems. This table represents those subjects.

aural/oral communicators. All the children in that study used traditional FM systems, which is not unusual considering that technology for adaptive coupling (direct audio input, induction loop) was not yet commercially available.

More recently, Maxon, Brackett, and van den Berg (1991) described children using FM systems in the 1980s. Table II presents the description of two samples (1981–82, 1988–89). In those two time periods the range of hearing loss was also wide, and a majority of the students were fully or partially mainstreamed. When compared to the UConn Mainstream Project data, there were more children in the two 1980s groups using total communication as the primary mode of communication. This may be a result of the method of data collection (statewide in the former and nationally in the latter). Table II also shows an increased use of adaptive coupling from the beginning to the end of the decade. That shift is concurrent with the change in available technology. The

Table II.   Children Who Use FM Systems*

Item	Sample	
	1981–82 (N = 638)	1988–89 (N = 350)
Age:		
Range	1–18 years	1–21 years
Majority	7–12 years (52%)	5–10 years (56%)
Grade:		
Range	Pre K–12th	Pre-K–12th
Majority	3rd–9th (49%)	Pre-K–2nd (49%)
Hearing Loss:		
Range	Mild–Profound	Mild–Profound
Majority	Severe + (68%)	Severe + (56%)
Full-time FM Users	81%	73%
Traditional Models	75% (21% waist-mounted,	62% (17% waist-mounted,
	4% ear-level mikes)	10% ear-level mikes)
Adaptive Coupling	15%	38%
Ear Level Hearing Aids	72%	74%
Communication Modes:		
Oral/Aural	25%	29%
O/A + Speechreading	31%	25%
Cued Speech	1%	2%
Total Communication	42%	39%
Educational Placement:		
Mainst7ream	83%	84%
Program for HI	17%	16%

Percentages are rounded to the nearest whole number.
*Maxon, Brackett, and van den Berg (1991).

difference in number of children between the two samples is a result of data collection and does not reflect a decrease in the number of FM users over time.

These data indicate that across the United States and Canada, school-age children with varying skills and needs were using FM systems over a fifteen year period. Specific illustrations of children in mainstream settings who were successful FM systems users demonstrate that point.

Figure 1 shows the unaided audiogram of a 17-year-old girl with a congenital bilateral profound sensorineural hearing loss, mainstreamed in a twelfth-grade class. She had used an FM system since preschool. In the tenth grade this student demonstrated an interest in changing from a traditional system (chest-mounted, cords, and snap-on transducers) to one that incorporated her own ear-level hearing aids through direct audio input. Although this student had little residual

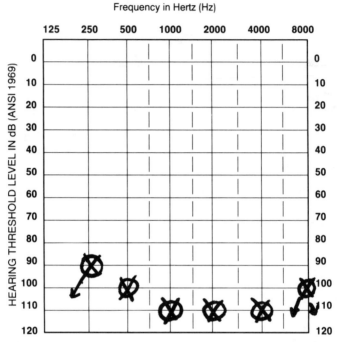

Figure 1.   Unaided audiogram of a 17-year-old who was a successful FM system user.

hearing, she benefited from the use of an FM system in the classroom because it could provide the requisite gain and output she needed to function. Furthermore, the system allowed her to separate information presented by the teacher from ambient noise and the voices of her peers.

There are professionals who would not consider recommending an FM system for a child with this degree of hearing loss because of the erroneous assumption that there is not enough usable residual hearing. Careful assessment demonstrated that this particular child, even with minimal measurable residual hearing, was indeed a candidate. She made good use of the system in the classroom and had good access to information presented in her regular classroom.

Figure 2 is the audiogram of a seven-year-old boy who also might not be considered an FM candidate because of the amount of residual hearing he displays. He has a relatively flat mild sensorineural hearing loss and receives good functional gain; aided speech discrimination shows great benefit from his binaural ear level hearing aids. Those benefits, demonstrated in optimal listening conditions, would not be replicated in his regular second-grade classroom. With only his personal hearing aids, he would have to work to "get by."

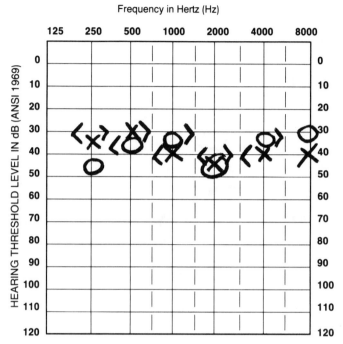

Figure 2. Unaided audiogram of a 7-year-old who was a successful FM system user.

Too often, for a child with mild hearing loss, little attention is paid to the fact that he or she could do much better in difficult listening conditions when afforded the good signal-to-noise ratio provided by a wireless FM system. Children with a lot of residual hearing will suffer great negative effects from distance and noise. Once again, through careful assessment, professionals can demonstrate the true advantage of an FM system over hearing aids for regular classroom use.

The child with the hearing loss shown in figure 3 presents the problem of fitting amplification when the hearing loss is asymmetrical. This eleven-year-old boy, who is mainstreamed in the fourth grade, needs an FM system that allows for individual ear gain, frequency response, and output settings. What cannot be seen directly is that his needs are further compounded by the recurrent middle ear disease that adds a fluctuating conductive component to his sensorineural hearing loss. During episodes of middle ear disease, his low and mid-frequency air conduction thresholds are reduced and greater gain is needed in those frequency regions.

This student's atypical problems are handled by using a traditional FM system in which the electroacoustic characteristics of each channel

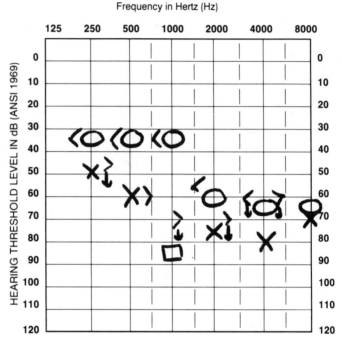

Figure 3. Unaided audiogram of an 11-year-old with asymmetrical hearing. This child was a successful FM system user.

are set individually. Further, since the controls for those settings are readily accessible, they can be adjusted easily to accommodate changes in hearing levels caused by the fluctuating conductive component. When there is no middle ear disease, the unit is set so that there is maximum low frequency roll-off in the right ear and less low frequency roll-off in the left.

Electroacoustic flexibility must be considered by professionals making decisions about an FM system. For example, even a child with essentially normal low frequency hearing can use an FM system. This low frequency gain can be specially modified by the manufacturer, decreasing the chance of overamplifying those frequencies.

The most obvious candidates for FM systems are children with sensorineural hearing losses. Figure 4 is the audiogram of an eleven-year-old girl with congenital middle ear abnormalities that caused the severe, flat, purely conductive hearing loss. Although surgical treatment is planned for her when she reaches age sixteen, she must use amplification until then.

Like the child with mild hearing loss (see figure 2), her good per-

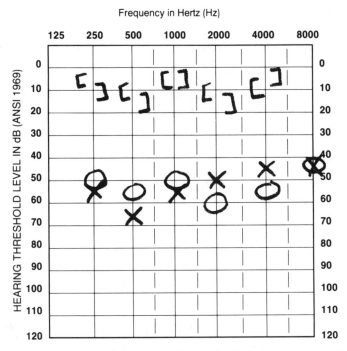

Figure 4. Unaided audiogram of an 11-year-old with structural conductive hearing loss. This child is a successful FM system user.

formance with ear level hearing aids made her family and teachers skeptical about her need for special classroom amplification. In order to demonstrate her candidacy, this student's audiologist recommended a monitored trial of an FM system in the first grade. The success of that trial resulted in the purchase and continued use through her present placement in fifth grade.

The children presented in these four cases are examples of the fact that every hearing-impaired child is a candidate for an FM system. No decision about need for and appropriateness of use should be made on the basis of the pure tone audiogram. It is the rare situation in which a child with hearing loss cannot benefit from the positive signal-to-noise ratio provided by an FM system.

The information presented in previous chapters discussed why an FM is needed, how it functions, what the electroacoustic features are, how they are set, etc. In order to select an appropriate FM system for a particular child, all of that information must be known, evaluated, and then integrated with the individual needs of the child and the demands of the educational setting.

SELECTION

There are two levels in the selection process. The first is to demonstrate a need for an FM system for a particular child and to establish candidacy. The second is to decide which specific make and model to purchase, the coupling method to use, and the electroacoustic settings that are necessary. The first level of decision making requires the input of a team.

Team

Demonstration of candidacy requires input from a variety of individuals. A typical team—an audiologist, school case manager (speech-language pathologist, educational audiologist, or teacher of the hearing impaired), parent(s), and child—is presented in table III.

The *audiologist*, whether clinic-based or school-based, is the professional who is most familiar with the child's hearing loss. Much of the information pertinent to FM system need is related to the type, degree, and configuration of the hearing loss, as well as speech reception and discrimination, and any possible tolerance problems. How much the child benefits from personal amplification and makes use of residual hearing should be well documented in the child's audiological records. The audiologist is best suited to explain to the team about the better signal-to-noise ratio afforded by an FM system versus personal hearing aids and why it is important to classroom listening. (The role of the audiologist in the selection of a specific FM configuration is presented later in this chapter.)

The school-based *case manager* is the team member who has the best access to and familiarity with the educational environment in which a particular child must function. The pertinent information includes the listening, communicative, and academic demands of the classroom. Although the child's speech, language, and academic abil-

Table III. The Team Members Involved in the Recommendation and Selection of an FM System

Team Member	Suggested Input
Audiologist	Hearing levels, tolerance levels, speech perception skills, personal amplification, earmolds, and recommendation of FM settings
Case Manager	Listening environment, teaching environment, and classroom demands
Parents	Possible areas of resistance and ways to increase acceptance
Child	Preferences about the unit and options

ities will be part of the child's school records, more performance-based information must be available to demonstrate the specific need for an FM system.

Classroom observation is the best way to document classroom demands and the child's difficulties in coping with them. Structuring an observation that directs attention to items presented in table IV will afford the case manager invaluable information.

The listening environment is particularly critical. Negative effects of noise and the need for determining ambient noise levels in the classroom were discussed in Chapter 2. Taking sound level meter measurements at different times during the school day, and in all classrooms in which the child must function, serves as good documentation of need. When noise levels are higher than desirable, it may be possible to reduce them by making physical modifications to the room. However, physical modifications that improve listening conditions should not be used in place of an FM system. An analysis of both internal and external noise sources is crucial. For example, a fish tank with an air pump can produce a low frequency hum that will increase ambient noise. Rooms that border on the gymnasium or playground or are on a much-used corridor may have a poor listening environment during high activity periods. Even classrooms that have relatively low ambient noise levels may produce listening conditions that are difficult for a child with hearing loss.

Problems may be related to the source of salient sound rather than background noise. For example, teaching style and flexibility of the classroom teacher may put the child in a less than optimal environment. If the teacher presents most of the academic information verbally with little visual support, an FM is crucial. The teacher's presentation style and movement around the room can change the signal-to-noise ratio, making an FM system critical.

The case manager must determine various input sources within each class. The amount of teacher-directed classroom interaction (e.g.,

Table IV. The Listening, Communicative, and Educational Demands of a Child's Classroom(s) that Should Be Evaluated

Condition	Information
Listening Environment	Noise levels, noise sources, speech sources, signal-to-noise ratios problems
Teaching Environment	Teaching style, teacher flexibility, use of A/V equipment, teacher-directed input problems
Classroom Demands	Need to depend on auditory input, amount of classroom discussion, level of language input, level of oral directions problems

large class discussions led by the teacher), student presentations, and use of audio-visual equipment are all important components of classroom communicative demands. The percentage of time that academic material is presented by the teacher, a videotape, an audiotape, or other sound source must be documented in order to demonstrate the need for an FM system and to plan for its appropriate use.

Finally, the case manager should determine a child's need to rely on auditory input to function in the classroom linguistic environment. The higher the level of language used in class, the more difficult communication is likely to be for the child with hearing loss. Any educational component that puts stress on the child can interfere with learning. Although an FM system cannot reduce all stress factors, and is not intended to overcome language-related problems, it can make listening easier. By making it easier for the child to receive linguistic information, some of the stress will be reduced and the child will be better prepared for learning.

In a class where there is reliance on audiotaped or videotaped presentations, the case manager will want to note the need for an auxiliary input to the FM transmitter. Also, it is important that the input sources (e.g., VCR) can accommodate direct coupling to the FM transmitter without interfering with output to other students.

When the child with hearing loss is in middle school, junior high, or high school, and typically interacts with a number of different teachers, observations must be made in all educational settings. The case manager must pay attention to special classes (art, music, physical education, etc.) as well as the basic academic classes.

Important information about potential acceptance problems can be provided by *parents*. They must understand the differing functions of special classroom amplification versus personal hearing aids. Informed parents are more likely to accept the unique benefit of an FM in the classroom for their child. They can then present their understanding to the child and, perhaps, ameliorate negative feelings the child may have. Parents can cope with concerns such as cosmetic issues more sensitively when they have a factual basis for supporting FM use.

Acceptance problems may be exacerbated when the *child* is not included in the decision making process. Like the parents, children should know why an FM is being recommended. Even young children can benefit from simple demonstrations of the purpose and ease of function. It is particularly important for older children to be a part of the team. Something as simple as soliciting an opinion about particular features of a unit can make children more knowledgeable and, in turn, more readily accepting of an FM system.

It is clearly important for a team—speech, language, and hearing professionals, the child, and family—to make the decision about the need for an FM system for a particular child. Unfortunately, such a con-figuration is atypical. In a national study conducted in 1981–82 and 1988–89, Maxon, Brackett, and van den Berg (1991) found that there was not consistent team involvement. Table V is a summary of a por-tion of the data they reported about the decision making process. It can be seen that in neither sample were speech, language, and hearing professionals always included. There was an increase in their inclusion over the decade, however; most recently, over twenty percent of the decisions to buy an FM system use information from professionals who were likely to be most knowledgeable about the needs of the child and the advantages an FM system could provide.

The potential for problems in use and acceptance is greatly in-creased by the fact that little child and family involvement was reported by professionals serving children with hearing loss in school settings. Slightly more than half the reports over the decade indicated that nei-ther the child nor parent was included in the process.

In another component of that same study professionals reported that parents appeared to be concerned about the cosmetic aspects of FM systems. Those concerns appeared related to a lack of knowledge

---

Table V.   Individuals Involved in the Selection and Purchase of FM Systems*

Sample 1981–82

Speech, language, hearing professionals participated in the decision to purchase an FM system 60.8% of the time.

Parents and children participated in the decision making process only 37% of the time.

Neither parent nor child was involved in 56% of the time.

The decision to select a particular make and model of FM unit was made primarily by:
consultation of special education personnel,
consultation with audiologists,
educators' previous experience, or
manufacturers' demonstration.

Sample 1988–89

Speech, language, hearing professionals participated in the decision to purchase an FM system 79% of the time.

Parents and children participated in the decision making process only 39% of the time.

Neither parent nor child was involved 56% of the time.

The decision to select a particular make and model of FM unit was made primarily by at least two of the following:
consultation with audiologists,
consultation with other schools, or
educators' previous experience.

*Maxon, Brackett, and van den Berg (1991).

about the purpose of the units and the benefits they provided (Maxon, Brackett, and van den Berg 1991). Observations made on the UConn Mainstream Project, showed that the more knowledgeable the families and children were about FM systems, the better the use and retention of the systems.

In summary, with good team input that has been carefully developed and documented there should be little problem in establishing need for an FM system.

Demonstrating Need for an FM System

Even when the team has carefully displayed evidence of a need, there may be administrators and other school personnel, including classroom teachers, who must be convinced that a particular child needs more than personal hearing aids, preferential seating, and physical modifications to survive and learn in the classroom. In those instances, it may be helpful for the team to conduct a demonstration of the benefits provided by a wireless FM system for that child.

Table VI is an adaptation of material presented in Ross, Brackett, and Maxon (1991). It demonstrates the primary purpose of classroom FM use: providing the child with a positive signal-to-noise ratio that remains consistent regardless of proximity of the listener to the sound source. Data should be collected in three conditions: distance, noise, and a combination of distance and noise. That a child receives the best possible reception and perception of the speech signal even when at a *distance* from the source can be demonstrated by measuring his or her speech perception at approximately 10 feet from the talker, first using personal hearing aids and then an FM system (Condition 1 in table VI). The difference (in percent of correct phonemes or words) between these two performance scores will demonstrate the FM advantage.

When there is *noise* in the background from internal or external sources, as well as reverberation, a child using only hearing aids will have a more difficult time discriminating among various speech sounds than when the environment is quiet. To demonstrate FM benefit in noisy listening conditions, a child's speech perception can be measured in a background of noise with hearing aids and then an FM system (Condition 2 in table VI).

The negative interaction effect of *distance and noise* can readily be shown by combining the two previous test conditions. Maintaining noise in the background and measuring speech perception at 10 feet from the talker shows the benefit of the FM system over hearing aids (Condition 3 in table VI). There is no question that the FM system will provide better listening with a higher score obtained than will hearing aids in any of these three conditions.

Table VI. Ways to Demonstrate the Need for an FM System (Adapted from Ross, Brackett, and Maxon 1991)

1. Demonstrate the improvement in receptive speech intelligibility or paragraph comprehension provided by an FM system over hearing aids when listening at a *distance* from the sound source.
2. Demonstrate the improvement in receptive speech intelligibility or paragraph comprehension provided by an FM system over hearing aids when listening in a background of *noise*.
3. Demonstrate the improvement in receptive speech intelligibility or paragraph comprehension provided by an FM system over hearing aids when listening at a *distance* from the sound source *and* when in a background of *noise*.
4. Compare the child's classroom performance/interaction when using an FM rather than hearing aids.
   a. Teacher's log before and during FM use.
   b. Child's log or report before and during FM use.
   c. Case manager's observations before and during FM use.
5. Demonstrate what speech sounds like when using an FM and hearing aids with the sound source at a *distance,* using a commercially available video- or audiotape.
6. Demonstrate what speech sounds like when using an FM and hearing aids in a background of *noise* using a commercially available video- or audiotape.
7. Demonstrate what speech sounds like when using an FM and hearing aids with the sound source at a *distance and noise* in the background using a commercially available video- or audiotape.

Speech material used for these demonstrations should be within the vocabulary of the child so that scores reflect speech perception errors with no influence of language. It is also beneficial to score responses on a phoneme correct basis. Using Boothroyd's isophonemic word lists (Boothroyd 1984) allows for this in-depth analysis of the effects of adverse listening conditions on different speech sounds and the relationship to the FM advantage.

To provide information that school personnel may readily generalize to classroom listening, short paragraph comprehension can be used. Replicating conditions 1–3 in table VI and using material such as is used for reading comprehension will provide the desired information. As long as the material is within the child's receptive language level, a purely auditory effect can be shown.

Classroom observation (Condition 4 in table VI) should be carried out when the child is using hearing aids. Difficult listening conditions should be carefully noted. When conducted by the case manager, the classroom teacher, and the child, and carried out over at least a two-week period, all possible problems in a variety of educational conditions should be observed. A second, parallel set of observations using an FM system for a trial period (at least one month) will yield comparable records. A comparison of the number and types of problems that arise during the two amplification conditions (hearing aid versus FM system) will demonstrate how an FM reduces the effects of difficult listening problems.

A quick method of demonstration is to use an *audio-* or *videotape* of speech recorded through a hearing aid and through an FM system in conditions of noise, distance, and a combination of the two. Such a videotape was previously described by Maxon (1990) and is commercially available (Communication Sciences, University of Connecticut). Although this demonstration is not specific to a given child, the impact made by listening in distance and noise, even with normal hearing, makes the demonstration quite powerful. It does not require an understanding of decibels, signal-to-noise ratios, reverberation time measures, or even speech discrimination measures. The tape is also valuable for inservice training of classroom teachers (Maxon 1990).

Specific FM Recommendations

Amplification requirements—including frequency response characteristics, output limits, gain requirements, and earmold modifications—all are essential pieces of information to consider when making decisions about the specific make, model, and coupling method of the FM. The initial decision relates to the type of system that is recommended, that is, traditional or alternative coupling.

In general, the greatest ease of fitting can be attained with traditional units. These units have enough electroacoustic flexibility so that they can be fitted to the mildest degrees of hearing loss as well as to asymmetrical losses. The use of ear-level microphones reduces the problems associated with chest-level environmental microphones. Young children do best with traditional units because complications in maintenance and troubleshooting found with alternative couplings are reduced. Specifications provided by the manufacturer can be used by the audiologist to select an appropriate make and model and to help in choosing settings.

In Chapter 3, Thibodeau describes the large number of system settings, couplings, and coupling settings that must be considered in order for a child with hearing loss to receive the greatest benefit from an FM system. That material clearly demonstrates how erroneous it is to assume that electroacoustic characteristics of hearing aids are maintained when any nontraditional coupling (direct audio input, induction loop, silhouette) is used (see Chapter 4).

Often electroacoustic settings of an FM system are determined by someone other than an audiologist. Maxon, Brackett, and van den Berg (1991) reported that this happens in up to 30% of cases nationally. This is particularly disconcerting when considering the errors in selection that can occur in setting various components of FM systems, particularly those with adaptive coupling.

It is obvious from information presented in Chapter 3 that great care must go into the selection of adaptive coupling. It is important that the team audiologist determines the exact model of boot, connector cord, or neckloop to accommodate the child's hearing aids and FM system. That information should be readily available from the hearing aid manufacturer. Some issues that must be taken into consideration in the selection process are presented in table VII.

Table VII.   Some Issues Audiologists Should Consider when Recommending Specific Makes and Models of FM Systems

Traditional unit	1.	Child's unit is sturdy.
	2.	Controls are accessible.
	3.	Easy to troubleshoot.
	4.	Easy to maintain.
	5.	Easy adjustment of electroacoustic characteristics.
	6.	Environmental signal is received at chest level.
	7.	Cords are a vulnerable component.
Traditional unit with ear-level mikes	1.	Environmental signal is received at ear level.
	2.	Other qualities of a traditional unit are maintained.
Neckloop coupling	1.	Environmental signal may be received at ear level.
	2.	No direct connection between child's unit and hearing aids.
	3.	Hearing aids must have a good quality telecoil.
	4.	An environmental microphone is needed if no M/T switch on hearing aids.
	5.	Output, gain, and frequency response of hearing aid's telecoil may be altered by the coupling (see Chapter 3).
	6.	FM to environmental microphone ratio may be altered by the coupling.
	7.	Troubleshooting is difficult. Must maintain hearing aid close to neckloop.
	8.	Hearing aid breakdown affects classroom amplification.
Direct Audio Input	1.	Environmental signal is received at ear level.
	2.	Hearing aids must allow for this coupling of boot/shoe, or direct cord input.
	3.	Boot/shoe must be appropriate for FM unit and hearing aids (see Chapter 3).
	4.	Connecting cord must be appropriate for hearing aid and boot/shoe (see Chapter 3).
	5.	Output, gain, and frequency response of hearing aids may be altered by the coupling (see Chapter 3).
	6.	FM to environmental microphone ratio may be altered by the coupling.
	7.	Troubleshooting is difficult. Two people are necessary to determine if FM transmitter is functioning.
	8.	Hearing aid breakdown affects classroom amplification.

In order to be sure that the chosen FM arrangement is providing appropriate electroacoustic characteristics, all components must be measured and set as a unit (see Chapter 4). For example, LeMay (1991) demonstrated that setting the boot level and FM ratio controls independently of each other greatly affects output. He found that output saturation was reached earlier than anticipated when those settings were not exactly right. Saturation at low input levels compromises the FM advantage.

Once specific settings that will accommodate a particular child and, in the case of adaptive coupling, allow for the best interface with hearing aids, have been determined by the audiologist, clinical assessment of the system should be conducted. Specific techniques that should be used are described in Chapter 4. This evaluation is the final stage of FM selection.

After an appropriate FM system has been selected, purchased, and set for the child, validation of the fitting must be conducted. This initial validation should occur within two weeks of the fitting.

Table VIII displays four basic components of the validation: clinical assessment, classroom observation, an objective evaluation of the child's performance, and the child's subjective evaluation. Appropriate electroacoustic measures were presented in Chapter 3. In addition, probe microphone, aided warble tone, and speech discrimination measures will demonstrate benefits provided by the FM system. Considering all of the potential difficulties in selecting and maintaining the appropriate settings, this type of evaluation should be a routine part of the child's clinical and audiological management. As recently as the late 1980s, however, only 48% of speech, language, and hearing professionals sampled indicated that the children with whom they worked brought their FM systems to their regular clinical audiological evaluations for an objective and subjective evaluation (Maxon, Brackett, and van den Berg 1991).

Classroom observation can follow the same plan as that originally developed by the team to show need for an FM system. Performance

Table VIII. Validating the FM Fitting

Component	Information Acquired
Clinical	Functional gain (environmental microphones, transmitter), real ear measures, receptive speech intelligibility.
Classroom Observation	Resolution of problems, better performance, ability to interact, appropriate use, inappropriate use.
Performance Assessment	Receptive speech intelligibility (distance, noise, interaction), receptive comprehension of connected discourse (distance, noise, interaction).
Child Report	Subjective indication of performance, use, problems.

assessment should follow the protocol presented in table VI, items 1–3. A particularly important component is the child's evaluation of the system. Any problems the child reports should be handled immediately. Validation is important initially and should be an integral component of the child's ongoing auditory management program.

CLASSROOM USE

If the FM system is not used properly in the classroom, it will not be successful.

Environmental Microphones

The primary purpose of an FM system is to improve the signal-to-noise ratio, but this should not be accomplished at the expense of all environmental sounds. Environmental microphones are the child's only access to any sound not reaching the transmitter. To hear his or her own voice for self-monitoring of speech and language, the child must be using environmental microphones. The only avenue for receiving questions, responses, and speech or language models of other children in the class (at a reasonable intensity level) is through environmental microphones. Announcements via a Public Address system or alarms, for example, are best accessed through these microphones.

Only rarely should environmental microphones be turned off. It would be inappropriate to turn them off even when working individually with a child. One obvious exception to this principle is in industrial arts class, when noise levels are high and there is little or no interaction between children. If dangers arise there, the teacher can warn the child through the transmitter.

Transmitter/Microphone

The transmitter should be functioning only when information it is receiving is to be heard by the child using the system. When the teacher is the primary sound source in a large group, the microphone/transmitter must be used. Common teaching situations will require flexibility in microphone technique in order to ensure that the child has access to all information. For example, if a question is asked and other students respond, the teacher should repeat the responses so that the child using the FM will hear them. During a large group lesson when students are providing a great deal of information, the teacher must decide if it is feasible to pass the microphone/transmitter to individual speakers in order to allow the child with the FM system equal access to spoken material. When that is not possible, the teacher can repeat the pertinent information. Another technique for a large group discussion is to call on the speakers by name; in this way the child with the FM system can direct attention to the speaker and be better able to follow the material.

Good use of the FM microphone/transmitter also includes the ability to incorporate other sound sources. Small group discussions readily lend themselves to passing the microphone/transmitter. For example, each reader in a reading group should use the microphone/transmitter, allowing all children to hear everything that is said. The child using the FM can then be held accountable for maintaining his or her correct place in the book. This will reduce uncertainty if the child is having difficulty: knowing that he or she can hear the material helps the teacher determine that an incorrect answer is the result of unfamiliarity with the information.

Other examples of situations in which someone other than the teacher should be using the microphone are: (1) an individual child giving an oral report, (2) an individual child presenting during "show and tell," (3) a guest speaker in class or an assembly, and (4) class trips narrated by someone such as a museum guide.

When the sound source is an audio-visual device such as a television, or audiotape deck, the microphone/transmitter should be directly coupled to the device. Typically, a hard wire connection from the audio-visual device to the auxiliary input of the FM microphone/transmitter is used. Such a coupling will override the microphone capabilities of the transmitter and deliver only the signal carried by the cord. If the teacher wishes to comment during the time the auxiliary input is being used, he or she merely has to switch back to "microphone" to do so.

The microphone/transmitter should not be functioning when it is inappropriate for the child using the system to hear what the teacher is saying. Specific examples of this are: (1) the teacher speaking privately to another adult or child, (2) the teacher talking to a group of students that does not include the child with the FM system, and (3) the teacher engaging in an activity other than teaching (at lunch, restroom, teacher's lounge).

A summary of these principles for classroom use is shown in table IX. As with any set of rules, there are exceptions, situations that are less than clear cut. It is important to use an FM microphone/transmitter during physical education classes that meet in a gymnasium. The physical construction of the room creates reverberations that increase noise levels, causing the child who is relying on hearing aids to have a great deal of difficulty hearing directions. However, using the FM system may interfere with certain physical activities, such as gymnastics.

Table IX.   Principles for FM Use in the Classroom

Principle: Improve the signal-to-noise ratio (S/N), but not at the expense of access
            to all environmental sound.
   Environmental microphones
     —Child's only access to his/her own voice.
     —Child's only access to other children's voices.
     —Child's only access to environmental sounds.

Principle: The transmitter should be functioning when the speaker is directing his
            or her voice to the child.
   Transmitter
     —Teacher is primary sound source for the child.
     —Teacher repeats what other children say.
     —Teacher passes the transmitter to other speakers.
     —Child giving a report uses the transmitter.
     —A speaker at an assembly uses the transmitter.
     —Guide on a class trip uses the transmitter.

Principle: The transmitter should be deactivated when the teacher is directing his
            or her voice to someone other than the child.
   Transmitter
     —Teacher is talking to another adult.
     —Teacher is engaged in a non-teaching activity.
     —Teacher is talking to a group of children in which child using FM is not
     a part.

Principle: The transmitter should be coupled to an electronic sound source.
   Transmitter
     —Child's access to audio track of television.
     —Child's access to audio- and videotape decks.

The child using the FM may also "cue in" to direction intended for others. For example, if the child with hearing loss is on third base in a baseball game and the PE teacher is yelling "go, go" to a child on first, the third base runner may think that those directions are being yelled to him or her and start running to home plate and be tagged out.

There are daily school-related situations in which an FM system cannot overcome listening problems. For example, when the child leaves the classroom and goes to lunch or recess, the benefit typically afforded by the FM system is greatly reduced. Although physical characteristics of the cafeteria make for extremely bad listening conditions, there are a number of speakers with whom the child will interact making remote microphone use impossible. In this particular situation the child must learn to cope in whatever manner best suits him or her because there is no practical way to decrease the ambient noise. A situation in which the use of the FM microphone/transmitter is, at best, difficult, occurs when the child relies on an interpreter (signed, cued, oral). If the child hears the teacher through the microphone but watches the interpreter in order to receive a portion of the speech signal, the spoken message will be heard before the visual representation (sign, hand signal and lip movement, lip movement) is seen. In this situation, it becomes extremely difficult for the child to integrate auditory and visual messages.

Principles of classroom FM use must be carefully considered when working with the child with hearing loss in preschool or kindergarten. The amount of time when the teacher is the primary sound source is generally quite low for these grades, yet noise levels are likely to be high, making it difficult for the child to receive speech information through personal hearing aids alone. Only through careful planning can an FM system be well integrated.

Inservice Training

There is a great deal to know about FM systems and how they can best be used, and thus a significant need for inservice training. Obviously the principles of classroom use will be an important part of any inservice program. Further, the case manager and teacher(s) should have information specific to a particular child's FM readily available.

Table X outlines the information with which direct service personnel should be familiar. That information should be maintained in the child's file and on an index card in the case manager's office for quick reference. It can be used to determine: (1) if the FM system is set correctly, (2) if the FM system is functioning according to specifications, (3) how to troubleshoot the equipment, (4) whom to contact in case of any problems, (5) how to remediate any problems, and (6) how to charge the system.

Table X.   Information About the Child's FM System that School Personnel Should Have Available

The Unit:	Settings (kept on a file card)
	Directions for charging (kept with unit)
	Directions for use (kept with unit, in child's classroom)
	Supplies (extra cords, etc.)
Troubleshooting:	Designated individual (knows complete troubleshooting protocol)
	Simple checking
	Simple parts replacement
	Where it is done
	Access to equipment for troubleshooting/checking
Problems:	Who to contact (varies by specific professional)
	How to make simple repairs
	How to send out for repair (designated individual)
Use:	The four principles of appropriate FM use (see table IX)
	Incorporate the use into regular classroom routine
	Change transmitter (frequency) when appropriate

FM systems can provide great benefit to the child with hearing loss. The speech signal can be readily accessed, even in difficult listening conditions. Although there is this potential to provide a quality auditory signal there is also the potential for problems. The latter will occur when care is not given to the determination of need, selection, setting, and daily use. Professionals involved in recommending, validating, and monitoring the function of an FM system carry a great responsibility.

REFERENCES

Boothroyd, A. 1984. Auditory perception of speech contrasts by subjects with sensorineural hearing loss. *Journal of Speech and Hearing Research* 2:134–44.

LeMay, M. 1991. The effects of coupling devices on FM system electroacoustic characteristics. Unpublished Masters thesis. University of Connecticut: Storrs, CT.

Maxon, A. B. 1990. Implementing an inservice training program. In *Hearing-Impaired Children in the Mainstream*, ed. M. Ross. Parkton, MD: York Press.

Maxon, A. B., Brackett, D., and van den Berg, S. A. 1991. Classroom amplification use: A national longterm study. *Language, Speech and Hearing Services in the Schools*.

Ross, M., Brackett, D., and Maxon, A. B. 1991. *Assessment and Management of Hearing-Impaired Children: Principles and Practices*, Austin, TX: Pro-Ed.

Chapter • 6

Troubleshooting FM Systems

Chris Hawrylak Evans

The full benefits of an FM system cannot be realized unless the entire system functions properly, from the microphone input to the acoustic output into the ear. This requires that troubleshooting procedures be conducted using the coupling mode employed by the child. Different coupling modes add their own variations and potential problems. All modes have to be considered to ensure that the child receives appropriately amplified signals from both the environmental microphone and the FM microphone. Components are pictured in Chapter 3, and selection and use considerations are discussed in Chapter 5. Because "real-life" troubleshooting procedures are not conducted in a vacuum, the information in this chapter overlaps all of these others in some respects. The focus, however, is on maintenance and operation of the entire FM system, from the time of purchase to classroom utilization.

This chapter is written with the orientation that the child, as the user, must be involved in maintenance of the equipment by kindergarten age. Try to recall your feelings as a child when mother "spiffed you up" for a picture or holiday occasion. You may have felt a lack of control. Hearing-impaired children have to endure this every day as we invade them with straps, cords, and switches, to be "spiffed up" for the day and ready to receive a better acoustic signal. Just as the ribbon Mom placed may have come untied before that special occasion, the cords, switches, and signal may not remain working throughout the day. FM equipment is not programmed to malfunction at the beginning of the school day. This emphasizes the importance of the child's ability to alert the teacher anytime there is a problem. This chapter is written to make the process of troubleshooting a logical, step-by-step procedure.

Too often, an audiologist, who must recommend personal amplification, has only basic knowledge of the FM apparatus. Access to auditory systems for instruction is the responsibility of the school system and is often removed from the clinical facility recommending personal amplification. Coordination between school and clinical facility is critical. If hearing aid coupling to an FM system is being considered for a child, the audiologist must make specific recommendations for cords and boots by part number to assure proper coupling. Greater complexity within new FM instrumentation requires electroacoustic analysis of the entire system (see Chapter 3). The same hearing aid coupled to two different FM systems may have very different harmonic distortion measurements. The audiologist should obtain electroacoustic measurements with the same FM instrument used in the educational program. This information will help the teacher to understand the student's capacity to receive instruction, to self-monitor, and to access classmates and the environment in general.

TIPS FOR GETTING STARTED

Purchase

If you are responsible for purchasing FM equipment, start by contacting companies listed in speech and audiology trade journals. Personal contact from the manufacturer should follow, setting an appointment date to meet the sales representative. Ask the sales representative to send equipment manuals for your review. Also request a list of customers in your area who use the specific equipment under consideration for purchase. Your sales representative is as important as the service you will need after the purchase is made. You will want a person who is willing to offer guidance in a friendly manner and will continue to educate you and your staff. Look for clear explanations of equipment and instructions for troubleshooting the various coupling arrangements in the manuals you receive. Reputable companies offer a toll-free telephone number for your convenience. Call that number in advance of any purchase to acquaint yourself with the people most accessible to you if a purchase is made. Your contact person should know all the equipment and the parts by number and cost. Your equipment is only as valuable as the service offered by the company manufacturing it.

After the equipment has been selected, review the manuals in depth with your sales representative and the audiologist with whom you will be working. Invite the sales representative to join you when the instrumentation is first introduced to the students(s). This will assist you later if there are problems with a specific student's arrangement because your representative is aware of the FM coupling used in your program. Have the sales representative contact the audiologist who will provide on-going evaluations of equipment settings. Technology changes every year. A good company representative will alert you and the audiologist to changes coming, not only from their company but industry-wide.

Record-Keeping

Begin a student file card (figure 1) and a classroom chart (figure 2) immediately, with the assistance of the representative. A student card should indicate: child's name, hearing aid manufacturer and model, ear(s) amplified, volume settings for each volume control (e.g., hearing aid volume, FM receiver volume, FM microphone volume), and part

---

name _____ hearing aid: brand _____ model: _____
serial# R _____ L _____ battery # _____
*internal settings R _____ L _____
hearing aid volume R _____ L _____
*if the settings are different, mark one aid with tape or a sticker so it is fit to the correct ear
FM coupling—check one
_____ transducer _____ neckloop _____ DAI _____ silhouette
receiver # _____ model _____ crystal(RO) _____
FM volume settings: FM / Teacher _____ Environmental / Self _____
Internal trimmer settings: ___ SSPL; ___ Tone; ___ FM; ___ balance
other:
Coupling parts
Transducer # _____ cost _____ purchase from _____
Neckloop Loop # _____ cost _____ purchase from _____
       Connecting Cord # _____ cost _____ purchase from _____
DAI: Boot # _____ cost _____ purchase from _____
     Cord # _____ cost _____ purchase from _____
     other: _____

Figure 1. The student file card can be made on index cards. The back of the card can be used to keep track of repairs, dates that earmolds were made, etc.

Name	Hearing Aid Volume R	L	Receiver Volume FM R	L	Environmental mic R	L	Coupling Mode	Accessories
D.B.	2½	----	3	off	off	off	DAI	AT388 cord A 4 boot
K.C.	----	----	6	6	5	5	BTE mics	
J.R.	6	6	4	4	3	3	Silhouettes	AT385 cord
L.A.	3	3	5	5	off	off	DAI	AT388 cord Unitron boot
C.J.	----	----	7	7	5	5	Button Transducer	
R.H.	3½	2½	4	4	off	off	DAI	DT30 cord AP302 boot

Figure 2. The information on the classroom chart may be dictated by the way FM is used in your program. If all students are on transducer buttons, the volume control and coupling modes would not need to be part of your chart. If, however, you are using a variety of coupling arrangements, including different FM receivers, it may be necessary to expand the chart to include the receiver number. Most coupling-to-hearing aids will be with receivers that have only one volume control for the FM signal. If there is an additional volume control, it is most likely for the environmental microphone on the FM receiver.

numbers of accessories such as boots, cords, silhouette style, and neckloop. If students are using direct audio input and have different hearing aid models from a variety of manufacturers, expect that they will also need different boots (audio shoes) and cords. You may need a more extensive address file than you ever imagined. Cords, boots, etc., for each hearing aid may need to be ordered from the hearing aid manufacturer rather than the FM manufacturer. Invite the audiologist to assist in recording the data on your original file card and create a duplicate file card for the audiologist. You will want to share responsibility with the audiologist and sales representative for securing the proper cords.

On the back of your card you can indicate the dates that parts were issued. This will assist in predicting the consumption rate and your budget needs. You also may want to indicate dates that earmolds were made and FM receivers were sent for repair. Most educational programs assume responsibility for a specific number of earmolds, e.g., two per year for each ear during the preschool primary years and one per year for each ear during the secondary years. Any additional earmolds are the responsibility of the family. Batteries are always the responsibility of the family.

The student file card can be made on half sheets of paper, large note cards, or the information can be put into a computer database. For programs serving hundreds of students it is important that it be accessible to a variety of personnel quickly.

It is important to make sure that substitute teachers and other staff people have access to specific amplification information for each child. Efforts to make the student file card or classroom chart accessible will help everyone know each student's requirements and will remind students that they have different arrangements because they have different needs.

Storage

Identification and storage of equipment parts and accessories can become confusing. Maintenance issues are different for programs serving one or two hearing-impaired students than for a classroom with eight to twelve students. Keeping a utility box in classrooms serving several students is an effective way of managing personal batteries, spare cords, etc. (figure 3). For older students or programs serving one or two students, use of the popular waist pouch (figure 4) gives the students primary responsibility for managing their own spare batteries, cords, and so forth. Programs serving hundreds of hearing-impaired students need storage on a much larger scale: cords can be

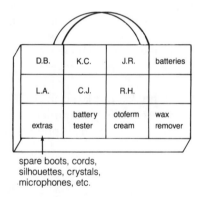

D.B.	K.C.	J.R.	batteries
L.A.	C.J.	R.H.	
extras	battery tester	otoferm cream	wax remover

spare boots, cords,
silhouettes, crystals,
microphones, etc.

Start-up accessories you will need (see Appendix B) include:
Stenoclip for listening
Dedicated listening cord and transducer
Spare batteries for FM and hearing aids
Spare charger for 9V batteries
Jeweler's screwdriver
Spare crystal (RO)
Spare auxiliary microphone
Spare cords
Tone hooks for hearing aids or BTE microphone/transducer
Troubleshooting forms (figure 7)

Wax remover
Earmold cream
Hand bulb blower
Spare tubing
Tubing threader
Battery tester

Figure 3.   A utility box can accommodate most of your accessories. You can often find plastic hooks that mount on the side of the box to hold the stenoclip. An envelope can be mounted on the other side of the utility box to hold the troubleshooting forms seen in figure 7.

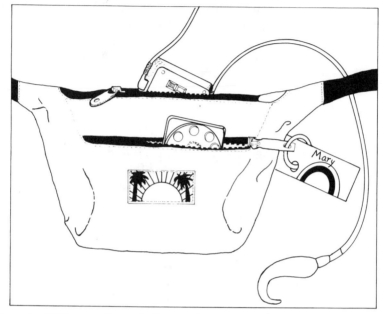

Figure 4. Waist pouches, which come in a variety of colors, can make a personal statement about the student. Students can learn to be responsible for spare batteries and cords as they can manage all needs from their seats, rather than having to move through the room to retrieve whatever they need from the utility box.

hung on peg boards with hooks, or placed in plastic bins with clearly marked labels indicating the coupling components. Plastic bins are also useful for storage of spare receivers, microphones, headphones, and so forth.

TROUBLESHOOTING FUNDAMENTALS

Microphones

You should have a spare lapel microphone if you are using a transmitter that accepts auxiliary microphones. If you are not sure what kind of microphone you have currently, refer to figure 5 and also Chapter 3. If budget constraints will not allow a spare, then try to have your transmitter retrofitted to include an internal microphone that will transmit with the addition of an antenna tail, and without the lapel microphone. The cost of a retrofit is approximately fifty dollars. Order new transmitters that have an internal microphone. The antenna/connecting cord from the microphone to the transmitter can break with every-

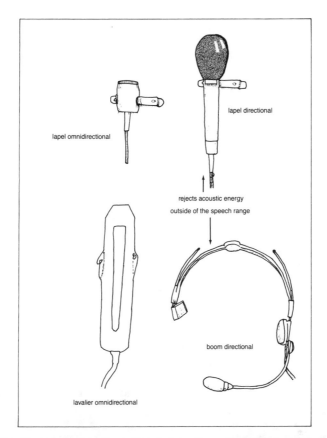

Figure 5. Transmitters and auxiliary microphones have changed through the years. The addition of a directional microphone has allowed an improved signal-to-noise ratio because the microphones tend to reject information outside of the speech range and only transmit information coming directly into the microphone port.

day use. Internal microphones are most often mounted on the top of the transmitter and will require the transmitter to be worn at the neck, lavalier style.

Any time your students start receiving static, noise, or radio stations in the middle of the day, be suspicious that your FM transmission is faulty. There could be a break in your antenna/connecting microphone cord. Remove the microphone from the transmitter. If you have an internal transmitter microphone, the students will be back on the air and you can teach the rest of that day and as many days as necessary while the original lapel microphone is repaired or replaced. If you have a spare label microphone, replace the defective part and continue teaching. If this fails, the problem may be with the FM transmission. If you have a spare transmitter and sufficient crystals (ROs) to match the new frequency, change frequencies and continue teaching.

Batteries and Chargers

If your FM equipment uses 9V batteries, keep spare batteries in your utility box. Most often the batteries in use are rechargeable. It is possible to obtain a charger for rechargeable 9V batteries separate from your group FM charging apparatus designed for the receivers and transmitter. Rotate two to four spare batteries in your auxiliary charger. If your equipment uses a 2.7V enclosed battery pack, charge extra batteries in your charger during the day while you are teaching. If the FM circuitry starts to consume excessive battery power, you will be prepared with spares. Note that rechargeable 9V batteries will provide five to eight hours of operating time, depending on the quality of the batteries. Enclosed 2.7V battery packs will give you eighteen to twenty teaching hours between charges. If the units are recharged before the battery charge is gone (for example, if they are returned to their chargers during physical education and lunch), you may be giving your batteries a "memory" for the number of hours they will remain charged before they need to be charged again. This most likely will be under five hours. A real problem could occur during an all-day field trip, because your batteries may only remember to hold a charge for three to four hour-use cycles. If you are using the FM receivers all day on a field trip, you may need to charge additional batteries in advance and have students place them in their pouches for emergency use. If your batteries have developed a four hour "memory," for instance, you need to keep the units on until all the battery power is consumed. Recharge the batteries in the receivers overnight. Do not return the receivers to the charger until the end of your teaching day. New rechargeable batteries or batteries that have not been charged for some time may need a 48 hour charge before you can expect to get a full day's use. The 2.7V enclosed battery packs have less of a "memory" problem because they have more capacity. Check with the manufacturer for specific recommendations on charging during the day, when the units are not in use.

Always write the date of purchase on your batteries. This will alert you to their age. Old batteries are susceptible to charging problems and reduced battery energy. Disposable alkaline batteries may not be cost effective for everyday use. They do, however, have twice the use life of the rechargables. If you are going on a weekend trip, you may find it convenient to leave your chargers at home and instead use the alkaline disposable batteries.

Do not trust lights located on the charger to tell you the battery is charged. The original purpose of the lights was merely to let the user know that the battery was no longer accepting a charge. A green light, for instance, may provide false security that the battery is charged. As batteries age, their ability to accept a charge is reduced. If the FM is used through the day, the batteries may, in fact, need to be replaced in two- to three-year cycles. The battery may be the least expensive and most important part of your FM equipment. The power source it provides is often the cause of FM equipment failure, so check the battery first when equipment is not working properly.

Charging the receiver should be the student's responsibility at the end of a day. Charge all units in the same charging position routinely. This will assist in determining if your charger could possibly have a bad charging pocket. If the batteries are consistently not charged when you place them in a specific pocket, try charging your unit (transmitter or receiver) in a different charging pocket. If this solves your problem, the breakdown is in the charger. If your batteries remain uncharged, place them in a spare unit and charge them a full day in their usual pocket. If they accept a charge, then your FM unit (receiver or transmitter) is not allowing the recharging cycle to occur. Send your unit for repair. If you have no spare units or effective way to charge spare batteries try charging a new set of batteries.

Volume Controls

Listen to the student receivers on a daily basis. A personal earmold will not allow you to explore an adequate volume range if you have normal hearing. A stenoset will permit you to listen at a higher volume setting, enabling you to determine if the volume control emits static or has a "flat spot" resulting in a reduced signal to the student at one place in the volume rotation. The "flat spot" is often located at the volume setting used most of the time. It is a result of dirt and debris that are deposited at a specific place in the volume wheel rotation.

Originally the receiver volume controls offered no balance between the environmental signal received through the environmental microphone(s) on the receiver and the FM signal sent from the teacher transmitter. As receivers were upgraded, manufacturers began to offer an option of balancing the signals; this was managed by a discrete trimmer, usually set by the sales representative, or by a switch hidden in a control panel. Some of the newer equipment may have separate volume controls for the FM signal and the environmental receiver microphone. The most recent practice allows the audiologist or user to choose the signal-to-noise or message-to-competition ratio desired, with a discrete trimmer screw with stops for specific settings located behind the receiver control door. This assures that any volume rotation maintains the ratio between the teacher's voice (FM input) and the environmental microphone input of the receiver. With most receivers there are two volume controls—one for the FM signal, and another for the receiver microphone to regulate the environmental signals. The user adjusts each until the signal-to-noise ratio sounds appropriate. This may be difficult to determine for young children. You will need to check with your sales representative on how to adjust these volume controls. This is important for checking the equipment properly; you may think you are listening to your voice transmitted from the transmitter, but in reality you may be listening to yourself via the environmental microphone(s) of the receiver. It will be confusing at first if there is a volume control on each side of the receiver, with one side controlling both ears for the FM and the other side controlling both ears for the environmental microphone (figure 6). It may be wise to mark the FM side with a sticker or colored electrical tape, so you and the student can know quickly which volume wheel controls the loudness of your voice or the loudness of any other signal (e.g., tape player) you choose to send via the FM transmitter. The original personal FM receivers had only one volume control at the receiver for S/N, because the hearing aid volume control was supposed to adjust the environmental acoustic information, such as one's own voice or other students' voices. The assumption was that a positive S/N would result with the loudness of the teacher's voice independent of the hearing and volume setting. This is not true with most hearing aids.

Switches

Study the placement of the switches on your equipment before beginning to troubleshoot. You can waste time changing batteries and microphones, only to discover the switch was on environmental microphone rather than FM. Also you may overlook a real problem with the FM transmission because the environmental microphone is on, resulting in hearing your own voice via the receiver's environmental microphone rather than via FM transmission. These problems are more easily identified when the transmitter is placed near a music source for the initial checking of FM transmission to the receiver. Listen to the student receiver in the environmental mode only, as well as the FM mode only. If the student is actively using the receiver as a personal hearing aid but is not actively using the FM circuitry to receive instruction over distance, it will be important to deactivate the FM reception at the receiver with the switch. Turning the transmitter off is not a solution when the student should not be hearing the teacher. If the transmitter is turned off, the crystal (RO) in the receiver will continue to search for an FM signal thereby causing static noise or reception of an unwanted signal

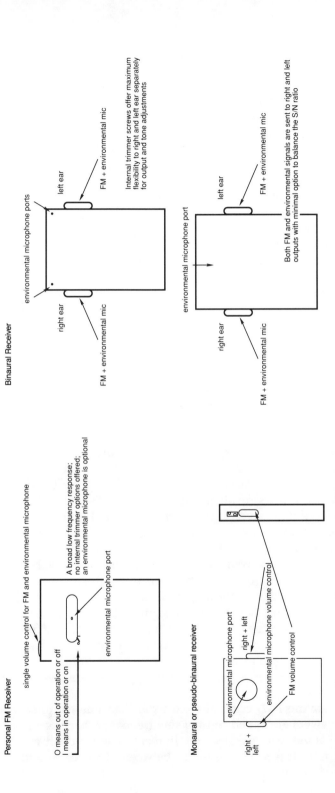

Figure 6. Receivers may come in similar sizes, but you cannot depend on the case or color alone to know which receiver offers what options. Receivers with one volume control have no trimmer screws to modify the frequency, tone, or output. Locate the microphone on the receivers you are using, especially if they are active with telecoil coupling or transducer buttons. Your harnesses, desks, and clothing should not contribute to any unwanted sound being transmitted to the ear. Receiver microphones at the waist should always be turned off.

near the frequency of the crystal. FM reception should be turned "off" at the receiver to avoid this interference.

Cords

Cords that look the same may not be the same. Cords that are used for direct audio input have different resistance ratings. Some even attenuate the hearing aid microphone. Storing and labeling cords is important whether you have one student or 100 students using FM coupling to the hearing aid. If the FM reception does not sound good at the hearing aid, the cord may not be appropriate. Colored electrical tape on the cord with the part number inscribed may provide you with a quick reference check. This also will identify any replacement cords as they are needed.

The Environmental Medium

Little attention is given to the environment where you plan to use your FM until the system arrives and there are problems with FM reception. The environment includes the room, the building, and the location within the city. If there is one position in the room where the FM consistently "cuts out" with intermittent or no FM reception, evaluate the construction in the room. You may find that there are areas of concentrated metal within your room, such as heating units, file cabinets, and air conditioning ducts. This may be worse in a room directly under the roof. Once the problem areas are identified and the "dead spots" determined, you can avoid these areas when teaching with FM technology. If there is an unusual amount of construction, a business complex, or a hospital nearby that has numerous paging and cellular phones in operation, the interference will be frequency specific. In this case it will be advantageous to use a transmitter that can transmit multiple frequencies. It will be wise to keep track of the frequencies in use in your school. If two transmitters are used on the same frequency, they "beat against each other," cancelling each other out. This can also happen with adjacent frequencies if the transmitters are only slightly off frequency.

FM Compatibility

You may be integrating FM receivers from more than one manufacturer. If both receivers are tuned to the same frequency, logic would dictate that they would work side by side. In reality that is not always true. Chapter 1 introduced the difference between broad band and narrow band transmission. It is clear that narrow band is more limiting and therefore a better choice for rejecting adjacent FM frequencies.

Some of the newer FM technology, using narrow band frequency transmission, limits reception of the transmitted signal to narrow band crystals that are compatible with the FM circuitry specific to that receiver. This will make it important for you to check the crystal in the receiver closely for potential incompatibility when mixing existing equipment with new equipment. Accept all new equipment only after trial in your program before a purchase is made.

Logical Progression for Troubleshooting

The following is the logical order for proceeding with troubleshooting. It is best to begin with items 1 and 2 before students arrive at school in order to maximize your teaching time.

1. The receiver should have a good sound quality in the environmental microphone position.
2. The transmitter should be transmitting the desired signal to each receiver.
3. The hearing aids should have a good sound quality on "M." This should be checked even if the student is not wearing a hearing aid coupled to the FM receiver.
4. The student should be receiving a quality FM signal and a quality environmental signal with the recommended coupling arrangement.

Table I shows a one page overview of FM troubleshooting. Figure 7 shows a troubleshooting form that can be completed each time a problem cannot be solved. This form should be attached to any equipment sent out for repair. The company can recommend additional problems to look for. Table II lists thirteen points for troubleshooting the transmitter and receiver.

CHECKING COUPLING MODES

Traditional Coupling

The round transducer button receiver was the way of delivering an amplified signal via an earmold to the ear. Transducers are made in different sizes. They also are designed to modify the frequency response from the receiver. Before internal FM tone settings were an option, the transducer played a primary role in modification of the signal to the ear. The smaller transducers generally have slightly reduced power and frequency range. They are very often the best choice for tiny ears because they are lighter in weight, creating less strain on an earmold that does not want to stay inserted into an ear. Also, larger transducers

Table I. How FM Works

Signal is transmitted (The transmitter and auxiliary microphone)	→ through a medium (The specific room and building as well as location within the city)	→ to a receiver (The student receiver and coupling paraphernalia)
What can go wrong!	*Symptoms! (at the receiver)*	*Solutions!*
Signal is transmitted		
batteries	dead; reduced, transmitting time	try a new battery
electronic failure	dead; intermittent	requires factory repair
frequency drift (FM failure)	distortion; intermittent; no transmission	try several crystals; may need factory adjustment
accessories—antenna / auxiliary / microphone	intermittent; dead; noise	try a new auxiliary microphone
through a medium		
radio frequency interference	intermittent; distortion; stray voices, beeping / paging systems; radio stations	check for transmitters on the same or adjacent frequencies; try contacting the interfering parties; move to different place in the room and recheck
electromagnetic interference	distortion; buzzing	
to a receiver		
batteries	dead; reduced receiving hours	try a new battery
electronic failure	dead	requires factory repair
FM failure (internal or bad crystal)	distortion; music; another teacher	try another crystal; may need factory adjustment
accessories—cords / neck loops / silhouettes / boots / transducers / hearing aids / BTE microphones	intermittent; dead; distorted	try replacement accessories—*one at a time*

earhooks	feedback	Hold your finger over the earmold canal opening, *if feedback continues*, look for a hole in the tubing of the earmold or a loose tone hook; *if feedback stops*, the earmold is too small or the ear canal has wax blocking the amplified sound; *if there is no sound*, check the earmold canal for wax or water
earmolds	no sound; feedback	*If feedback is not solved* with tubing, remove the earhook from the hearing aid and place your finger over the exposed nozzle; *if feedback stops*, replace the earhook *If feedback does not stop*, replace the BTE microphone/transducer or send the hearing aid for repair

```
TROUBLESHOOTING FORM
Date _____ Student _____ Teacher/Tester _____
ITEM (circle one)   FM receiver   hearing aid   charger   transmitter
DESCRIPTION OF PROBLEM _____
_____

TROUBLESHOOTING TRIED   _____ changed battery
                        _____ changed crystal
                        _____ listened to receiver without aid
                              (only listening cord)
                        _____ changed FM cord
                        _____ changed boot/silhouette
                        _____ changed neck loop
Model # _____ Serial # _____
```

Figure 7.   Attach this form to equipment being sent out for repair. This will assist the engineer in knowing how you tried to troubleshoot the equipment. A good sales representative will communicate with the engineers to give you any additional tips you may need that will make your troubleshooting more effective.

interfere more with the tragus and antitragus of the ear, causing irritation.

Coupling to the Hearing Aid

Troubleshooting the FM coupled to a personal hearing aid involves additional listening situations. Review the information in table III that discusses checking receiver transmission to the ear. These steps will require some modifications when a hearing aid is added to the system. You will have completed troubleshooting the FM receiver before students arrive. Now you will need to check the hearing aid and FM reception at the hearing aid. You will need a stenoclip that will accept the earmold to assure that you are listening to the entire system.

Complete the Ling Five Sound Test (see Appendix C) with only the hearing aid on the student's ear. Stand directly in front of the student and request that he or she close both eyes. Check each ear separately. If the student is not performing up to expectations with the hearing aid alone, then troubleshooting of the hearing aid will need to be done. If hearing aid and earmold are in good working condition, then a referral should be made to an audiologist for evaluation of the hearing thresholds and middle ear status. If the student's ability to perform on the Ling Five Sound Test is within expectations, then you will need to make sure the FM signal is arriving at the earmold tip with good sound quality.

Table II.   Troubleshooting Specifics

CHECKING **TANSMITTER ━━━━▶ RECEIVER**

CHECKING **TRANSMITTER ━━━━▶ RECEIVER**

This should be completed for each student receiver before the students arrive for school.

1. Check the transmitter for proper transmission. Remember to charge your transmitter in the same charging position routinely.
2. The crystal (RO) should be the same frequency as the transmitting signal. Keep spare crystal in the classroom; if the crystal has been dropped or damaged, it may no longer receive the frequency that it was designed to receive originally.
3. Turn the transmitter on, and place it near a sound source such as a tape player or radio.
4. Plug your listening cord into the receiver and the stenoset. If the student is using a transducer button, you may prefer to check the equipment with the cord in use. Contacts on the receiver plug can loosen when cords are plugged and unplugged many times, negatively affecting cord retention.
5. Turn the receiver on, using volume 1. Turn the switch to environmental microphone only.
6. Put the stenoset to your ears. (Caution: Some volume controls send a strong click as the volume wheel is rotated from the "off" position to the "on" position. It is important, therefore, to turn the receiver "on" before placing the stenoset to your ears.)
7. Gradually move the volume control wheel to a comfortable loudness. Recite the Ling Five Sound Test (Appendix C) to insure that the receiver is working.
8. Turn the receiver to the FM only switch position.
9. Gradually move the volume control wheel to a comfortable loudness. You can repeat the Ling Five Sound Test or place the transmitter near an alternate sound source such as a radio or tape player.
10. Manipulate the plug of the cord at the receiver to test the plug retention for intermittency.
11. Move the antenna on the transmitter to check for intermittency.
12. If your signal is intermittent and you are using an auxiliary microphone, change microphones. You may have an internal omnidirectional microphone built into your transmitter. If this is the case, unplugging your auxiliary microphone will activate the internal microphone and the "tail" type antenna from your transmitter. Remember, if you are transmitting with the internal microphone, you will need to check the antenna tail for intermittency by moving it gently between your fingers.
13. If your signal is distorted or sounds like noise, you do not know if you have a transmitting problem or a receiving problem. Try a different crystal. If this does not help, change receivers. If this does not help, you may need to change the batteries in both the transmitter and the receiver because the problem could be related to charger malfunction or battery energy.

Troubleshooting an FM system coupled to a cochlear implant is similar to troubleshooting a hearing aid, except that you cannot listen to sound quality. In the case of a cochlear implant, the volume setting of the FM receiver may need to be determined by the child because electroacoustic measures and listening checks cannot be obtained.

Table III.   Checking Receiver Transmission → Ear

This can be accomplished after students arrive. With students age five and up, plan an approach that involves students in the checking procedure.

1. Charge the receiver in the same charging position routinely. This will assist in determining if your charger could possibly have a bad charging pocket or cord. You have already identified any receiver that is not receiving the FM signal during your transmission check completed before students arrive.
2. Earmolds need to be checked daily for wax or debris that could clog the earmold canal bore, reducing sound audibility. You can waste a lot of time troubleshooting a unit that emits no sound, only to discover the earmolds are plugged with wax. Encourage students to wash their earmolds regularly. It is best if the molds can remain removed overnight, or have all the water in the sound bore blown out with a hand bulb before snapping the mold back on to the transducer or on to the earhook. Never blow with your mouth because your breath contains moisture.
3. Place the transmitter near a sound source. Better yet, assign a different student each week to choose a listening tape and place the transmitter near the tape recorder speaker with the tape recorder volume low. The music should not be audible at a distance of 3 or 4 feet. This will assure you that you are hearing the music via the FM.
4. Each student should insert his or her earmolds or learn to ask for assistance with the earmold insertion, and listen for the signal from the tape player via his or her receiver.
5. Turn the receiver to *FM only*.
6. Each student should be responsible for moving the cords, especially at the plug, to the receiver, to check for intermittency. The Listening Chart in figure 8 is an example that you can post to help students describe inappropriate sound qualities. For younger students and multiply handicapped students, an adult may need to assist in the listening procedure. Put one earmold to the stenoset and proceed to 7 and 8 below. Put the other earmold to the stenoset and repeat.
7. Now it is time for the student to listen to your voice. The receiver should remain on *FM only*.
8. Proceed with the Ling Five Sound Test (Appendix C) wearing the teacher microphone on your chest just below the chin. Stand two to three feet behind the student. (*Be sensitive to the fact that different students will have different abilities on the Five Sound Test. Performance on auditory tasks does not reflect intellectual functioning. Deflated egos may result for profoundly hearing-impaired children if daily attempts at impossible auditory tasks are required in front of more auditory peers*). Speak in a normal conversational voice. A loud voice will send the equipment into compression, distorting the FM signal.

*If a student's abilities fluctuate, you need to refer back to the audiologist. Hearing levels can fluctuate for a variety of reasons, including middle ear fluid.

Magnetic Induction Coupling

Neckloops and silhouettes.   Silhouettes and neckloops convert amplified electrical signals at the output to a magnetic signal. This magnetic signal is transmitted to a coil embedded in the hearing aid

Listening Chart

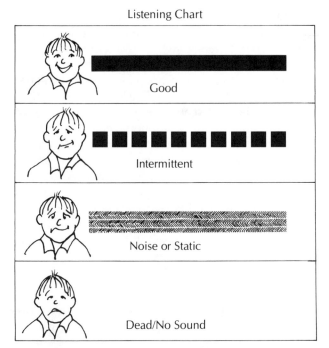

Figure 8.   This listening chart will assist young children in explaining to you any sounds they experience that may suggest a problem in the FM or hearing aid reception.

that detects the magnetic signal. This is then converted back to electrical energy and amplified by the hearing aid. A silhouette is worn adjacent to the hearing aid, thereby providing a stronger, more consistent signal for telecoil reception. Each manufacturer offers a similar size silhouette with its instrumentation. An alternate, smaller silhouette is available from Rastronics company for students with ears that are small or close to the head.

Activation of magnetic pick-up is made by placing the hearing aid on "T" for telecoil. This means deactivation of the hearing aid microphone. Some hearing aids are marked "MT" or " + ," which means the hearing aid is responding to both acoustic and magnetic signals simultaneously. Environmental information is collected at the hearing aid microphone port, and the FM signal is collected on "T" from the neckloop or silhouette. If the hearing aid microphone is inactive, the opportunity to receive environmental acoustic information can be accomplished with an environmental mircophone on the FM receiver. Balancing the environmental signal and FM signal to create a positive signal-to-noise ratio is challenging (see Chapter 3).

Listening to the hearing aids of older, reliable students every day may suggest to them that you lack confidence in their ability to judge for themselves. Once a week may be a sufficient check of listening to the actual hearing aid with your stenoset. This will not be the case with young students or multiply handicapped students. It will be necessary for you to enact your entire Ling Five Sound Test (Appendix C) routine with the hearing aid earmold attached to the stenoset on a daily basis (figure 9). If a student is using a silhouette, couple it on the side of the hearing aid that complements placement on the head. If a student is using a neckloop, it will be important to hold the hearing aid at the approximate distance from the loop. You may need to rotate the volume control of the hearing aid to deliver additional gain. Check with your audiologist if the transmitted signal is not loud enough. The student's responses to the Ling Five Sound Test alone will not be sufficient to alert you that the signal-to-noise ratio is appropriate for a student with a mild-to-moderate hearing loss.

Hearing aid microphone inactive and FM environmental microphone active (hearing aid on "T"). When an FM receiver environmental microphone is active, two signals are sent to the loop or silhouette: a transmitted signal and an environmental microphone signal. It

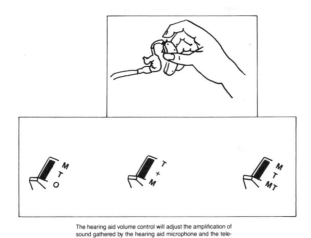

The hearing aid volume control will adjust the amplification of sound gathered by the hearing aid microphone and the telecoil magnet. Few hearing aid models allow the telecoil amplification to override the microphone amplification resulting in a poor signal-to-noise ratio.

Figure 9. It will be important to examine the switch on the hearing aid before beginning to listen to your voice amplified through the hearing aid. Also, examination of the volume control will be equally important to save your own hearing. Always begin in the off position with the volume on zero. The off position may not be available with any switch notation. Some off positions operate only when the battery door is open. If you are not sure what the letters on the hearing aid switch mean, check with the audiologist.

is important to identify the volume control for each of these signals in troubleshooting the equipment. This is important as you try to create a positive signal-to-noise ratio for your students. There may be a single volume control on the receiver, with no way to balance the loudness levels between the two signals sent to the loop or silhouette. Some of the equipment may have separate volume controls for the FM signal and the environmental receiver microphone. It is important to have a full understanding of which signal(s) each volume wheel will alter when checking the equipment. As mentioned earlier in this chapter, you may think the auditory signal is being transmitted from the transmitter, but in reality you may be hearing yourself via the environmental microphone on the receiver, or in other coupling modes, the hearing aid.

The environmental microphone may be activated by a toggle switch. The international symbol, "**I**," means "in operation." The symbol, "**O**," means "out of operation" (figure 10). These symbols are common on computer instrumentation. When the "I" is active and located at a students waist, environmental noises such as feet shuffling may be louder than a teacher's voice. Therefore, it may be advantageous to keep the environmental microphone inactive for directed group instruction. This will give the best FM advantage.

To proceed, first be sure that all environmental microphones on the receiver and the hearing aids are turned off. The environmental microphone may be turned off with a switch, trimmer screw, or with a dial. Read your manual closely if you cannot identify a switch to deactivate the environmental microphone on the receiver. The hearing aid should be on "T." Perform the Ling Five Sound Test with *only* FM transmission while standing behind the student. Repeat the exercise 2 to 3 feet in front of each student with *the FM environmental microphone active* and *the receiver inactive for FM reception*. The hearing aid should remain on "T" because you are checking the receiver environmental microphone.

For some students you will need to listen to the FM transmission with your stenoset attached to the hearing aid (figure 11). Remember you will have *three listening conditions*, "T" with FM only, "T" with the

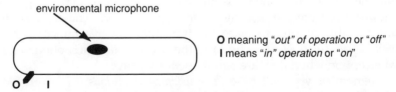

environmental microphone

O meaning *"out"* of operation or *"off"*
I means *"in"* operation or *"on"*

O I

Figure 10.   Often teachers misunderstand these symbols. Think of the "O" and "I" as international symbols, just as those on all computers and printers in your school.

FM environmental microphone of the receiver active and the FM reception inactive, and "M" with the hearing aid microphone active.

Hearing aid on "MT" or " + " with the hearing aid microphone active and the FM receiver environmental microphone inactive. The purpose of the FM receiver with the "MT" or " + " on is to bring the transmitted signal to the student's hearing aid. Environmental information will be received at the hearing aid microphone port. The receiver should, therefore, be on "FM only." Environmental acoustic information will be picked up by the microphone port of the hearing aid.

Complete the Ling Five Sound Test with only the FM transmission active, standing behind the student. This requires the hearing aid to be on "T" and the environmental microphone on the receiver to be off. When a student is using the "MT" position, it will also be important to check FM reception in that position. It is rare that the "T" would fail to operate on "MT" if it worked on "T." However, it is possible that this could be the case, suggesting that when the hearing aid was placed in the "MT" mode, the student would not hear the transmitted signal very loud. The student may hear your voice through the microphone port of the hearing aid but much of your volume will be lost over distance. Checking the FM reception on "MT" will require that the student move to the other side of the room so your voice arrives clearly via FM transmission rather than through the hearing aid microphone. Environmental information will be picked-up by the microphone port of the hearing aid or cochlear implant. The addition of the FM receiver is to bring the transmitted signal to the student. Repeat the Ling Five Sound Test behind the student without visual cues.

For some students you will need to listen to the FM transmission with your stenoset attached to the hearing aid (figure 11). This can be difficult with the hearing aid microphone active. Some hearing aid microphone ports are cylindrical and allow the tester's finger to be placed over the microphone port (figure 12). This will allow the "MT" to remain active but reduce acoustic information that enters the hearing aid microphone port. If it is impossible to keep the hearing aid on "MT" and reduce the signal on "M," then the listener will need to move away from the transmitter. The transmitted signal will need to be a significant distance from the hearing aid microphone port. The suggestion earlier in this chapter to place the transmitter near a music source works very effectively for checking the hearing aid microphone and FM reception when they are simultaneously active.

Remember you will have *three listening conditions,* "T" with FM only, "MT" or " + " with the FM only from the receiver and the hearing aid microphone active, and "M" with only the hearing aid microphone active and the FM receiver turned off.

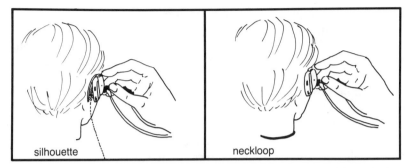

silhouette   neckloop

Figure 11.   Placing the hearing aid on the child's ear with the neckloop in place assists in listening at the correct distance from the loop. Listening with the silhouette in place is also best, because sometimes the silhouette can slip out of position or fit poorly between the ear and the hearing aid. Correct placement on the head may be the only way to know which size silhouette is best.

ELECTRICAL COUPLING

Hearing aid on "M" with the direct audio input coupling (or BTE microphones) and the hearing aid microphone active.   Direct audio input (DAI) to a hearing aid can be both wonderful and a nightmare at the same time. DAI can give a student a consistent frequency response for both the hearing aid microphone and the FM signal (see Chapter 4). It is possible, however, that DAI may produce loud static. If you are not confident about the student reporting static, listen to the hearing aid coupled to the FM via your stenoset at least once a day. A loose boot

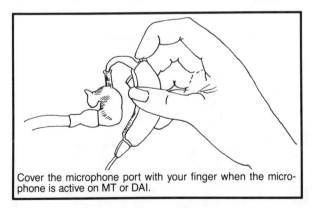

Cover the microphone port with your finger when the microphone is active on MT or DAI.

Figure 12.   Some cylindrical microphone ports allow the listener to cover them with a forefinger. This reduces contamination by environmental noises, or the tester's voice, from entering the hearing aid microphone when checking with the DAI or MT positions.

may be the source of the static or intermittency (figure 13). Keep a spare boot in your utility box for troubleshooting. Try this boot, which you know is good. If the problem is solved, inspect the original boot. Some boots have a screw at the base that holds both sides together. Tighten the screw, and try the boot again. If the problem is solved, you saved your program the cost of replacing a defective part. If your problem is not solved, try using an eraser on the contacts at the hearing aid. Moisture can create corrosion that you cannot see. If this does not help, the contact may need to be replaced, which you can do on some hearing aid models. Keep spare contacts in case any student has a hearing aid that will accept a replacement contact. If there is still a problem, replace the cord. Make sure the cord sits snugly into the receiver plug. If no solution is found, check to make sure you are using the correct cord and the correct FM receiver.

Just as the "MT" setting for magnetic coupling is not easy to troubleshoot, the direct audio input system can also be difficult to troubleshoot when the hearing aid microphone cannot be deactivated in any way. Unfortunately this is the case for most hearing aids. Some microphone ports allow the tester's finger to be placed over the microphone port. This assists in reduction of acoustic energy entering the hearing aid microphone. (See Hearing Aid Coupling on "MT," this chapter.) Some boots use a switch to deactivate the hearing aid microphone.

Completion of the Ling Five Sound Test with only the FM transmission active requires the hearing aid to be on "M" and the environmental microphone of the receiver to be off. Environmental information will be picked-up by the microphone port of the hearing aid or

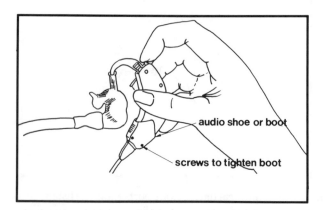

Figure 13. When DAI is intermittent, check to note if the boot or shoe has screws on the sides. Often, the screws can be tightened, improving the fit on the hearing aid, and eliminating the intermittent problem.

cochlear implant. The same situation exists as discussed previously in this chapter regarding "MT" coupling.

Remember you will have *two listening conditions*: "M" + "FM" and "M without FM."

Hearing aid on "A" or boot on "M" with the direct audio input coupling with the microphone inactive. This arrangement may be recommended in order to prevent confusion caused by noises in the learning environment. It may be especially helpful for a student who is easily distracted by extraneous acoustic stimuli or has unusually poor figure-ground auditory abilities. It is not available with every model of hearing aid. "Audio only" may be indicated by a variety of different symbols such as T, A, E, M, or B. Audio only may also need a special boot or cord before the environmental microphone of the hearing aid can be deactivated. An audiologist should be familiar with the options for each hearing aid model and company.

Troubleshooting techniques will be very similar to those for troubleshooting in the "T" position. All environmental microphones on the receiver and the hearing aids are turned off. The hearing aid should be on "audio only." Recite the Ling Five Sound Test via the FM transmitter out of the student's visual field.

Remember you will have *two listening conditions*: "Audio only" with FM, and "M" without FM.

SUMMARY

Troubleshooting can become an automatic procedure that teacher and student proceed through every morning. It may be helpful to post a reminder near the charger that follows the logical progression described in this chapter. The Listening Chart can be used with young kindergarten children to teach and explain good and poor sound qualities. Children will need to become familiar with poor sound quality and feel comfortable reporting it at any time during the teaching day. You will be performing auditory training and listening experiences daily with the children as you proceed with suggested activities. Listening to transmitted music from a tape player that the children chose themselves will involve them in a positive way. Introduction of joint responsibility between teacher and student, however, may be the most positive outcome.

APPENDIX A   DEFINITIONS OF TERMS

FM: frequency modulation
Transmitting frequency: frequency carrying the FM signal

RO/Crystal: receiving oscillator; or crystal

Transmitter: device that sends the radio waves through the air; the transmitter sends the radio signal to the antenna which, in turn, sends the signal out into the air for reception at the student receiver

Microphone Options for Transmitters

Internal microphone: microphone located within the transmitter; usually omnidirectional

Auxiliary microphone: a microphone option that can be plugged into a transmitter and used instead of the internal microphone

  Omnidirectional microphone: collects sound from 360 degrees

  Directional microphone: collects sound from the direction to which it is pointed

  Boom microphone: directional microphone worn on the head or around the neck with a wand type microphone positioned at the mouth

Pass Microphone: omnidirectional microphone that can be passed from child to child; very sensitive to distance in that it picks up sound from several feet; it is plugged directly into the teacher transmitter with a five foot cord

Conference microphone: omnidirectional microphone that is stationary, usually in the middle of a discussion area; very sensitive to distance in that it picks up from several feet and transmits the information via a transmitter

Lavalier microphone: omnidirectional microphone (worn around the neck) that is an integral part of the transmitter (internal microphone)

Lapel microphone: omni- or directional microphone worn at the neck or clipped to the front of clothing, and plugged directly into the transmitter

Receiver: receives the FM signal

  Receiver volume controls: a wheel on the side or top of the student receiver to adjust volumes of the FM signal and environmental signal

    FM volume control: volume control wheel that adjusts the loudness of the transmitted signal (i.e., teacher's voice or tape player)

    Environmental microphone volume control: volume control wheel that adjusts the loudness of acoustics within the environment

  Trimmer screws: screws located on the back of the receiver, usually under a control cover that adjusts output, frequency response, and gain of the receiver

Discrete trimmer screws: screw adjustments with stops that dictate the specific variable that is being adjusted; −6 dB means that at that specific setting the signal is 6 dB softer

Continuously variable trimmer screws: screw adjustments without any stops (which makes it difficult to find specific settings)

Coupling Options for Receivers

Transducer: standard button that fits on the earmold

Headphones: a band that fits over the head with transducers on each side placed over the ear

Magnetic inductions: telecoil reception

    Neckloop: magnetic induction from the neck

    Silhouette: magnetic induction at the HA

    T: only the telecoil is active

    T-shoe: telecoil boost shoe or boot

    "MT" or " +": hearing aid microphone and telecoil active simultaneously

Electrical induction: direct audio input reception

    DAI: direct audio input

    M: active hearing aid microphone

    A or M: audio only; hearing aid microphone is inactive

    MA: active hearing aid microphone and direct audio input simultaneously

    Boot: sleeve connector from the hearing aid to the cord from the receiver (also called audio shoe)

Sound field or free field system: an FM system that transmits to speakers in a room, rather than to individual body worn receivers

Cords: wire used to couple the FM to the ear

    Receiver cord: cord from the student receiver to the button transducer

    Audio-input cord: cord from the boot to the FM receiver; cords have different resistance therefore the specific cord number is critical for proper transmission from the FM receiver

    Audio patch cord: plugs the receiver or transmitter into an auxiliary sound source such as a tape player

    Audio jack adapter: an adapter put on the end of a male plug to change or adapt the size of that plug, making it smaller or larger

APPENDIX B   START-UP ACCESSORIES

Battery tester: Used to check the voltage of batteries.

Dedicated listening cord and transducer: A cord and transducer that is in good working condition. It should be used exclusively for listening to FM at the receiver. This is very important to have handy during the day when a problem occurs with hearing aid coupling. Check FM reception at the receiver before wasting valuable time checking cords, boots, or neckloops.

Earmold cream: Baby oil or Otoferm® are the two best lubricants for earmold insertion.

Hand bulb blower: This will remove moisture in the tubing and earmold assembly after cleaning. (See figure 14.)

Jeweler's screwdriver: This will accompany any FM purchase for receivers that have trimmer screw options. It can also be used for some hearing aid adjustments if they are necessary.

Spare auxiliary microphone: This may seem to be an expensive luxury. With transmitters that use auxiliary microphones integrated with the antenna, the only way to know if the lack of transmission is in the FM transmission circuitry, or the microphone assembly, is to change the microphone. (See figure 5.)

Spare batteries for FM and hearing aids: Expect the family to provide spare batteries for their child. If you are using rechargable 9V batteries, you may also want to keep a charger and rotate batteries that are not in use in a wall charger for emergencies.

Spare cords: There may be many different cords if students are using a variety of coupling arrangements. If some students are coupled with DAI and others with neckloop, you will need to organize the cords systematically so you have the proper backup when you find one intermittent or broken.

Spare crystal (RO):   If FM transmission cannot be detected with the dedicated listening cord but you hear a broad frequency noise, the crystal may have been damaged. Changing to a spare can solve that problem quickly. Some crystals can be repaired by the FM manufacturer. (See figure 14.)

Spare tubing: Children by grade 5 can be taught to change tubing in some earmolds. An audiologist can assist the classroom teacher in learning how to replace most tubing, at least on an interim basis, until the family can visit the audiologist.

Stenoset or stethoset for listening: A plastic device that resembles a physician's stethoscope. The hearing aid earmold, or receiver button can be coupled to the device for listening by the normal hearing ear. (See figure 14.)

Tone hooks for hearing aids or BTE microphone/transducers: The tone hook takes the amplified sound from the hearing aid to the earmold tubing. It may not be possible to have a spare for all hearing aids. Most hearing aids that have a screw-on hook will accept a standard hook until the child can visit an audiologist for the

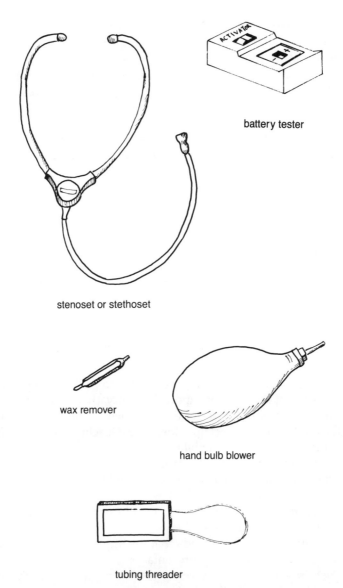

battery tester

stenoset or stethoset

wax remover

hand bulb blower

tubing threader

Figure 14.   The above items should be part of your start-up kit. Check with your FM manufacturer for the best wholesale house from which you can order the items you need. The stenoset sketched above can be used with the transducer button after removing the tube to which earmolds can be coupled from the hearing aid. You may find, however, that listening to the transducer coupled to the earmold through the tube is the best way to identify any wax plugs. The hand-held bulb blower should be used routinely after each earmold is cleaned. Also it may assist in removing wax plugs, if time does not permit washing the mold.

proper part. The tone hook can be the cause of many feedback problems, so it is important to have spares if possible.

Troubleshooting form: See figure 7, this chapter.

Tubing threader: A handle-like device that has nylon line on one end to create a closed loop. It is inserted into the earmold sound bore and used to pull the new tubing in through the earmold. (See figure 14.)

Wax remover: A small instrument with a wire loop on the end that can be managed by young children to remove wax from the earmold sound bore. (See figure 14).

APPENDIX C   LING FIVE SOUND TEST

The purpose of the Five Sound Test is to identify the acoustic access a student enjoys for the speech frequencies. Ling has suggested that the vowels /u/, /ɑ/, and /i/ coupled with the consonants /s/ and /ʃ/ provide low, middle, and high frequency components of speech. The ability to hear all five sounds suggests that the student has auditory access to the acoustic parameters included in most speech.

There are two ways in which the Five Sound Test can be administered.

1. **Detection:**   Students raise their hand to indicate they detect the presence of teacher phonation. In reality, this shows awareness of presence or absence of voice. Awareness of phonemes that cover the entire speech spectrum does give a teacher valuable insight for auditory training and habilitation.

    a.   For the profoundly hearing-impaired student, begin with visual plus auditory cues. Success should be good, because each sound looks different on the lips.

    b.   As the student progresses, introduce visual plus auditory cues alternating with auditory cues alone.

    c.   Choose only the sounds that the student can successfully detect for an auditory only presentation.

2. **Discrimination:**   This level of testing suggests that the student can identify auditorily which sound the teacher is speaking. Each sound should be presented two or three times in random order for student identification.

Covering your mouth with your hand is not a good way to deliver the test. The hand will change the acoustic energy arriving at the student's hearing aid or FM receiver. It is much better to ask students to close their eyes, and, then speak directly in front of their hearing aid microphone ports for hearing aid testing. When testing with the FM *only* mode, it would be acceptable to stand behind students, expecting performance at the detection or discrimination level that each student can perform with the hearing aid.

RELATED READINGS

Benoit, R. 1989. Home use of FM amplification systems during the early childhood years. *Hearing Instruments* 40:8–12.

Hawkins, D. 1984. Comparisons of speech recognition in noise by mildly-to-moderately hearing impaired children using hearing aids and FM systems. *Journal of Speech and Hearing Disorders* 49:409–418.

Hawkins, D. 1988. Options in classroom amplification. *Hearing Impairment in Children*, ed. Fred Bess. Parkton, MD: York Press, Inc.

Hammand, L. 1991. *FM Auditory Trainers: A Winning Choice for Students, Teachers and Parents*. Minneapolis, MN: Gopher State Litho Corp.

Lewis, D., Jeigin, J., Karasek, A., and Stelmachowicz, P. 1991. Evaluation and assessment of FM systems. *Ear and Hearing* 12(4):268–80.

Ling, D., and Ling, A. 1978. *Aural Habilitation*. Washington, DC: Alexander Graham Bell Association for the Deaf, Inc.

Ross, M., and Giolas, T. 1971. Effect of three classroom listening conditions on speech intelligibility. *American Annals of the Deaf* 116:580–84.

Chapter • 7

FM Systems For Children Birth To Age Five

Jane R. Madell

LANGUAGE LEARNING IN THE PRESCHOOL YEARS

A great deal of research has demonstrated that children develop sophisticated auditory skills during the first year of life. As early as one month of age, infants are capable of perceiving acoustic cues that enable them to develop the complex adult language system (Fry 1978; Mischook and Cole 1986). Children as young as two months of age are able to distinguish the language spoken in their home from another language (Mehler et al. 1988). By eighteen weeks, children are able to associate facial movements with the appropriate vowel production (Kuhl and Meltzoff 1988.) Seven-month-old children have the ability to recognize the acoustic cues that identify syntactic boundaries (Hirsh-Pasek et al. 1987). Obviously, even before a child begins to speak, he or she has developed many auditory skills that are critical for the development of verbal language.

Birth to age three is the critical age for language development. Language stimulation during this period is most frequently provided at home, with the parents and caregivers functioning as the primary language models. It is, therefore, critical that the child be able to receive as much language input from parents and other caregivers as possible if we are to maximize the child's language skills. For the hearing-impaired child this becomes more difficult because the hearing loss will limit the amount of language stimulation the child can receive. Appropriate amplification is the only avenue parents have for providing their child with the necessary access to auditory information.

Audition is considered the most efficient avenue for learning language (Fry 1978; Hasenstab 1983, 1987; Oller et al. 1985; Taylor 1985; Davis and Hardick 1986). Even before the advent of auditory language development, however, the child uses audition to maintain and expand elaborate babbling (Oller et al. 1985; Oller and Eilers 1988). It is not difficult to predict the effect of auditory deprivation on language development during the critical language learning period. The need for early appropriate amplification and auditory stimulation should be obvious.

There is every reason to believe that hearing-impaired children are capable of the same sequence of auditory language development as normal-hearing children, although at a somewhat slower rate, provided that they are exposed to appropriately amplified speech at an early age. For this reason the selection of amplification is critical. We do not know at exactly what age it would be too late for hearing-impaired infants to take advantage of the normal auditory development sequence nor do we know the specific impact of auditory sensory deprivation. What we can say with certainty is that a delay in exposure to auditory information or inadequate auditory information will have a negative effect on the child's potential to use audition for learning language.

Thus, there is a clear rationale for early auditory management of hearing-impaired children. Regardless of the educational method used, all children should have the opportunity to maximize their use of audition. If children are not supplied with an amplification system that provides sufficient access to auditory information, they will miss this opportunity. The combination of the hearing loss and the effects of distance and acoustical condition on the speech signal limits the adequacy of conventional hearing aids (see Chapter 2). For that reason FM systems should be considered as a potential first and primary amplification device for young deaf children. In brief, FM systems will provide the acoustic raw material for language and speech development at a time when children are most ready to take advantage of it.

WHY CONSIDER FM SYSTEMS AS PRIMARY AMPLIFICATION?

The purpose of any amplification system is to provide access to amplified information. The more severe the hearing loss, the more difficult it is to accomplish this task. Standard behind-the-ear hearing aids may be adequate for children with hearing losses ranging from mild to moderately severe but they probably do not provide sufficient access to acoustic information for those children with severe and profound hearing losses.

Distance between the listener and the talker affects the perception of speech. The greater the distance, the less information received by the listener. The ideal distance for children with hearing aids is about three to six feet in a quiet environment with maximal acoustic information available at less than one foot (Chapter 2). Under noisy conditions, the ideal listening distance may be less than this. Infants may frequently be within three to six feet of the person primarily responsible for their language input but once children begin to crawl they will spend a great deal of time at distances that are less than ideal from the primary speaker.

Because it is not possible to control the environment so that the talker is always within a few feet of the child's hearing aids, various techniques must be used to improve the listening environment. The primary advantage of FM systems for severely hearing-impaired preschool children is to increase the loudness of the speech signal during the frequent times when the primary speech source is at a distance of more than a few feet. For very young children with severe and profound hearing losses, a FM system should be considered as the primary amplification system because it will effectively reduce the effect of distance.

The second critical problem for the reception of auditory information is the presence of noise and reverberation. Noise and reverberation have a more serious negative effect on speech perception for hearing-impaired children than for those with normal hearing. Work by Finitzo-Hieber and Tillman (1978), Tillman, Carhart, and Olsen (1970), Bess and McConnell (1981), and others has demonstrated the negative effect that poor acoustical conditions have on the perception of speech.

The benefit of FM systems in the classroom is well recognized. By producing a radio link between the listener and the talker, an FM system will overcome the effects of distance and reduce the impact of noise and reverberation. FM systems are used in school to overcome poor classroom listening conditions; a fact which has been well documented (Finitzo-Hieber 1981; Olsen 1988; Ross 1978; Ross and Giolas 1971). It has been assumed that the home does not provide the same kinds of listening problems and, therefore, does not require the same kind of solution. However, careful evaluation of the acoustic environment in which very young hearing-impaired children live suggests that this is not the case. Distance and noise can be as much of a problem in the home as in the classroom. Even the quietest home is noisy. Noise comes from many sources. Open windows let in street noise; TV, radio, and the stereo provide additional noise; appliances are noisy; voices of other children or of adults add to the din. The home is not an ideal acoustic environment. While signal-to-noise problems are usually not as serious at home as in school they do still exist and the FM will be beneficial in overcoming those difficulties.

Benoit (1989) demonstrated the benefit parents feel when using FM systems with their children. He loaned FM systems to six children between the ages of one and four years for one year. At the end of the year parents were asked to comment on their experience. They reported that when their children were using FM systems they were able to talk to their children from a greater distance, that it was more "convenient" to talk because it was not necessary to be close, that background noise was not perceived as an obstacle to communication, and that the microphone transmitter worn by the parent served as a "reminder" of the need to provide language stimulation. The benefits derived from the FM system went beyond the acoustic advantages. They improved communication from parent to child and were viewed as being a factor in improved language stimulation.

WHAT CAN WE EXPECT FROM FM SYSTEMS IN PRESCHOOL YEARS?

Because the FM transmitter is worn within a few inches of the mouth of the person talking, we can expect that the child will receive a louder signal with less interference than the signal that would be received with a hearing aid. Our experience in the audiological test room indicates that children receive a signal that is 10 to 15 dB greater with the FM microphone/transmitter than that received with the environmental microphones alone. This means that the child hears more of the important acoustic features of speech. Our experience indicates that FM systems enable children with severe and profound hearing losses to function auditorily more like children with moderate and moderately-severe hearing losses.

Figures 1, 2, and 3 show typical examples of preschool children who use FM systems as primary amplification. While the advantage of the FM transmitter may seem relatively minor when looking at the difference between warble tone thresholds obtained with and without the use of the FM transmitter, the effect on improved speech perception is clear in the speech recognition results. Consider the effect over time of this improved speech signal on the use of audition and the learning of language!

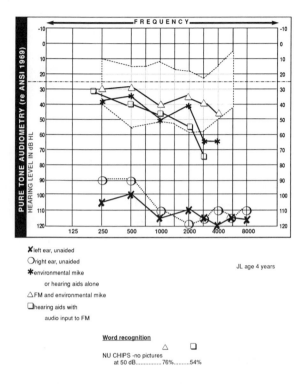

Figure 1.   FM benefit received by a four-year-old with a profound hearing loss.

SELECTION CONCERNS FOR PRESCHOOL CHILDREN

The Receiver

(See Thibodeau, Chapter 3 for pictures of all the FM components discussed in this section.) The FM receiver selected for preschool children must be extremely flexible because the audiologist may initially have only a limited amount of information about the child's auditory capabilities. At the time of the initial fitting, the audiologist will have information about degree of hearing loss in each ear but will not yet have information about the child's ability to use his or her residual hearing for the perception of speech. In addition, the possibility that hearing thresholds will change needs to be considered and the amplification selected should allow for that possibility.

The FM receiver should have adjustable frequency and output controls so the response can be modified as more information about the child's hearing levels and speech perception skills becomes available. It

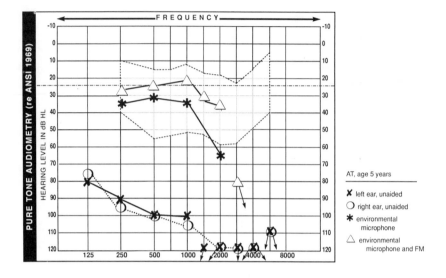

Figure 2. FM benefit received by a five-year-old with a profound hearing loss.

should have separate adjustments for each ear to allow for maximal flexibility, and should allow the audiologist to select a variety of coupling options. For example, a system that only permits the use of direct audio-input or a neck loop and does not permit the use of button transducers may limit the child's options. Finally, the controls on the receiver should permit the user to turn on the hearing aid/environmental microphone without FM transmission, FM without hearing aid/ environmental microphone, and FM and hearing aid/environmental microphone at the same time. This maximum flexibility will allow the system to be used optimally in a variety of listening situations, maximizing the auditory signal available to the child.

Microphones

The three types of FM microphones available have different advantages for the preschool child. The *boom microphone* is always in the ideal acoustic position directly in front of the speaker's mouth, but this position can interfere with speechreading. In addition, it is very difficult to pass from one speaker to another, which may limit the way the microphone is used and reduce the input that the child receives.

The *clip-on microphone*, while often viewed as cosmetically more

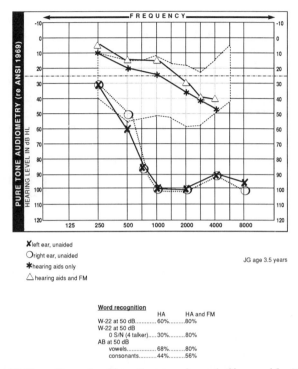

X left ear, unaided
O right ear, unaided
✱ hearing aids only
△ hearing aids and FM

JG age 3.5 years

Word recognition

	HA	HA and FM
W-22 at 50 dB	60%	80%
W-22 at 50 dB		
0 S/N (4 talker)	30%	80%
AB at 50 dB		
vowels	68%	80%
consonants	44%	56%

Figure 3.   FM benefit received by a three-and-one-half-year old with a sloping (moderately severe-to-profound) hearing loss.

appealing, is frequently misused. When we do a school or home visit, we frequently find the clip-on microphone tilted over to the side, upside down, or attached inside the jacket rather than in the optimal acoustic position six inches from the speaker's mouth. This microphone is also difficult to pass from speaker to speaker because it needs to be unclipped, removed from the pocket or belt, and reattached to the person who is taking it over. While this is certainly possible to do, speakers who view the process as complicated may not pass the microphone around as needed.

The *lavalier microphone*, because of the way it is worn around the neck, is always in the ideal acoustic position, six inches from the speaker's mouth. It is easy to pass this microphone from one speaker to another because it is one piece and easier to handle. This ease increases the likelihood that it will be used correctly.

Coupling Systems

Button transducers are the easiest coupling system to use with preschool children. The FM receiver functions as a body worn hearing aid with cords attaching it to the button transducers. They stay in place more easily than other coupling systems do. They provide less feedback because of the increased distance between the microphones on the unit on the child's chest and the earmold at the child's ear. The chest worn microphone takes advantage of the body baffle effect and provides increased low frequency stimuli because sound reflecting off the body is enhanced as it is reflected back into the environmental microphones on the FM receiver worn on the chest. For children with severe and profound hearing losses, the increased low frequency information is significant because the initial information that the child needs in the development of auditory skills is in the low frequencies, specifically alerting to the presence of speech, rhythm, intonation and inflection, and vowel recognition.

Of all coupling systems available, this one seems the easiest for young children to manipulate, which increases the probability that they will take responsibility for maintenance of their own amplification. Because our goal is to provide children with sufficient auditory information to allow them to use audition as a significant avenue of input, it is important that they learn to accept responsibility for management of their amplification.

Behind-the-ear (BTE) transducers provide ear level microphones that have the acoustic advantage of providing an improved high frequency response. Most consonant information is in the high frequencies, and is critical for recognition of such linguistic features as verb tense, pluralization, possession, and contractions. In addition, ear level microphones facilitate localization of the speech signal. Work by Maxon and Brackett (1989) and Byrne and Dermody (1975) have demonstrated that children with body worn amplification are able to localize sound as long as it is loud enough to be detected. While localization is important, in my view it is secondary to the ability to understand speech, which is greatly enhanced by the improved acoustic signal available from a body worn FM system.

A disadvantage of ear level microphones, especially for young children, is that they cause more feedback problems than button transducers due to the decreased separation between the microphone and the ear and the soft cartilage in the pinna. This may require that the child turn down the volume to control the feedback, resulting in a reduction in the amount of auditory information received by the child. Because of the size of BTE transducers, these systems may be somewhat more difficult to keep in place on young children with small ears.

BTE hearing aids with direct-audio-input allow the child to have hearing aids to use when they do not want to use the FM system. For children with mild-to-moderately severe hearing losses, there may be situations when hearing aids should be worn alone, and for those children this may be a good coupling system. However, the additional equipment means that there are more pieces to break down. The cords and boots used to couple the hearing aids to the FM system are very fragile and breakdown is not uncommon, especially for young children who are not careful. This type of coupling system is difficult for young children to manage on their own, which means that they will always need a knowledgeable adult available to provide assistance. Preschool children cannot always report equipment failure, which may present some problems. If equipment failure is frequent, both parents and children will become frustrated with the equipment and will cease to use it, which, of course, defeats the purpose of having amplification fitted early.

Neckloops and silhouettes are not recommended for use by preschool children. Their electroacoustic responses are more variable and poorer than other coupling modes and are, thus, less suitable for these children. Cosmetic concerns, the major advantage of neckloops, should not be a significant concern for this age group.

EVALUATION OF FM SYSTEMS

Test Stimuli

To be certain that the FM system selected is the best one for the child, the system must be tested both electroacoustically and behaviorally. Both frequency specific stimuli and speech stimuli should be used in the evaluation. Frequency specific stimuli may consist of frequency modulated warble tones or noise bands to measure threshold level stimuli and real ear measures for supra-threshold testing.

Speech stimuli should be part of every evaluation. For very young children who do not have sufficient language for standardized tests, the Ling Five Sound test (Ling 1978) can provide some information to demonstrate that the child is receiving auditory information throughout the frequency range necessary for reception of speech. When the child has some vocabulary, words that the child knows can be used to obtain a nonstandardized speech reception threshold. Many standardized tests are available. The *Early Speech Perception Test* (ESPT) by Moog and Geers (1990) is a useful test of speech recognition for young children with limited vocabulary. As a child's vocabulary increases, more standardized closed set tests are available. These include the NU-CHIPS (Elliott and Katz 1980), the WIPI (Ross and Lerman 1970), and the Alphabet Test (Ross and Randolph 1990).

When the child's skills are such that he or she does very well with closed set testing, open set testing should be tried; this will increase the level of difficulty of the task. Test materials may include the words from the NU-CHIPS or the WIPI without pictures, the Isophonemic Word Lists (Boothroyd 1984), or the PBK, the CID W-22 or the NU-6 lists. We have successfully conducted these tests with children as young as two and three years of age.

Test Protocol

To demonstrate clearly the advantage of the FM system, testing should be conducted under different conditions: in quiet using the hearing aids/environmental microphone without the FM transmitter, and then with the addition of the FM transmitter. If the child is capable of cooperating, testing also should be conducted in the presence of background noise such as four talker babble. This can usually be accomplished once a child can easily perform word recognition testing—usually by age three or four years. By testing in a number of different conditions and using a variety of stimuli, it is possible to get an accurate picture of the child's level of functioning. We can demonstrate to families and therapists the advantages obtained from the FM microphone, and we can provide information to speech-language therapists and preschool classroom teachers regarding areas of speech perception needing additional work. Figure 4 is an example of a useful test form on which to record the information from an FM evaluation.

Audiologic Test Room Set-up

The test room evaluation should be as close to real listening situations as possible. To accomplish this the child should be seated at the position in the test room calibrated for soundfield testing, facing the loudspeaker. Testing with the environmental microphones should be accomplished just as it would be when testing standard hearing aids (see figure 5.) When testing with the FM microphone, the microphone should be hung six inches in front of the loudspeaker, typical of normal use where it is six inches from the mouth of the person talking. When background noise is used, it should be presented at 90 degrees from both sides of the child. This will stimulate the situation outside the test room in which noise is coming from all directions, and will allow the audiologist to measure FM benefit when noise is present.

HELPING PARENTS LEARN TO USE FM SYSTEMS WITH THEIR CHILDREN

At the New York League for the Hard of Hearing we have been fitting FM systems as primary amplification on preschool children with se-

NAME		**FM EVALUATION**
TEST DATE	BIRTH DATE	**New York League for the Hard of HEARING**
RELIABILITY	TEST METHOD	71 West 23rd Street, New York, NY 10010
AUDIOLOGIST	AUDIOMETER	VOICE 212-741-7650 • TDD 212-255-1932 • FAX 212-255-4413

			UNAIDED	AIDED			FM 1			FM 2			FM 3		
				R	L	B	R	L	B	R	L	B	R	L	B
WARBLE/NBN		250 Hz													
		500 Hz													
		1000 Hz													
		2000 Hz													
		3000 Hz													
		4000 Hz													
	SAT	ba/sh/s													
	SRT														
WORD RECOGNITION	QUIET	50 dB													
		35 dB													
	NOISE	dB S/N													

NOTES:

Figure 4. Form for recording test results during an FM evaluation.

vere and profound hearing losses for about nine years, and we have been very impressed by the way parents have received this type of amplification. The first step is to convince parents that an FM system will help their child. This can be done by demonstrating the benefit the FM provides in the test room, by lending an FM system to the family to try at home, and by having the parent talk to other parents who have successfully used FMs with their children. Once we have demonstrated to parents that FM systems provide significant benefit for their hearing-impaired child they have no difficulty accepting them. There is an advantage at our facility, because parents coming into the League see other children wearing FM systems and find other parents with whom they can discuss their concerns. Parents see that FM systems are a part of the total therapy package. FM use is taken for granted, and there is no real problem getting them to accept the need for it.

There are two groups of parents who hesitate about using FM systems. The first group comprise those who arrive at our center after

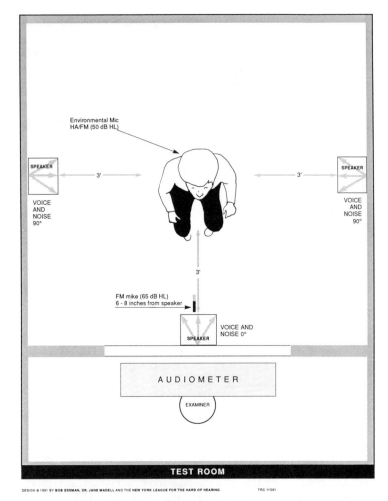

Figure 5.   Test room set-up for FM evaluations.

their child has already been fitted with BTE amplification at another facility. These parents have adjusted to the need for amplification but they are accustomed to seeing their child using the smaller hearing aids and have difficulty accepting the larger and more visible FM systems. However, after seeing the way other children in the program respond to sound with their FM amplification and after a trial period with an FM system, no parent has refused to make the switch.

The second group are families whose children are receiving therapy at another facility in which their child is the only one using an FM system and in which there is limited professional support for full-time FM use. The loan or rental of an FM system for a two or three month period may help the parents feel comfortable with a decision to use FMs full time. In this case, it is important to counsel parents to use FMs full time during the trial and not to alternate back and forth between FMs and hearing aids. If the child is alternating back and forth between different amplification systems it will be difficult for the child to adjust to different auditory signals provided by two systems and parents will have a difficult time developing realistic auditory expectations. In addition, full-time use will allow more opportunity to demonstrate benefit. Many parents who elect to use FM systems part time use them only during "therapy" or "story time" considering this to be the most critical learning time. They have not recognized that language learning takes place all day and that the FM will be most beneficial during times not traditionally thought of as "teaching" time, when the child will be farther away from the parent and when the acoustic environment is less than ideal.

During the early stages of adjusting to FMs, it is important that parents be comfortable with the FM system. If there are equipment breakdowns that parents cannot handle, they will stop using the system.

QUESTIONS AND ANSWERS

Concern About The Use of Equipment

Almost all parents begin any amplification program with a fear of the amplification equipment. These fears are exacerbated by the grief they feel in having a hearing-impaired child, and this will complicate the adjustment. They are afraid that they will not know how to use the amplification, that they will not be able to get the earmold into the child's ear, or that they will hurt the child when inserting it. The fact that the child is frequently uncomfortable in the beginning, when parents have difficulty inserting the earmolds, does not help to ease parents' fears. They do not know how the child will respond to sound and are concerned about the amplification working properly. A positive approach by the audiologist, despite his or her own concerns, and the passage of time always work, and in a week or two parents are usually able to get the earmolds in and are on the way to becoming experts.

Troubleshooting

Parents need to learn very early how to check out FM systems and to make minor repairs. Initially parents, and later the child, need to be shown how to do a listening check of the FM system. As soon as parents are comfortable with the equipment, the child needs to begin assuming responsibility for it. As part of the troubleshooting process, parents need to be told what to do if something seems wrong. We try to make them feel that they are capable of managing the equipment, and we find that they usually are. For more information on troubleshooting, see Chapter 6.

Using the Transmitter/Microphone Correctly

The FM transmitter transmits auditory information to the hearing-impaired child. If the child is going to learn to use audition maximally, it is important that information presented be meaningful to him or her. Older children learn to distinguish between meaningful speech and background conversation, but that is not possible for very young children who are learning to use auditory information for the first time. The environmental microphones on the FM receivers will allow the child to hear his or her own voice and the voices of those close by. This will be meaningful because the child can see the person talking and hear what is being discussed. The FM transmitter will help the child hear the parent or caregiver when he or she is a few feet away or in the next room and is speaking to the child. The child should not hear conversation that is intended for others (e.g., talking on the telephone or talking to someone in another room), because it will only be confusing. This can be managed by turning the transmitter on and off appropriately. Parents are encouraged to keep the transmitter off and to turn it on when they want to direct their conversation to the child. In that way, the child quickly learns to attend to speech sounds that are coming from the FM transmitter. Our experience indicates that parents learn this skill quickly.

How Long Will the Child Use the FM System?

Parents are frequently concerned about how long the child will need to use the FM system. They are willing to accept its use in preschool years when language learning is their first concern, but they would like to think that something less visible will be available when the child reaches school age. We assure parents that their children will eventually wear ear level hearing aids but that good acoustic information needs to be the primary concern during the early years.

Once children begin to use high frequency information consistently we begin to evaluate use of BTE transducers with the FM system or BTE hearing aids. This usually happens at about age six. In fact, we find that we delay this as long as possible because the acoustic information available appears to be significantly poorer without the FM system, and both children and parents have become resistant to giving up the FM. Eventually social pressure takes over. By age five or six most children with severe hearing losses have BTE hearing aids and by age seven most children with profound hearing losses have BTE hearing aids.

An intense period of auditory training is necessary after the child has switched to BTE hearing aids to "re-educate" him or her to use the reduced acoustic information that he or she is now receiving to the maximum. Fortunately, the improved acoustic information obtained with the FM gives the child sufficient auditory skills and language to enable him or her to learn to listen with a reduced signal.

What about Cost?

FM systems cost more than BTE hearing aids. This is more frequently expressed as a concern by other professionals than by parents. When the benefit of the system is demonstrated, parents do not object to the extra cost if they can afford it. Unfortunately, some state agencies who pay for hearings aids will not pay for FM systems, which they have classified as educational devices and not medical devices such as hearing aids. It is important that we educate these agencies to understand that an FM system is simply another kind of amplification system which should be viewed in the same way as any other. For this reason it may be useful to refer to the FM transmitter/microphone instead of a teacher's microphone and to refer to evaluations of hearing aids and FM systems as amplification evaluations to make clear that both systems are providing the same function—that of amplification of sound.

CONCLUSION

FM systems provide an excellent means of providing auditory access to preschool infants and young children with severe and profound hearing losses. This improved access to auditory information will permit these children to use audition for language learning and for improved speech production. If we believe that amplification is valuable for hearing-impaired children, then we are obligated to provide them with the best possible amplification. For many hearing-impaired children, this means the use of FM systems as primary amplification.

REFERENCES

Benoit, R. 1989. Home use of FM amplification systems during the early childhood years. *Hearing Instruments* 40:3:8–12.

Bess, F., and McConnell, F. 1981. *Audiology, Education and the Hearing Impaired Child*. St. Louis: C.V. Mosby.

Boothroyd, A. 1984. Auditory perception of speech contrasts by subjects with sensorineural hearing loss. *Journal of Speech and Hearing Research* 27:134–44.

Byrne, D., and Dermody, P. 1975. Localization of sound with binaural body-worn hearing aids. *British Journal of Audiology* 9:107–115.

Davis, J., and Hardick, E. 1986. *Rehabilitative Audiology for Children and Adults*. New York: Macmillan Publishing Co.

Elliott, L., and Katz, D. 1980. *Development of a New Children's Test of Speech Discrimination*. St. Louis: Auditec.

Finitzo-Heiber, T. 1981. Classroom acoustics. In *Auditory Disorders In School Children*, eds. R. Roeser and M. Downs. New York: Thieme-Stratton.

Finitzo-Heiber, T., and Tillman, T. 1978. Room acoustics effects on monosyllabic word discrimination ability for normal and hearing impaired children. *Journal of Speech and Hearing Research* 21:440–58.

Fry, D. B. 1978. The role and primacy of the auditory channel in speech and language development. In *Auditory Management of Hearing Impaired Children*, eds. M. Ross and T. G. Giolas. Baltimore: University Park Press.

Hasenstab, M. S. 1983. Child language studies: Impact on habilitation on hearing-impaired infants and preschool children. *The Volta Review* 85: 88–100.

Hasenstab, M. S. 1987. Auditory learning and communication competence: Implications for hearing-impaired infants. *Seminars in Hearing* 8:175–80.

Hirsh-Pasek, K., Nelson, D., Jusczyk, P., Woodward, A., Piwoz, J., and Kennedy, L. 1987. The perception of cues to major phrasal units by prelinguistic infants. Unpublished manuscript.

Kuhl, P., and Meltzoff, A. 1988. Speech as an intermodal object of perception. In *Perceptual Development in Infancy*, ed. A. Yonas. Hillsdale, NJ: Lawrence Erlbaum Associates.

Ling, D. 1978. Auditory coding and recoding: An analysis of auditory training procedures for hearing impaired children. In *Auditory Management of Hearing Impaired Children*, eds. M. Ross and T. G. Giolas. Baltimore: University Park Press.

Maxon, A., and Brackett, D. 1989. Children's localization abilities: Effects of age, hearing loss, and amplification. Convention of the American Speech-Language-Hearing Association, St. Louis.

Mehler, J., Jusczyk, P., Lambertz, G., Halsted, N., Bertoncini, J., and Amiel-Tison, C. 1988. A precursor of language acquisition in young infants. *Cognition* 29:143–78.

Mischook, M., and Cole, E. 1986. Auditory learning and teaching of hearing-impaired infants. *The Volta Review* 88:67–78.

Moog, J., and Geers, A. 1990. Early Speech Perception Test for Profoundly Hearing Impaired Children 1990. St. Louis: Central Institute for the Deaf.

Oller, D. K., and Eilers, R. E. 1988. The role of audition in infant babbling. *Child Development* 59:441–49.

Oller, D. K., Eilers, R. E., Bull, D. H., and Carney, A. E. 1985. Prespeech vocalizations of a deaf infant. A comparison with normal metaphonological development. *Journal of Speech and Hearing Research.* 28:47–63.

Olsen, W. 1988. Classroom acoustics for hearing-impaired children. In *Hearing Impairment In Children*, ed. F. Bess. Parkton, MD: York Press.

Ross, M. 1978. Classroom acoustics and speech intelligibility. In *Handbook of Clinical Audiology, second edition*, ed. J. Katz. Baltimore: Williams & Wilkins Co.

Ross, M., and Giolas, T. G. 1971. Effects of three classroom listening conditions on speech intelligibility. *American Annals of the Deaf* 116:580–84.

Ross, M., and Lerman, J. 1970. A picture identification test for hearing impaired children. *Journal of Speech and Hearing Research* 13:44–53.

Ross, M., and Randolph, K. 1990. A test of the auditory perception of alphabet letters for hearing impaired children: The APAL test. *The Volta Review* 92:237–44.

Taylor, I. G. 1985. Hearing impaired babies and methods of communication. *Ear and Hearing* 6:25–28.

Tillman, T. W., Carhart, R., and Olsen, W. O. 1970. Hearing aid efficiency in a competing speech situation. *Journal of Speech and Hearing Research* 13:789–811.

Chapter • 8

Effects of Early FM Use on Speech Perception

Diane Brackett

FM systems make it possible for hearing-impaired infants and preschoolers to be exposed to the raw material of language learning—an audible speech signal. Noise enhanced by reverberation and speaker-listener distance disrupts the child's access to auditory information. Early FM use reduces the impact of these negative listening conditions on the child's ability to receive the speech input needed to learn language. Having access to increased intensity levels of speech input sets up the expectation that "sound" is important and that it should not be ignored. Given that premise, the child is more likely to extract acoustic cues from even the most minimally audible speech signal. Conversely, a child who has continually experienced only minimal access to sound will be unaware both that speech is present and that it should be responded to.

Typically FM units are utilized in schools where the classroom acoustics are poor (Ross, Chapter 2 this volume). The home environment also has widely varying acoustic conditions resulting from internal and external noise sources and reverberation. Those rooms with hard, shiny surfaces such as bathrooms, basements, laundry rooms, and kitchens are most susceptible to reverberation-enhanced noise. A poor listening environment occurs in the home when background noise is created from appliances, TV, street, and siblings (table I). Also, due to the unstructured nature of communication in the home, noise is generated by competing conversations that are the norm during meals

Table I. Potential Interference from Noise and Distance in the Home

Noise	Distance
Appliances	Inside
Kitchen	Upstairs
Laundry	Another room
Bathroom	Hallway
Street noise	Outside
Horns	Playground
Cars	Street
Police/fire sirens	Beach
Street maintenance	
Large group	
Family dinners	
Holiday gatherings	
Birthday parties	
Gymboree	
Circus	
Restaurant	
Media	
Record player	
TV	
VCR	
Radio	
Siblings	
Play	
Meals	
Conversation	
Car	
Motor	
Air conditioner	
Passengers	
Radio	
Workshop	
Tools	
Pets	

and other family interactions. To further complicate matters, daily routines often place the infant and parent in separate rooms, such as in meal preparation or laundry, or at distances of more than three feet, such as at the playground or bike riding.

Unlike a classroom where potentially interfering situations can easily be predicted due to the routine nature of activities, the home breeds flexibility and spontaneity—a nightmare for parents who are concerned with providing their child with audible speech. An appropriately used FM unit can enhance the parent's ability to stimulate language in this rich, learning environment despite the interfering factors of noise and increased speaker-listener distances.

Infant and toddler "out of school" activities may extend to settings other than the home, whose reverberant qualities should be recognized—gym class, mother/child art classes, shopping, cars, and fast food restaurants. Organized daycare and play groups include individual and group activities that vary in the noise generated (table II). Any setting that is designed to accommodate large numbers of unrelated people tends to be constructed with hard, shiny surfaces that are easy to maintain but detrimental to speech reception.

To understand fully the benefits of using FM units with young profoundly hearing-impaired children, it is important to understand that language learning takes place within an interactive framework, with parental speech providing the raw material from which the language system derives. This language learning equation shows the prerequisites that are needed for language learning to take place.

Audible Speech + Repeated Exposures + Meaningful Context = Language Learning

AUDIBLE SPEECH

Parents of normally hearing children take the audibility portion of the equation for granted. Even in the worst acoustic conditions, most normally hearing children can receive a speech signal that is audible enough that they can decode its elements. While this prerequisite is often ignored by parents of normal-hearing children, its importance for language learning is in no way diminished. Because it is not possible to make all aspects of speech audible to a profoundly hearing-impaired child using the most powerful hearing aids or to control the listening environment effectively, the equation is unbalanced, with the audibility of the speech signal compromised.

Figure 1 depicts a parent/child interaction in which the audibility of the mother's speech is reduced. The mother is talking to the infant at

Table II. Analysis of Potential Noise Generated in Individual and Group Activities in Group Child Care

	Individual	Group
Quiet	{ Reading Arts & crafts Puzzles	Circle Cooking Story Show and tell
Noise	{ Blocks Carpentry	Housekeeping corner Trucks Snack Songs Musical instruments

Figure 1. The audibility of the mother's speech is decreased due to the distance between the speaker and the listener.

a distance greater than the optimal three feet, resulting in a decrease in intensity of the speech signal as it reaches the microphone of the hearing aid. Distance between talker and child is not the only factor that may reduce audibility. A poorly adjusted amplification system may make only part of the potentially audible speech spectrum available to the child. Even in situations where speaker and listener are in close proximity and the amplification is appropriately adjusted, the caregiver must be sure to gain the child's attention, in order for the rich language input to fall on attentive ears. To repeat, maximizing audibility is a prerequisite condition for acquiring an auditory-based spoken language system.

REPEATED EXPOSURES

Repeated exposure to language occurs when the parent reiterates a word, phrase, or sentence in similar situations over time. Parents of children with normal hearing unconsciously label objects in the environment ("Here's your bottle.") and comment on frequently occurring events ("Your diaper's wet.") many times before first words are learned.

Because profoundly hearing-impaired children do not overhear the speech of others, they do not experience this rich and redundant exposure to language. Their parents must deliberately increase the amount of input to compensate by repeated exposures for the variability and reduction in audibility. Creative repetition is the key to exposing the child effectively to the lexical, semantic, and syntactic aspects of spoken language. If parents find multiple uses for words in many situational and linguistic contexts, their child will readily attach meaning to input he or she hears.

MEANINGFUL CONTEXT

Most children, hearing-impaired or otherwise, lead lives that are full of the contexts necessary for learning language. Their daily routines, daycare activities, and social interactions provide meaningful contexts that are the framework to which the words, phrases, and sentences are attached. Narrating a shoe-tying scenario (a frequently occurring event) can be as effective as a discussion of the circus (seasonal involvement at best).

Figure 2 demonstrates a parent/child interaction that ignores the

Figure 2. This mother and child have not established joint attention on a common object causing the mother's input to lack relevance for the child.

meaningful context prerequisite. Because the mother and baby are not looking at the same object, the child will not understand the references to the speech he or she hears. In this naturally occurring situation, the parent has inadvertently selected a topic that does not follow the child's interest at the moment. She has two choices to remedy this situation: (a) drop the subject and follow the child's lead; (b) gain the child's interest by an attention-getting movement, facial expression, or sound.

Because, by definition, the audibility component of the language learning equation is reduced, it is vitally important that the remaining components are emphasized by parents in the home with the support of a parent/infant program.

An FM unit can be used to help balance the equation. To encourage language learning, the parents are instructed to activate the microphone only when they are talking directly to the child or to a group of people that includes the child. Thus, for a large portion of the child's day, he or she relies on the environmental microphones on the FM receiver for amplification. As long as the parents learn appropriate use of the on/off switch on the transmitter/microphone, the child continues to get practice listening to softer speech emanating from far away or speech occurring within a three feet radius during these nonadult directed interactions.

Overuse of the transmitter/microphone can result in children who are highly dependent on the intense, clear signal for all their verbal interactions. While it is not the method of choice, the result is not all negative, because the child will have acquired minimally a more advanced linguistic system than would have been possible without such a consistently high speech-to-noise ratio. Ideally, however, the child will reap greater benefits if both the FM-transmitted and environmentally transmitted inputs are used.

An environmentally transmitted signal at a conversational distance of three feet (65 dB SPL) may lack the acoustic saliency of an FM-transmitted signal (84 dB SPL), but it is no less important, especially for peer-to-peer learning. The environmental microphones play a major role in the reception of conversational cues, distance listening, and locating sound in space. Maxon et al. (1988), in studying the effects of hearing loss on localization ability, found that profoundly hearing-impaired subjects using body-worn FM units with environmental microphones activated were able to localize stimuli placed at 90 degrees right and left and immediately in front of them (0 degrees). Admittedly, the degree of localization was less refined than that demonstrated by children with lesser degrees of hearing loss who wore ear-level hearing aids. Yet when degree of hearing loss was considered, the children with FM amplification were able to detect the signal at normal conversational levels; the other profoundly hearing-impaired peers, wearing hearing aids, required greatly increased stimulus levels before they were sufficiently aware of the sound to attempt the task.

The microphone/transmitter seems to have important psychosocial implications for parents. When parents begin using the microphone, they describe their relief at being in touch with the child during all their interactions. No longer do they feel that their input to the child is only minimally received. The mere presence of the microphone acts as a signal to parents that their input is important. When Korkes (1991) observed maternal input as a function of FM transmitter use, she found that the feelings of dependence expressed by these parents were not translated into acoustic or linguistic modifications. On a questionnaire, they expressed a lessening of stress, and a sense of relief when the microphone was activated, because verbal contact was assured.

Intuitively, one would assume that having increased access to sound through the microphone/transmitter would result in improved and rapidly developing perceptual skills. A study conducted at the New York League for the Hard of Hearing documented the phonemic recognition skills of young profoundly deaf children who wear FM units as personal amplification.

FM STUDY

Nineteen profoundly hearing-impaired children, ranging in age from 2½ to 7 years, participated in the New York League's long-term comparison study of young children with cochlear implants. Four children had pure tone averages (PTAs) of 90 to 100 dB; twelve children had PTAs between 100 and 110 dB; and three children had losses exceeding 110 dB. They had been enrolled in an auditory-oral communication training program at the New York League for the Hard of Hearing for at least one year. They had been fitted with FM systems as their personal amplification for a period of at least one year and a maximum of six years prior to the study.

Because no comparison hearing aid data were available on these same children, the data reported by Boothroyd (1984) on 120 profoundly deaf orally trained children at Clarke School for the Deaf were used. His subject pool included children between the ages of 8 and 15 years who wore hearing aids considered optimal for their losses as personal amplification. These older students who wore hearing aids were individually administered a CVC word list, without visual cues, and their responses were recorded. Each phoneme in the response was scored as accurate or inaccurate and percent correct was computed.

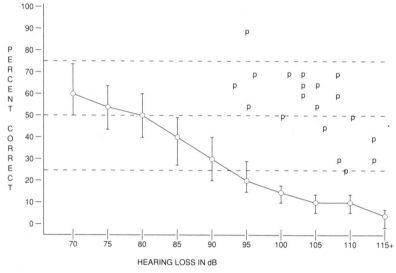

Figure 3. Comparison of the phoneme recognition scores for Boothroyd's (1984) 8–15 year old hearing aid users (o) and the nineteen preschool children (p) wearing FM units as primary amplification.

Results

Figure 3 displays the comparison between the Boothroyd data and those obtained in the League study. Hearing loss is represented on the horizontal axis; percent correct phonemes on the vertical axis. As would be expected, there is a decrease in the percentage of correct phonemes as the degree of hearing loss increases. An advantage to phoneme scoring, as Boothroyd emphasizes, is that it shows *how much* information *is* perceived instead of how little. For example, under conventional whole word scoring procedures, students with hearing loss in excess of 110 dB would have received scores of 0%, implying that they were unable to recognize any of the phonemes in the words. It is clear from the scores that this is untrue. Given the degree of loss, one would assume that the correct phonemes were those having the greatest intensity, that is, voiced consonants or vowels. For the profound group (90 dB +), all the subjects fell below the 50% level for phonemes, with those children having losses greater than 100 dB falling below the 25% level.

The young subjects using FM systems in the League study were tested with the FM transmitter/microphone and the environment microphones activated. They were asked to repeat a list of CVC words (AB List) presented without visual clues. Their responses were immediately transcribed and scored according to the total number of phonemes repeated accurately, with care taken to eliminate those phonemes compromised by articulation difficulties. As with the Boothroyd data, there is a decrease in phoneme recognition as the degree of hearing loss increases. The scores of the young FM users remain fairly consistently above the 50% correct level until 105 dB, where more variability is noted. There are even a few children with hearing losses approaching 110 dB who have sufficient access to acoustic information to perform similarly to children with 95 dB losses. What is most encouraging is that all these children performed above the 25% correct phoneme level—at better levels than children with the same degree of hearing loss from the comparison group.

Segmental Analysis

In order to analyze further the potential of these young FM users to perceive the segmental aspects of speech, frequency counts of the total number of correct vowels and consonants were obtained. The children perceived 84% of the vowels correctly. All but one child repeated vowels at the 50% level or better. For children with losses from 90 to 104 dB, all scores fell at the 75% level or better. While the scores were good for the remaining children, more variability in vowel perception was noted for children with greater degrees of hearing loss (figure 4).

The children perceived 44% of the consonants correctly. Variability

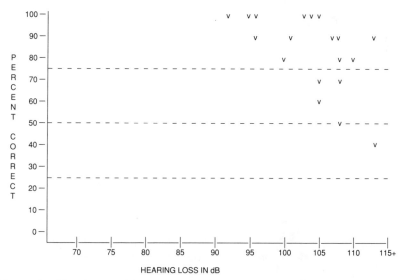

Figure 4. Vowel recognition scores (v) for nineteen preschool children using FM units as primary amplification.

in consonant performance was evident at all degrees of loss. Nine out of twenty children scored at the 50% level or higher (figure 5).

Error Analysis

To determine if there was a pattern to the consonant errors, we completed a speech feature analysis, looking specifically at voicing, manner, and place of articulation. Table III displays the consonants of English categorized across speech features necessary for this analysis. For 44% of the consonants, acoustic cues that distinguish all the speech features—voicing, manner, and place of articulation—were perceived accurately. The remaining 56% of the responses were errors in that the child's response omitted one or two speech features. Of the errors that were made, voicing errors were the least frequent at 7% of the total, manner errors were next at 65% of the total, and place errors were the highest at 88%.

These responses indicate the amount of acoustic information received by the child. A correct response is obtained when all features (voicing, manner, and place of articulation) are the same in the stimulus and response. An error is considered *Good* when two features in the stimulus and response are shared (e.g., voicing and manner match, but place of articulation does not, as when /g/ is recognized as

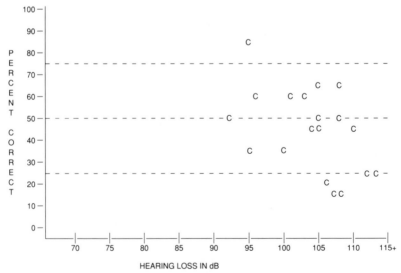

Figure 5.   Consonant recognition scores (c) for nineteen preschool children using FM systems as primary amplification.

Table III.   English consonants classified according to manner of articulation, place of articulation, and voicing.

MANNER OF ARTICULATION

PLACE OF ARTICULATION	STOPS and AFFRICATES				CONTINUANTS					
	STOPS		AFFRICATES		NASALS		QUASI-VOWELS		FRICATIVES	
BILABIAL	b	p			m		w			hw
LABIODENTAL									v	f
LINGUADENTAL									ð	θ
LINGUA ALVEOLAR	d	t			n		j	l	z	s
LINGUAPALATAL			dʒ	tʃ			r		ʒ	ʃ
LINGUAVELAR	g	k			ŋ					
GLOTTAL	ʔ									h
	VOICED	VOICE-LESS	VOICED	VOICE-LESS	VOICED	VOICE-LESS	VOICED	VOICE-LESS	VOICED	VOICE-LESS

VOICING

/d/). The example below demonstrates a typical speech feature analysis applied to actual errors that occurred on the AB Lists.

Response/Target		Common Features
bish/fish	/b/ for /f/	none
shib/hive	/sh/ for /h/	voicing, manner
	/b/ for /v/	voicing
dole/bone	/d/ for /b/	voicing, manner
	/l/ for /n/	voicing, place
mag/log	/m/ for /l/	voicing

For these young FM subjects, 41% of the errors shared at least two features in common, making them acceptable. For example, when /d/ was the stimulus and /b/ was the response, voicing and manner were maintained since both phonemes are voiced plosives; only the place feature was incorrect because a bilabial was substituted for an alveolar.

The most glaring error is one in which all features of the stimulus and response differ (e.g., if /s/ was the stimulus and /m/ was perceived, then voicing, manner, and place have all been violated). In this group of young children, only 7% of the error responses had no common features. These results further support the premise that these profoundly hearing-impaired early FM users have access to important speech information.

These children demonstrate excellent use of the low and mid-frequency information that carries the cues for *voicing* and *manner* of articulation. These features are the ones most effectively gained through audition. *Place* of articulation remains illusive because much of the energy distinguishing this feature falls above 2200 Hz. Fortunately, place cues are readily visible for easily confused pairs such as in the lips closing for /b/ as contrasted with /d/ which has an alvelar placement for the tongue.

TRAINING

Just putting on the FM system is not enough. Worn as primary amplification, it potentially provides the child with access to the speech signal to the degree permitted by the hearing loss. Through training, parents can help their child use speech input for developing spoken language. At one end of the continuum is the child with a mild to moderate hearing loss who is able to develop spoken language from exposure to speech from peers and adults. However, it requires more than exposure to linguistic forms and vocabulary for children with the more severe hearing losses to deduce the rules of language. For these children, adults must conscientiously organize their own speech input to facilitate the sequential, integrated development of the child's auditory, speech, and language skills. Critical to auditory learning is that auditory skill does not develop in isolation in normally hearing children

Table IV.   Integrated Speech/Language/Listening Targets for Two Children Who Use FM Units as Primary Amplification

Child A (Early language learner) Context: Baby's daily routine		
Audition	Language	Speech
Where's the baby? (intonation)	Baby Play with baby	Imitates "baby" (listen only) if /ee/ is bad, see if it im-
Baby vs. cat (syllable #)	Where's baby Baby's crying	proves when stressed the second time ("baBEE")
Sound association (wahwah vs. meow)	Baby fell down	Contrast with "mommy" to show the difference with
Baby vs. mommy (vowel difference) (plosive-nasal)		/m/ + /b/, using props if needed.

Child B (Adding grammatical morphemes) Context: Packing a suitcase		
Audition	Language	Speech
Singular vs. plural (sock vs. socks) (shirt vs. shirts)	Socks 5 shirts	Production of /s/ phoneme in final position
Recognition of plurality, denoted by /s,z,ez/	Formulation of plurality dependent on phonological context	Adult selects sock or socks based on the child's production

and, therefore, should not be expected in hearing-impaired children. Auditory skills must be integrated with language and speech acquisition and not viewed as a separate activity. Table IV displays an intermeshing of auditory, speech, and language goals for two children, one at a beginning level of language acquisition and the other having more advanced communication skills. Within age-appropriate activities, these plans sample the child's auditory perception of suprasegmental and segmental aspects of speech and provide gradually more difficult acoustic contrasts, expose the child to unfamiliar vocabulary or linguistic forms as well as situations that obligate their use, and train auditory monitoring of speech skills. For Child A, the situational context may be the daily routines of sleeping and eating for a baby doll and a stuffed cat. Plurality as a listening, language, and speech goal is targeted for Child B within the context of packing a suitcase. While activities and targets change, the integration of listening, language, and speech remains constant.

In addition to helping the child learn and practice specific forms, sounds, and words, the rehabilitation specialist must constantly re-evaluate the child's auditory learning and adapt the management plan accordingly. Flexibility and individualization make this approach to auditory learning especially effective.

Incidental verbal learning is negligible for these profoundly hearing-impaired children in early stages of language learning. For learning to occur, the child needs many meaningful opportunities to use or act on what is being said. For example, using a stimulating context such as a hospital theme, /s/ or /s-blends/ can be heard or used multiple times during the session in the words *hospital, nurse, sick, stethoscope, stretcher, tongue depressor*. While the situational context is critical to sustain the child's interest, it should remain the framework for the target, not overshadow the lesson. Most important is that the target repeatedly occur in situational contexts relevant to the child's life experience, such as those that occur daily during home routines.

SUMMARY

Children who are only barely able to detect the loudest parts of speech with hearing aids can increase their access to parental speech through the use of an FM unit worn as personal amplification. Over time, their ability to hear more of the speech signal results in improved auditory perceptual skills that, with training, can be used for environmental awareness, speech recognition, and self-monitoring of speech. With the language learning equation balanced, the acquisition of a functional spoken language system can be a reality for profoundly hearing-impaired children.

REFERENCES

Boothroyd, A. 1984. Auditory perception of speech contrasts by subjects with sensorineural hearing loss. *Journal of Speech and Hearing Research* 2:134–44

Korkes, N. 1991. The effect of FM microphone use on maternal input. Kiamesha, New York State Speech-Language-Hearing Association Annual Convention, New York.

Maxon, A. B., Brackett, D., Zara, C., and Ross, M. 1988. Children's localization abilities: Effects of age, hearing loss, and amplification. American Speech-Language-Hearing Association Annual Convention, Boston, MA.

Chapter • 9

FM Classroom Public Address Systems

Carol Flexer

How long would you listen to a lecture that you couldn't quite hear? How long would you strain to hear the words of a speaker at a conference? How much effort, self-discipline, and focused concentration are you, as an adult and competent learner, willing to put into a group listening situation? What is the level of stress and the magnitude of learning that occur under difficult listening situations? What do we do to young children when we place them in typical large, noisy, reverberant classrooms at some distance from the teacher and expect them to listen, attend, and learn from group instruction? Perhaps the most critical question is, why are we surprised when many young children appear distracted, unfocused, undisciplined, and overwhelmed by the demands of classroom listening?

One simple way to enhance the amount of information that children are able to obtain from classroom instruction is *to enable the children in the class to hear the teacher better.* As discussed in previous chapters, all we have to do is make sure that the teacher remains consistently close to every child at all times so that each child receives a clear and complete speech signal. Since consistent physical proximity of pupils and teacher is obviously not possible, one alternative is to amplify the entire classroom through an FM Public Address (PA) system (soundfield amplification).

The technology of soundfield amplification is employed when the teacher's speech is transmitted through a wireless FM microphone to two, three, or four wall- or ceiling-mounted loudspeakers to provide an improved signal-to-noise ratio (S/N) throughout the classroom (Berg 1987). Thus, the teacher's or primary speaker's voice is amplified for the benefit of all children in the class. Soundfield amplification can be viewed as an assistive technology; it is an interface between children and their environment that enables children to extract information from their environment in order to learn (Flexer and Berg 1990).

The purpose of this chapter is to examine classroom amplification from many perspectives. Issues will be raised and questions will be asked because classroom amplification is a relatively new concept and data are scarce; assumptions regarding use and effectiveness of class-room PA systems are evolving as experience and research add new information to our knowledge base. Accordingly, the following topics will be discussed in this chapter: rationale for enhancing audition in the classroom; populations who might benefit most from soundfield

Figure 1.   An example of a soundfield amplification unit showing the micro-phone/transmitter and three loudspeakers. (Used with permission of Audio Enhancement, Salt Lake City, Utah.)

Figure 2.   A classroom amplification system used during group instruction; note the teacher/worn microphone/transmitter and two visible loudspeakers. (Used with permission of Audio Enhancement, Salt Lake City, Utah.)

amplification; practical issues to consider when selecting and installing classroom amplification; ways of convincing school systems of the value of amplifying classrooms; and some suggested techniques for effective use of classroom amplification.

RATIONALE FOR ENHANCING AUDITION IN THE CLASSROOM

Mainstreamed classrooms are auditory-verbal environments (Simon 1985). Instruction is presented through verbal communication, with the underlying assumption that children can hear and attend to the teacher's speech. That is, children must be able to hear the teacher in order for learning to occur. If children cannot hear the teacher clearly, then the entire premise of the educational system is undermined!

Elliott, Hammer, and Scholl (1989) tested children with normal hearing and found that the ability to perform fine-grained auditory discrimination tasks (e.g., to hear "pa" and "ba" as different syllables) classified 80% of the primary-level children in their study either as progressing normally or as having language-learning difficulties. The point is that auditory discrimination is associated with the development of basic competencies that are essential for success in school. The young child who cannot "hear" phonemic distinctions is at extreme risk for academic failure.

The ability to discriminate individual phonemes, to hear word/sound differences, is defined as *intelligibility*, as distinguished from *audibility*, which is the ability to detect the presence of speech. If, because of a mild hearing loss, poor classroom acoustics, and/or poor attending skills, a child cannot discriminate *wave* from *raise*, for example, he or she will not learn appropriate semantic distinctions unless deliberate intervention occurs.

Acoustic Filter Effect

The "power" of hearing tends to be underestimated because hearing loss itself is invisible; thus, the effects of hearing loss are ambiguous and difficult to conceptualize. The ambiguity of hearing loss is magnified by the tendency to categorize hearing loss into the dichotomous classifications of "normally hearing" or "deaf" (Ross and Calvert 1984). Because children with a mild to moderate hearing loss are obviously not "deaf" (about 94 to 96% of the population of persons with hearing loss is functionally "hard-of-hearing" and not "deaf"), their hearing loss is often erroneously believed to present only a minor barrier to classroom performance (Bess 1985; Davis 1977).

Davis (1977) and Ling (1986) describe hearing loss as an invisible acoustic filter; the negative effects are obvious, but the causal filter itself is hidden. The primary negative effect of the invisible acoustic filter of hearing loss is its detrimental impact on verbal language development. If one does not hear, then one does not speak unless intervention occurs (Ling 1989). If ones does not hear "clearly," then speech and language skills will not be clear either, unless deliberate intervention occurs (Ling 1989).

A secondary negative effect of the invisible acoustic filter of hearing loss is its destructive impact on higher-level linguistic skills of reading and writing (Wray, Hazlett, and Flexer 1988). If a child does not hear clearly enough to discern word/sound distinctions, then clear verbal language concepts will not develop. If verbal language is deficient, then reading skills also are likely to be deficient because reading is built upon speaking (Simon 1985). To carry the concept of negative effects of the acoustic filter further, if a child has poor reading skills, then academic options are likely to be limited (Wallach and Butler 1984). The cause of this entire unfortunate chain of events is the ambiguous, invisible, underestimated, ignored acoustic filter effect of hearing loss. Until the core problem of hearing loss is recognized and treated, intervention at the secondary levels of verbal language, reading, and academics is likely to be ineffective.

School personnel often misinterpret the cause of a child's behaviors that result from the acoustic filter effect. For example, a teacher in a mainstreamed classroom once said, "I know that Mary has a bit of a hearing loss, but her problem is not hearing loss; her problem is that she has reading difficulties." Mary's problem *is* her hearing loss; the effect of her hearing loss is its negative impact on Mary's language and reading skills. Until Mary's hearing is enhanced through technology to allow her to hear and subsequently to learn word/sound distinctions, she may have limited success in improving her reading skills. Hearing cannot be bypassed in the chain of intervention.

The relationship between hearing loss and academic failure is well known (Berg 1986a; Bess 1985; Brackett and Maxon 1986; Davis 1977; Ross and Giolas 1978). Indeed, Bess (1985) has documented that even a "mild" hearing loss or a unilateral hearing loss can cause significant academic difficulty.

Data input precedes data processing. A child must have information/data in order to learn, and information is entered into the brain through the ears/hearing. If data are entered inaccurately, rather like having one's fingers on the wrong keys of the keyboard, then the child has incorrect and incomplete information to process. To carry the keyboard analogy further, once the fingers are placed on the correct keys and data are entered accurately (likened to using amplification technology that enables a child to detect word/sound distinctions), what happens to all of the previously entered inaccurate and deficient information? Does that wrong, fuzzy, and incomplete information automatically convert to complete and accurate data? Or does all of the information have to be re-entered into the system? Remember, hearing is the crucial and necessary *first* step. Once hearing has been accessed, the child has an opportunity to learn language as the basis for acquiring knowledge about the world. All levels of the acoustic filter need to be understood, respected, and accessed. The longer a child has inaccurate data entry, then the more destructive the acoustic filter effect will be on the child's overall life development. Conversely, the more clear and complete the entered data are, the better opportunity the child will have to acquire language, to learn reading skills, and to develop academic competencies.

Signal-to-Noise Ratio (S/N)

It is unfortunate but true that children are expected to extract meaning-ful word/sound distinctions in unfavorable acoustic environments, in the presence of background noise. They face the necessity of listening to a speaker who is not close and who may be moving in an unpredict-able fashion (Berg 1987).

S/N is the relationship between the primary input signal, typically the teacher's speech, and background noise. Background noise is ev-erything that conflicts with the auditory signal of choice and may in-clude other talkers, fans, heating or cooling systems, classroom and traffic noises, computer noise, internal biological noises, television, playground and gym noise, hall noise, wind, etc. The more favorable the S/N (the louder the primary auditory signal relative to background sounds), the more "intelligible" that auditory signal will be for the child and the better opportunity the child will have to learn the word/sound differences that underlie the development of basic academic competen-cies. The further the listener is from the sound source, the poorer the S/N (see Chapter 2).

For people with normal hearing, an S/N of +6 dB typically allows for the reception of intelligible speech. Because of internal auditory dis-tortion, persons with any degree of hearing loss need an S/N of +20 dB (Finitzo-Hieber and Tillman 1978). Due to noise, reverberation, and changes in teacher location, the S/N in an average classroom is only +4 dB (and may be 0 dB S/N); less than ideal even for children with normal hearing (Berg 1986b).

RASTI

The negative effects of a typical classroom environment on the integ-rity of the speech signal have quite likely been underestimated. The fact that sound is degraded as it is propagated across a space has long been known, but the magnitude of that degradation has been difficult to determine because of the problem of relating the physical compo-nents of high fidelity sound (dynamic range, frequency, intensity, re-verberation, and S/N) to speech perception.

Leavitt and Flexer (1991) used the new Bruel and Kjaer Rapid Speech Transmission Index (RASTI) System to measure the effect of a listening environment on a speech-like signal. The RASTI signal con-sists of amplitude-modulated broadband noise centered at 500 Hz and 2000 Hz. The signals are transmitted from the RASTI transmitter to the RASTI receiver (Houtgast and Steeneken 1985). The RASTI score is a measure of the integrity of signals as they are propagated across the physical environment; a perfect reproduction of the RASTI signal at the receiver is noted by a score of 1.0. The issue in question was, how much speech information is lost as the teacher's speech travels from his or her mouth to the ears of children who are seated around the room? The RASTI score provides this information.

In order to evaluate the loss of critical speech information at various sites in a typical, occupied classroom, Leavitt and Flexer (1991) obtained RASTI measures at 17 different seating locations (see figure 3). Results revealed that significant sound degradation occurred as the RASTI receiver was moved away from the RASTI transmitter; the magnitude of the loss of critical speech information was reflected in a significant decrease in RASTI scores. Note that even in seating location 3, which was the best seat in the house, the RASTI score dropped to .83.

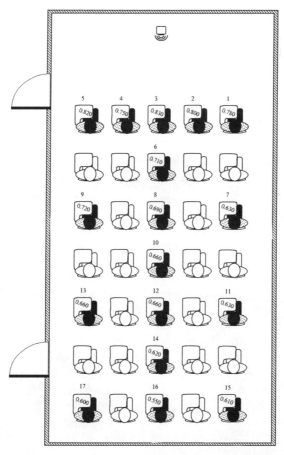

Figure 3.   Schematic representation of classroom (top view) with RASTI score at each seating/test location. (Reprinted with permission of *Ear and Hearing*.)

By the time the signal reached the back row (seating location 16), the RASTI score decreased to .55; a loss of 45% of equivalent speech intelligibility in a quiet, occupied classroom.

These results represent only the loss of speech fidelity that might be expected at the child's ear or hearing aid microphone in a quiet classroom environment. The negative effect that the child's central processing deficit, or hearing loss (even a "minimal" hearing loss), or attention problem will have on speech intelligibility must be added on to the effects of the degraded speech signal. It should be noted that a perfect RASTI score of 1.0 was attained only at the six-inch reference position. Even in a front-row center seat, the loss of critical speech information was significant. Obviously, the most sophisticated of hearing aids cannot re-create speech fidelity that has been lost during transmission across the classroom.

The RASTI study emphasized the importance of being close to the speaker, either physically or through the use of a remote location microphone, in order to obtain a complete speech signal. As soon as any child in the classroom moves further away than six inches from the teacher's mouth, the speech signal begins to degrade. To the extent that a child does not receive a complete speech signal, that child is being denied access to instructional information.

The Logic of Classroom Amplification

Classroom amplification can, if properly adjusted, counteract weak teacher voice levels and ambient noise interference by: (1) increasing the overall speech level; (2) substantially improving the S/N; and (3) producing a nearly uniform speech level in the room that is unaffected by teacher position (Flexer, Millin, and Brown 1990; Ray, Sarff, and Glassford 1984; Worner 1988).

The advantages of soundfield amplification are obtained through the use of a teacher-worn transmitter microphone that is positioned 4 to 6 inches from the speaker's mouth, thereby avoiding loss of critical speech elements. An additional advantage is that all children in the class are consistently closer to the speech source, in the form of a loudspeaker (usually three loudspeakers are positioned around the classroom, on the walls or ceiling), than they could be to a mobile teacher. That is, the speech signal is not only *louder* when amplified through the classroom system, but each child is *closer* to the signal (loudspeaker), thereby reducing the magnitude of the degradation of the speech signal as the signal travels across the physical environment. Note that any given child could not be as close to a loudspeaker as a child could be to a personal FM receiver channeling sound directly into the ear; therefore, a personal FM could provide a superior speech signal. Said another way, soundfield amplification would facilitate the reception of a consistently more intact signal than that received in an unamplified classroom, but not as good a signal as that received by a personal FM unit (Leavitt 1991).

Logic would suggest that if children received a louder, more intact speech signal, they would be able to determine word/sound distinctions better. Flexer, Millin, and Brown (1990) found that nine children who attended a primary-level class for children with developmental disabilities made significantly fewer errors on a word identification task when the teacher presented the words through soundfield amplification than they made when the words were presented without classroom amplification. During the same study, informal observations revealed that the children responded more quickly and seemed more relaxed in the amplified condition.

The MARRS (Mainstream Amplification Resource Room Study) National Diffusion Network Project, directed by Helen Ray, investigated classroom amplification as a means of enabling children with mild or fluctuating hearing losses to remain in the mainstream without expensive referral procedures. Following the original three year study in Illinois, data were analyzed for three different treatments of identified target students: (a) those in typical classroom settings without special provisions, (b) those receiving regular classroom instruction supplemented by resource room instruction, and (c) those educated in classrooms with soundfield amplification. Classroom amplification resulted in significant improvement in academic achievement test scores for the students with "minimal" hearing losses (Ray, Sarff, and Glassford 1984). Furthermore, academic gains were achieved to a higher level, at a faster rate, and with lower costs than gains achieved by students in the more traditional resource room model.

The Putnam County, Ohio school system has approximately 50 soundfield units in place, and the staff has been collecting data on soundfield effectiveness for five years. The data have revealed the most dramatic results in amplified kindergarten classes as compared to unamplified kindergarten classes, with significantly higher scores on the listening, language, and word analysis portions of the IOWA TBS (Flexer 1989). Perhaps kindergartners demonstrated more benefit than older children because younger childen tend to have more episodes of hearing loss caused by middle ear dysfunction, and typically have more problems attending to the teacher's speech. Amplified first grade classrooms also demonstrated better IOWA TBS scores on word analysis and vocabulary, and amplified second grade classrooms showed better scores on math concepts and computation. Teachers reported that when children used the soundfield system in instructional activities, they displayed better voicing, longer utterances, and more confidence when speaking. Formal classroom observations in amplified and unamplified classrooms showed that students in amplified classrooms had better on-task behaviors, and kindergarten teachers in amplified classes tended to speak more consistently, with less need for repetition and rephrasing. School principals reported fewer teacher absences due to fatigue and laryngitis when teachers taught in amplified classrooms.

Classroom amplification, making the teacher's speech louder and clearer throughout the classroom, can increase children's opportunity to obtain an appropriate education. Hearing is not tangential to learning but, rather, is at the heart of the educational system.

Populations Who Might Benefit Most From Soundfield Amplification

There is evidence to suggest that all children benefit from listening to an improved speech signal; some children, however, seem to benefit more than others. It should be noted that classroom amplification is not a replacement for all other forms of S/N enhancing technology. Soundfield amplification is a new technological option that adds another decision-making piece to the riddle of how children, with and without hearing loss, can have the most efficient access to clear and complete auditory information. The choice of equipment depends on the child in question, the classroom environment, and the needs of other children in the classroom. A classroom might have both soundfield and personal FM systems in use. The following populations seem to benefit most from classroom amplification:

1. Children with past and current histories of otitis media with effusion (OME).

The universal consequence of OME is conductive hearing loss, leading to the previously discussed acoustic filter effect. The degree of hearing loss caused by OME varies with the volume of fluid in the middle ear space (Northern and Downs 1991; Wiederhold et al. 1980). Hearing loss may occur even if fluid is not present but significant negative pressure exists in the middle ear (Bluestone et al. 1983). The duration of the hearing loss may vary from 2 weeks to 3 months following a single episode of OME (Northern and Downs 1991).

The magnitude of hearing loss ranges from 10 dB (mild) to 50 dB (moderate), with an average loss of 25 dB (Paradise 1981). Nozza et al. (1990) determined that infants and young children who have the typical 20 dB hearing loss caused by OME, experience more negative consequences than older children with the same degree of hearing loss. It seems that infants and young children need a more favorable S/N and better hearing sensitivity than older children and adults in order to be able to discriminate word/sound differences. Thus, children with a history of recurrent OME in their first year of life may have developed a significant auditory deficit.

The incidence of OME-caused hearing loss may be much higher than school screenings lead us to believe. Due to the typically less-than-favorable screening environments that exist in schools, hearing tends to be screened at 20 to 35 dB depending on ambient noise (Anderson 1991). Because even a 15 dB hearing loss may pose a significant problem for the young child who must learn crucial word/sound distinctions (Dobie and Berlin 1979; Northern and Downs 1991), school screenings miss many children who may be at risk for academic failure (Anderson 1991). Indeed, Flexer, Millin, and Brown (1990) found that only one of the nine children in their study had thresholds of 15 dB or better when tested in a soundroom; yet none of the children had been identified by the school as having hearing difficulties. The Putnam County study found that in primary grades, when a 15 dB criterion was used, 43% of the students failed the hearing screening on any given day and 75% of the primary-level children in a class for children with learning disabilities failed the hearing screening (Flexer 1989). In addition, the MARRS study found that approximately 30% of the children in grades 3 through 6 failed a 15 dB hearing screen (Ray, Sarff, and Glassford 1984).

The point is, the incidence of educationally significant hearing loss is tremendously underestimated, and many children with fluctuating or minimal hearing loss will probably *not* be identified by school hearing screenings. Classroom amplification, if appropriately installed and used, can provide approximately 10 dB of gain and a consistent and improved S/N throughout the classroom, thereby affording children with OME the opportunity to hear clear speech.

2. Children with unilateral hearing losses.

Children with unilateral hearing losses are at significant risk for educational failure due to difficulty in hearing crucial word/sound differences that are essential for the development of basic academic competencies (Cargill and Flexer 1989; Oyler, Oyler, and Matkin 1988). Classroom amplification allows the child with a unilateral hearing loss to have his or her good ear favorably positioned at all times.

3. Children with "minimal" sensorineural hearing losses who do not wear hearing aids.

Children with "minimal" (15–25 dB) sensorineural hearing losses may *not* be identified in a typical school hearing screening. Or, if identified, it may be determined that the child discriminates words very well in relatively quiet one-to-one situations but has significant difficulty in a typical classroom listening environment. Furthermore, the child may resist the initial fitting of hearing aids. Thus, a child with a minimal sensorineural hearing loss may not wear hearing aids but undoubtedly will have difficulty hearing the teacher's speech clearly, and therefore will be at risk for academic failure. The enhanced S/N provided by soundfield amplification can overcome the negative effects of a minimal hearing loss in a dynamic classroom environment.

4. Children with mild to moderate sensorineural hearing losses who are aided.

No matter what the degree of hearing loss, hearing aids alone are not enough to provide access to intelligible speech in classrooms (Flexer, Wray, and Ireland 1989). Children need an improved and consistent S/N in order to learn word/sound distinctions. For most children with mild to moderate hearing losses who are aided, soundfield amplification seems to provide enough of an improvement in S/N to facilitate academic performance; however, a given child might need the more favorable S/N obtained through a personally worn FM unit. How do we know which form of S/N enhancing technology would be best for a child? At this time, the only way to determine the performance effectiveness of a given piece of S/N enhancing technology is through observation of classroom performance.

5. Children with auditory processing or attentional difficulties but with normal peripheral hearing sensitivity (most of the time).

For this population of children, an improved S/N seems to facilitate attention to task and improved response time. That is, when the teacher's speech is made clearly audible, children have an easier time focusing and concentrating on relevant input while ignoring competing stimuli. Once again, classroom observation as suggested by Anderson (1989) and Edwards (1991) provides the only current means of validating the effectiveness of FM technology, whether soundfield or personal FM, for a given child.

6. Preschoolers, kindergartners, and first graders with normal hearing sensitivity who are in the crucial stages of developing academic competencies.

Classrooms that are full of active, excited, energetic, and noisy young children typically provide poor acoustic environments for learning. Even if a child has normal peripheral hearing on a given day (about a 50-50 chance), and has the maturity to listen to the teacher (also about a 50-50 chance), the speech signal that actually arrives at the ear of the child is likely to be substantially degraded (Leavitt and Flexer 1991). For many young children, the new concepts and vocabulary introduced by the teacher must seem like nonsense syllables. Because the ability to detect word/sound differences clearly is essential for learning new information, young children should have access to an improved and consistent S/N. Thus, they would have a better opportunity to develop basic academic competencies, which could prevent later underachievement and potential failure.

Unfortunately, most school systems provide services according to a failure model (Flexer 1990). That is, children typically do not qualify for any special service until they fail one or two grades (Blair 1991). The proactive use of technology to prevent later failure is a novel concept for most school districts.

PRACTICAL ISSUES TO CONSIDER WHEN
SELECTING AND INSTALLING CLASSROOM AMPLIFICATION

There are many issues to consider when selecting classroom PA systems or when recommending a soundfield instead of personal FM units, and there are very few data currently available to guide these decisions. What follows are issues, questions, and suggested solutions based on the few available studies and on personal experience with soundfield technology.

Should We Recommend A Personal FM Unit or Classroom Amplification For A Given Child?

Good question; the answer is, "I don't know." The populations previously listed seem to benefit significantly from classroom amplification. Would they do even better with the superior S/N provided by personal FM units? Perhaps. Certainly children with more severe hearing losses require the favorable S/N provided by personal FM units.

A child with a permanent hearing loss is likely to require an enhanced S/N throughout his or her school career, including college (Flexer and Berg 1990). Because it is not reasonable for a child to take a soundfield amplification system to each class, a personal FM unit would be preferable.

Three substantial advantages of soundfield amplification are:

1. Classroom amplification requires no overt cooperation from the child. The child does not wear a receiver; he or she simply has to remain in the classroom. So, for the child who cannot or will not tolerate any personally worn technology, soundfield amplification might be a viable alternative provided that the unit delivers enough gain and a favorable enough S/N for the child in question.

2. Classroom amplification is not stigmatizing for any particular child (Anderson 1989). That is, all children in the class benefit from the visible teacher-worn microphone/transmitter and the loudspeakers;

the child or children who are targeted for particular benefit are not singled out in any way.

3. Equipment function or malfunction is immediately obvious to everyone in the room; therefore soundfield technology is easy to trouble-shoot. How often have we discovered, to our horror, that a child with a personal FM unit has not been receiving a signal or has been experiencing interference for hours/days/weeks/months!

The most common reason for soundfield equipment malfunction is a weak battery in the teacher-worn transmitter. The teacher should always have spare batteries. Another cause of equipment malfunction is radio wave interference from an outside source that is using the same frequency band as the soundfield unit. Different equipment manufacturers use different carrier frequencies for their units. If there is local interference, then the specific carrier frequency of the equipment may need to be changed by the manufacturer. For example, in one school, the soundfield unit was picking up a baby monitor and conversations from cellular phones. In another school, the soundfield unit was receiving the audio portion from a local television station.

How Does One Select an Appropriate Soundfield Unit?

There are currently several companies that manufacture soundfield equipment, and more are getting into the business all the time. Soundfield units also can be assembled from component parts sold by companies such as Radio Shack. The cost of current units varies from approximately $700 to $2000, depending on the quality of the equipment, number of speakers, fidelity, flexibility, extra features such as additional microphones, etc. A high quality, permanently installed PA system can cost thousands of dollars. Potential purchasers of classroom amplification equipment are advised to evaluate equipment options carefully. Issues to consider when investigating soundfield units include:

1. The carrier frequency of the radio signal

As mentioned above, manufacturers use different frequency bands, some of which are very "crowded" and, thus, are subject to a great deal of interference. Some of the equipment that can be assembled from component parts purchased from local outlets uses the same transmission/carrier frequency bands as AT&T; consequently, the unit may pick up pagers, cellular phones, etc. Be sure to find out if the carrier frequency of your unit can be changed by the manufacturer if you pick up local interference. You can imagine how distracting it would be to try to teach with intermittent static, buzzing, clicking, or random conversations being heard over the loudspeakers.

2. The number of available discrete channels within the frequency band used by the manufacturer

Some units have only 2 to 4 discrete channels available, which means that only 2 to 4 units could be used in a building without interfering with one another. On the other hand, the more discrete channels that the frequency band is divided into, the poorer the S/N might be. Thus, too few bands limit the number of units that can be used in a building, while too many bands per carrier frequency can cause interference and an unfavorable S/N within the equipment itself (see Chapter 1 for elaboration).

3. The number of loudspeakers

A typical classroom needs at least three loudspeakers in order to amplify the entire room and to provide a relatively uniform S/N improvement. Larger rooms may need four or more speakers, and a small room may need only one or two loudspeakers.

4. The durability/quality of the equipment

Equipment that breaks down easily is of no value to anyone. How robust is the equipment? What is the quality? How easily can the equipment be repaired? What arrangements can be made for equipment repair, turn-around time, and loaner units?

5. The fidelity of the equipment

How does the equipment sound? Certainly room acoustics shape the signal. However, it appears that a high frequency emphasis enhances the intelligibility of speech and enables children to better detect word/sound differences (Flexer, Millin, and Brown 1990). Does the equipment crackle? Is there interference? Does it sound on the verge of feedback when set to a "comfortable listening level"?

6. Portability/flexibility

Some units may be permanently installed in a room, others may need to be moved to other rooms or within a room as seating arrangements are changed. How easy is it to move the speakers and speaker wires?

Equipment quality, durability, flexibility, and function are all important issues. Classroom amplification is meant to be a valuable tool that facilitates teaching and enhances learning. If equipment malfunctions in any way or interferes with rather than reinforces teaching, then teachers will be likely to turn the units off rather than fix the problem.

How Should The Loudspeakers Be Positioned Around The Classroom?

There are no readily available guidelines for speaker placement. Speakers have been placed at ear-level on speaker stands, three-quarters of the way up a wall, positioned on available shelves or cabinets, or mounted in the ceiling. Various placement strategies include: making sound-level measurements (Flexer, Millin, and Brown 1990; Worner 1988), obtaining RASTI scores (Leavitt and Flexer 1991), and just listening to the sound of the unit—called "ear cuing." Speech heard through the unit should be easily and uniformly audible *from*, and *at*, all locations throughout the room, comfortably intelligible, and non-stressful. As Leavitt (1991) emphasizes, poor speaker placement could increase reverberation and poor room acoustics, thereby transmitting a *poorer* speech signal than that available without amplification! In other words, the use of soundfield amplification does not automatically guarantee a superior speech signal. Equipment fidelity, number of loudspeakers, and loudspeaker position all influence the quality of the sound transmission.

WAYS OF CONVINCING SCHOOL SYSTEMS OF THE VALUE OF CLASSROOM AMPLIFICATION

Following are issues and strategies that have been helpful in promoting the use of hearing technology in a school system:

1. Recognize that most school personnel have limited information about the relationship of hearing and hearing loss to academic performance (Ross 1991). Therefore, any discussion of S/N enhancing technology must be preceded by discussions about hearing, as presented in the first part of this chapter. The purpose of using technology is to promote the child's right to hear and to benefit from educational instruction.

2. "Hearing" is believing. Demonstrating the equipment and allowing an opportunity for a trial period are necessary strategies. Most people have no idea about the value of classroom amplification until they actually hear and experience the equipment.

3. Administrative support is essential (Flexer 1989). School superintendents, directors of special education, and building principals need to be informed and supportive.

4. Teachers need to volunteer and be enthusiastic about using the equipment. Equipment "forced" on a skeptical, frightened, or timid teacher will probably not be used. Some teachers will be excited about innovative strategies, while others will be intimidated by any change in classroom dynamics. Assuring teachers that the equipment will have a trial period and will be removed if not proven useful offers reassurance.

5. There needs to be a support/contact person within or easily available to the school district to install the equipment, to present in-service courses, and to monitor equipment use and function. Amplifying a classroom represents a significant change for the school system, both in philosophy and operation, and that change requires a facilitator (Blair 1991).

6. The cost of the soundfield unit can be divided figuratively by the number of children who will benefit from the unit and the number of years the unit will be used (Anderson 1991). Thus, classroom amplification might be represented as costing about $5.00 for each child who will benefit from the unit.

7. Local civic groups, PTAs, and individuals have donated soundfield equipment to school systems. In return, the donor's name is engraved on a plaque that is placed in the school or on the equipment (Sexton 1991).

8. Once the equipment has been installed, and if it functions appropriately and with high fidelity, and if there is an accessible support person, and if the school administration recognizes the value of hearing, then the benefits of S/N technology become obvious.

TECHNIQUES FOR EFFECTIVE USE OF CLASSROOM AMPLIFICATION

Technology is simply a tool; a means to an end. The purpose of classroom amplification is to enhance the primary signal of the teacher's speech by providing an improved and consistent S/N throughout the classroom. Once children can detect word/sound differences clearly, they have an opportunity to advance their language skills and to acquire knowledge of the world. There are many techniques that teachers can employ to assist children in attending auditorily. Following are a few examples:

1. Use the word "listen" to cue attention to verbal communication.

2. The microphone can be considered the "mother ear" of the children in the classroom. Where is that ear to be? That "ear" needs to be within 4 to 6 inches of the primary signal source. When worn by the teacher, the microphone needs to be placed facing up, at the midline and relatively high on the body. Beware of inappropriate mircophone placement; clothing style has a definite influence on microphone placement.

3. Soundfield amplification is most efficient for large group instruction. If a teacher is working with a small group, for example a

reading group, and the rest of the class is doing seat work, then the teacher might elect to disconnect all but the loudspeaker that is closest to the special group. Or, the teacher might leave all the loudspeakers functioning because he or she wants the entire class to "overhear" the lesson in order to provide redundancy of information.

4. Whoever is speaking ought to have access to the microphone. Some teachers work the room as Phil Donahue does his audience, permitting each student the opportunity to make a statement on a given topic through the microphone. Other teachers allow children to use the microphone for sharing or circle time, after teaching microphone etiquette. The person with the microphone has the floor and the attention of the class.

5. The teacher can use the microphone to draw attention to crucial word/sound differences. Fricatives could be elongated and plosives could be "bounced" to assist young children in hearing differences among speech sounds. For example, a teacher might say, "*Listen* Johnny, I said fffffffffffish—fish, not d-d-d-dish—dish. Did you *hear* the difference? Now you try it. Say *fish*. Now say *dish* (as the teacher moves the microphone from her mouth to the mouth of the child). Good, I *heard* you say those different sounds."

6. If media equipment are used (video, tape recorder, movie projector), the audio portion of the equipment can be patched either directly through the classroom sound system using a connecting cord, or the microphone of the soundfield system can be placed 4 to 6 inches from the media loudspeaker.

SUMMARY

The purpose of this chapter has been to discuss the current status of FM classroom public address systems. Information was presented about the rationale for enhancing audition in the classroom, populations who might benefit most from soundfield amplification, practical issues to consider when selecting and installing classroom amplification, ways to convince school systems of the value of amplification in classrooms, and techniques for effective use of classroom amplification.

Because the ability to hear is a prerequisite for the ability to benefit from verbal instruction, hearing is the cornerstone of the educational system. When appropriately selected, installed, and used, classroom amplification offers all children, with and without hearing loss, the opportunity to hear the teacher clearly and, thereby, to obtain an appropriate education.

REFERENCES

Anderson, K. L. 1989. Speech perception and the hard-of-hearing child. *Educational Audiology Monograph* 1:15–29.
Anderson, K. L. 1991. Hearing conservation in the public schools revisited. In *Seminars in Hearing; Current Audiologic Issues in the Educational Management of Children with Hearing Loss*, Vol. 12(4):340–64, ed. C. Flexer. New York: Thieme Medical Publishers, Inc.
Berg, F. S. 1986a. Characteristics of the target population. In *Educational Audiology for the Hard of Hearing Child*, eds. F. S. Berg, J. C. Blair, J. H. Viehweg, and A. Wilson-Vlotman. New York: Grune & Stratton.
Berg, F. S. 1986b. Classroom acoustics and signal transmission. In *Educational Audiology for the Hard of Hearing Child*, eds. F. S. Berg, J. C. Blair, J. H. Viehweg, and A. Wilson-Vlotman. New York: Grune & Stratton.
Berg, F. S. 1987. *Facilitating Classroom Listening: A Handbook for Teachers of Normal and Hard of Hearing Children*. Boston: College-Hill Press/Little, Brown.
Bess, F. H. 1985. The minimally hearing-impaired child. *Ear and Hearing* 6:43–47.
Blair, J. C. 1991. Educational audiology and methods for bringing about change in schools. In *Seminars in Hearing; Current Audiologic Issues in the Educational Management of Children with Hearing Loss*, Vol. 12(4):318–28, ed. C. Flexer. New York: Thieme Medical Publishers, Inc.
Bluestone, C. D., Klein, J. O., Paradise, J. L., Eichenwald, H., Bess, F. H., Downs, M. P., Green, M., Berko-Gleason, J., Ventry, I. M., Gray, S. W., McWilliams, B. J., and Gates, G. A. 1983. Workshop on effects of otitis media on the child [Special article]. *Pediatrics* 71:639–52.
Brackett, D., and Maxon, A. B. 1986. Service delivery alternatives for the mainstreamed hearing-impaired child. *Language, Speech, and Hearing Services in Schools* 17:115–25.
Cargill, S., and Flexer, C. 1989. Issues in fitting FM units to children with unilateral hearing losses: Two case studies. *Educational Audiology Monograph* 1:30–47.
Davis, J. 1977. *Our Forgotten Children: Hard-of-Hearing Pupils in Schools*. MN: National Support Systems Project and Division of Personnel Preparation. Bureau of Education for the Handicapped. Department of Health, Education, and Welfare.
Dobie, R. A., and Berlin, C. I. 1979. Influence of otitis media on hearing and development. *Annals of Otology, Rhinology, and Laryngology* 88:46–53.
Edwards, C. 1991. Assessment and management of listening skills in school-aged children. In *Seminars in Hearing; Current Audiologic Issues in the Educational Management of Children with Hearing Loss*, Vol. 12(4):389–401, ed. C. Flexer. New York: Thieme Medical Publishers, Inc.
Elliott, L. L., Hammer, M. A., and Scholl, M. E. 1989. Fine-grained auditory discrimination in normal children and children with language-learning problems. *Journal of Speech and Hearing Research* 32:112–19.
Finitzo-Hieber, T., and Tillman, T. 1978. Room acoustics effects on monosyllabic word discrimination ability for normal and hearing-impaired children. *Journal of Speech and Hearing Research* 21:440–58.
Flexer, C. 1989. Turn on sound: An odyssey of sound field amplification. *Educational Audiology Association Newsletter* 5:6–7.
Flexer, C. 1990. Audiological rehabilitation in the schools. *Asha* April:44–45.
Flexer, C., and Berg, F. S. 1990. Beyond hearing aids: The mystical world of

assistive communication devices. In *How the Student with Hearing Loss Can Succeed in College: A Handbook for Students, Families and Professionals*, eds. C. Flexer, D. Wray, and R. Leavitt. Washington, DC: Alexander Graham Bell Association for the Deaf, Inc.

Flexer, C., Millin, J. P., and Brown, L. 1990. Children with developmental disabilities: The effect of sound field amplification on word identification. *Language, Speech, and Hearing Services in Schools* 21:177–82.

Flexer, C., Wray, D., and Ireland, J. 1989. Preferential seating is NOT enough: Issues in classroom management of hearing-impaired students. *Language, Speech, and Hearing Services in Schools* 20:11–21.

Houtgast, T., and Steeneken, H. J. M. 1985. The MTF concept in room acoustics and its use for estimating speech intelligibility in auditoria. *Journal of the Acoustical Society of America* 77:1069–1077.

Leavitt, R. J. 1991. Group amplification systems for students with hearing impairment. In *Seminars in Hearing; Current Audiologic Issues in the Educational Management of Children with Hearing Loss*, Vol. 12(4):380–88, ed. C. Flexer. New York: Thieme Medical Publishers, Inc.

Leavitt, R. J., and Flexer, C. 1991. Speech degradation as measured by the rapid speech transmission index (RASTI). *Ear and Hearing* 12:115–18.

Ling, D. 1986. On auditory learning. *Newsounds* 11:1.

Ling, D. 1989. *Foundations of Spoken Language for Hearing-Impaired Children*. Washington, DC: The Alexander Graham Bell Association for the Deaf, Inc.

Northern, J. L., and Downs, M. P. 1991. *Hearing in Children* (4th ed.). Baltimore: Williams & Wilkins Company.

Nozza, R. J., Rossman, R. N. F., Bond, L. C., and Miller, S. L. 1990. Infant speech-sound discrimination in noise. *Journal of the Acoustical Society of America* 87:339–50.

Oyler, R. F., Oyler, A., and Matkin, N. D. 1988. Unilateral hearing impairment: Demographics and educational impact. *Language, Speech, and Hearing Services in Schools* 19:201–210.

Paradise, J. L. 1981. Otitis media during early life: How hazardous to development? A critical review of the evidence [Special article]. *Pediatrics* 68:869–73.

Ray, H., Sarff, L. S., and Glassford, F. E. 1984. Sound field amplification: An innovative educational intervention for mainstreamed learning disabled students. *The Directive Teacher* Summer/Fall:18–20.

Ross, M. 1991. A future challenge: Educating the educators and public about hearing loss. In *Seminars in Hearing; Current Audiologic Issues in the Educational Management of Children with Hearing Loss*, Vol. 12(4):402–414, ed. C. Flexer. New York: Thieme Medical Publishers, Inc.

Ross, M., and Calvert, D. R. 1984. Semantics of deafness revisited: Total communication and the use and misuse of residual hearing. *Audiology* 9:127–45.

Ross, M., and Giolas, T. G. (Eds.). 1978. *Auditory Management of Hearing-Impaired Children*. Baltimore: University Park Press.

Sexton, J. E. 1991. Team management of the child with hearing loss. In *Seminars in Hearing; Current Audiologic Issues in the Educational Management of Children with Hearing Loss*, Vol. 12(4):329–39, ed. C. Flexer, New York: Thieme Medical Publishers, Inc.

Simon, C. S. 1985. *Communication Skills and Classroom Success*. San Diego, CA: College-Hill Press.

Wallach, G. P., and Butler, K. G. (Eds.). 1984. *Language Learning Disabilities in School Age Children*. Baltimore: Williams & Wilkins.

Wiederhold, M. L., Zajtchuk, J. T., Vap, J. G., and Paggi, R. E. 1980. Hearing loss in relation to physical properties of middle ear effusions. *Annals of Otology, Rhinology, and Laryngology* 89:185–89.

Worner, W. A. 1988. An inexpensive group FM amplification system for the classroom. *The Volta Review* 90:29–36.

Wray, D., Hazlett, J., and Flexer, C. 1988. Strategies for teaching writing skills to hearing-impaired adolescents. *Language, Speech, and Hearing Services in Schools* 19:182–90.

Chapter • 10

Alternate Uses for FM Systems

Ellen B. Pfeffer

FM amplification systems generally have been accepted as valuable tools for students with severe hearing impairments in educational settings. There are, however, many other uses of FM systems that can help children and adults in educational, social, and vocational situations. In fact, the limitations of FM systems are most often in the minds of audiologists and those using the systems.

The FM systems described in this chapter were evaluated in the same way as conventional hearing aids, using a comparative method to determine which of the systems best met the needs of the person being fitted. Considerations included frequency response, power, coupling method, size of the unit, and cost. All clients were tested in the sound-field using both functional gain measures and word recognition tasks in quiet and in noise; they were tested at close range and at a distance of 25 feet. Test room procedures were set up with the subject wearing an FM receiver, and a transmitter microphone placed six inches in front of a loudspeaker (to simulate the distance of the FM microphone from the mouth of a speaker wearing the FM system). Noise was presented from the opposite speaker.

Children with mild hearing losses, unilateral hearing losses, normally hearing children with learning disabilities, college students, and adults in a variety of situations were tested. Results illustrate some of the alternate uses of FM systems.

MILD HEARING LOSS

The term *mild*, as applied to hearing loss, can be very misleading. Does the child with a mild hearing loss necessarily have *mild* problems? In a study of five children with mild to moderate hearing losses, Brackett and Maxon (1991) found significant improvements in speech perception when FM systems were used in addition to hearing aids, as opposed to hearing aids alone, when the speech signal was at a distance of ten feet. An average improvement of 16% was seen when FM systems were added. In addition FM systems improved speech perception when noise was introduced into the background.

This is relevant for real-life classrooms, where noisy backgrounds are a fact of life. Children with very mild hearing losses are frequently in mainstream classes (with or without standard amplification). While standard audiological test procedures may show that these children function well auditorally in the confines of a quiet test room, the average classroom does not duplicate the sound conditions in a sound treated room! (See Chapter 2.) Even with "preferential seating" the hearing-impaired child will be at a disadvantage when sitting in a noisy classroom without the benefit of FM amplification.

Figure 1 is an audiogram of a six-year-old mainstreamed child with a mild sensorineural hearing loss. "T.C." has a word recognition score of 100% at a normal conversational level at a distance of three feet, however this score decreases to 84% when the volume is reduced to 35 dB HL, simulating a normal voice level at a distance of 12 feet, and the score decreases further when increasing amounts of noise are added to the background.

With the addition of an FM system, in this case coupled to loosely fitting personal-stereo style headphones, the scores improve in all conditions. Word recognition was 100% while using the FM system at 35 dB HL with no noise in the background, 100% with a signal-to-noise ratio of +6, and 92% with a signal-to-noise ratio of 0. The headphone coupling does not significantly impede the student's monitoring of his or her own voice or the ability to hear other students' comments.

UNILATERAL HEARING LOSS

Children with unilateral hearing losses are at a disadvantage in noisy situations (Bess, Klee, and Culbertson 1986; Cargill and Flexer 1989). They experience reduced intelligibility of speech when noise is present. Without the advantage of binaural listening, auditory figure/ground discrimination is reduced, making it more difficult for the child to determine where the teacher's voice is coming from in the class-

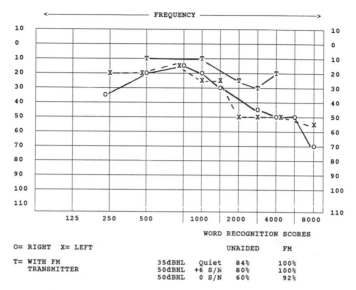

Figure 1.   T.C. is a six-year-old boy with a bilateral, mild hearing loss. A Com Tek FM was fitted binaurally, coupled to personal-stereo-style headphones.

room, as well as what the teacher is saying. This will often result in increased distractibility and reduced academic performance.

Cargill and Flexer (1989) describe two case studies of children whose unilateral hearing losses had been identified early (one at age 2½, one at age 4) and whose primary intervention strategies had been annual audiological monitoring and preferential seating in the classroom. Both children had experienced consistent difficulties in the classroom and had been identified as "problems" by teachers due to attention deficits and distractibility. Eventually both children were fitted with FM amplification for classroom use and almost immediate improvements in both behavior and academic performance were noted. Students, parents, and teachers were all reported to have positive reactions to the classroom use of the FM units. Bess, Klee, and Culbertson (1986) report similar findings with two 6-year-old unilaterally hearing-impaired children who were given two-week trials with FM amplification. Their teachers evaluated the children's classroom performance on various auditory tasks (e.g., understanding in small groups, understanding in large groups, ability to concentrate) before and after the FM trial period. Improvement was seen in every category in both cases with use of the FM system.

Figure 2 illustrates the audiogram of a six-year-old child with normal hearing in one ear and a severe-to-profound (unaidable) second ear. In quiet, ideal situations, this child hears very well; however, test

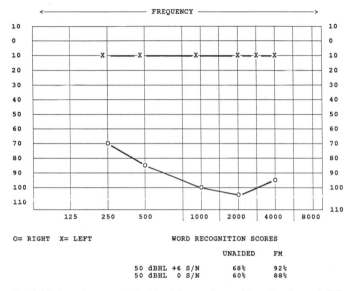

Figure 2. M.F. is a six-year-old girl with a unilateral hearing loss. A Telex TDR 3A/TW 3 FM system was fitted to the left ear coupled to a BTE transducer with an open earmold.

scores indicate a significant deterioration in auditory reception when noise is introduced into the background. The FM system, in this case utilizing a monaural BTE transducer with a nonoccluding earmold (to the normal ear) helps the child to compensate very well in the difficult listening conditions. Also, the open earmold will not block sounds that the ear can hear normally, such as the child's own voice or those of classmates.

NORMALLY HEARING STUDENTS WITH LEARNING DISABILITY OR CENTRAL AUDITORY PROCESSING DISORDERS

Learning disabled children with normal peripheral hearing have also used FM systems effectively (Blake, Torpey, and Wertz 1986; Loose 1984). Loose's study (1984) involved learning disabled children from six to twelve years of age who used FM systems for 30 minutes to 2 hours per day, for three to six weeks. Teachers' reports indicated increases in attention, productivity, and accuracy. Blake, Torpey, and Wertz (1986) reported on forty normal-hearing children, from five to ten years old, with "attention problems." Twenty of the children were given FM systems during academic classes for six months, while the other twenty were considered the control group. Ninety-five percent of the experimental group demonstrated improved attending behaviors as measured by increased eye contact with the teacher, increased rate of correct responses in class, increased ability to follow directions, and increased awareness of verbal cues, body position, and body control.

Stach, Loiselle, and Jerger (1987) described a project in which children with central auditory processing disorders (CAPD) were fitted with FM systems, and improved academic achievement and behavior were noted following fitting. It was found that FM amplification increased attention span, reduced distractibility, and increased sound awareness and discrimination. These favorable results were attributed to the increase in the signal-to-noise ratio provided by the FM system. However, only 40% of the children with CAPD showed enough improvement to warrant the continued use of an FM system.

Figure 3 is the audiogram of a sixteen-year-old student with normal hearing bilaterally, who was diagnosed as having a learning disability and who receives appropriate support services in school. The student reported significant difficulty concentrating in class. There was no indication that an FM system would be helpful because standard noise testing at a signal-to-noise ratio of zero yielded excellent word recognition scores. However, when the auditory system was put under stress (i.e., a signal-to-noise ratio of −10), the student exhibited a breakdown in scores. While it may seem that this is "pushing a

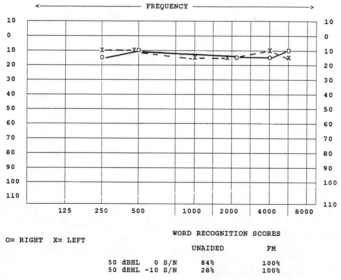

Figure 3.   L.B. is a 16-year-old learning disabled student, with normal hearing sensitivity bilaterally. A Phonic Ear® Easy Listener FM system was fitted binaurally, coupled to personal-stereo-style headphones.

point," it is not unheard of for noise in a classroom to reach a level of −10 S/N. In this condition, the word recognition scores dropped to 28%; with the use of an FM system the score reached 100%, and the student reported much greater ease in following classroom instruction after the fitting.

The audiogram shown in figure 4 indicates normal peripheral hearing and excellent word recognition scores in quiet. When noise is introduced into the background, significant decreases are noted. The history of this 35-year-old subject includes a closed head injury. Following the injury, she reported extreme adverse reactions to any sort of noise; even a piece of paper falling to the floor could completely distract her. She had plans to return to college and could not imagine how she was going to cope with the challenges of that environment in addition to the challenges of learning. She was originally fitted with an FM system and headphones but found it difficult to have both ears involved, so she was later switched to a monaural "earbud." The test scores are impressive in that under all noise conditions she was able to achieve word recognition scores of 100%. However, although the client reported an increased ease in auditory functioning, she was still having significant difficulty in the classroom and other situations. She is currently enrolled in a program of auditory training to help her function more effectively in a variety of listening situations and is making good progress.

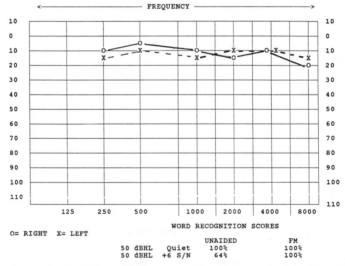

Figure 4.   A.A. is a 35-year-old woman with a history of a closed head injury and an apparent central auditory processing disorder. She has normal peripheral hearing sensitivity, bilaterally. She was fitted with a Com Tek unit to a monaural earplug on the left side.

COLLEGE STUDENTS

The lament is often heard from parents, teachers, and audiologists that students "just won't wear" the FM systems by the time they are 15 or 16 years old. This is known as the "disappearing FM" phenomenon. FM systems may disappear at that age, but requests for their reappearance occur quite frequently after the freshman year at college. Some universities will provide equipment for students through their offices for students with disabilities. State vocational rehabilitation agencies may be able to provide funding for the units for eligible students. In addition to preparing students to wear the FM systems, audiologists must prepare the students to teach their teachers how to use the units appropriately. This can be a critical factor in the successful use of the units in a university setting.

In their study of the effectiveness of amplification devices for moderately hearing-impaired college students, Flexer et al. (1987) found that FM systems are likely to provide "substantial improvement in speech intelligibility in the college classroom" (p. 356). They further concluded that hearing-impaired students must be convinced of the necessity for FM use and that this can most effectively be done in a non-threatening environment.

Figure 5 is an audiogram of a 26-year-old college student enrolled as a mortuary science major. It was important for him to hear his instructors in both classroom and in laboratory situations. He was afraid that the audio-input cords, which were the coupling method of choice for him, would interfere in the movement of lab equipment. He was therefore fitted with a unit that would accept direct audio-input and a neckloop. He could easily switch the coupling, depending on the situation. Although his scores did not improve to the 90 or 100% ranges seen in some of the other examples, the improvement wrought by the FM system was, nevertheless, very significant for him, especially in the laboratory. After one year of FM use, this student reported an increase in his grade point average and greater ease in functioning in the classroom.

FM SYSTEMS FOR ADULTS

FM systems do not have to be limited in use to academic areas. Hearing-impaired adults can benefit from FM amplification whether they use it as an addition to their standard amplification or as the primary mode of amplification.

Stach et al. (1987) evaluated 339 adults for possible FM candidacy. Of these, 108 were identified as meeting the criteria for successful can-

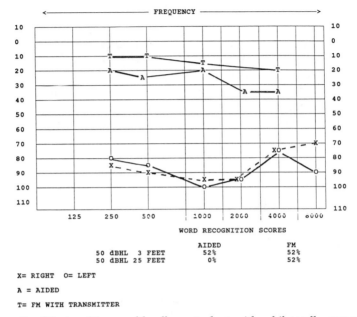

FREQUENCY

WORD RECOGNITION SCORES

	AIDED	FM
50 dBHL 3 FEET	52%	52%
50 dBHL 25 FEET	0%	52%

X= RIGHT   O= LEFT

A = AIDED

T= FM WITH TRANSMITTER

Figure 5. P.L. is a 26-year-old college student with a bilaterally severe sensorineural hearing loss. He wears a binaural Oticon E38P post auricular hearing aid. He was fitted with a Phonic Ear System 4 FM system that is coupled to a neckloop for some applications and to direct audio input boots for other applications.

didacy. These criteria include: the most severe hearing losses; communication demands related to occupational and social activities; new, rather than long-term, hearing aid users; and motivation to improve listening skills. Thirty-five of these subjects purchased FM systems as assistive listening devices, 16 without a trial and 19 after a trial. The major reason the other 231 adults gave for rejecting an FM system was financial. Another reason was that they were "too much trouble" to use. The clinical experiences of these authors clearly indicate that hearing-impaired adults represent a large group of potential users of FM systems.

Adults with progressive hearing losses meet special frustration, because they have "been through it all" in terms of audiological rehabilitation. One might progress from in-the-ear hearing aids to post-auricular hearing aids to body aids, through speechreading classes and auditory training and, if the hearing loss progresses to profound levels, may eventually be told that little else can be done, especially if a cochlear implant is not an option. Figure 6 is the audiogram of an 85-year-old man whose hearing loss progressed in just this fashion, and due to other health problems, he was not a candidate for cochlear im-

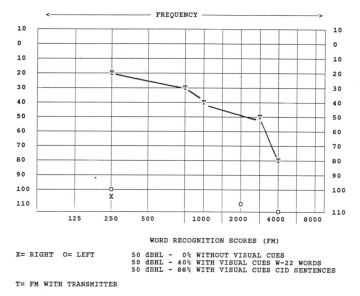

WORD RECOGNITION SCORES (FM)

X= RIGHT   O= LEFT

50 dBHL - 0% WITHOUT VISUAL CUES
50 dBHL - 40% WITH VISUAL CUES W-22 WORDS
50 dBHL - 88% WITH VISUAL CUES CID SENTENCES

T= FM WITH TRANSMITTER

Figure 6.   R.S. is an 85-year-old man with a bilateral, profound sensorineural hearing loss. He was fitted with a Telex TDR 5/TW 3 coupled to button receiver transducers, binaurally, as his primary amplification system.

plant surgery. He was having significant difficulty functioning in virtually all communication situations and was becoming increasingly withdrawn. When an FM system was suggested he agreed to try it. While the speech discrimination scores are poor they are a significant improvement over those that could be obtained with even the strongest of body aids. He is wearing the system with the most powerful binaural button transducers and uses the transmitter microphone whenever possible. He is very dependent on visual cues for optimal communication, but he is now able to participate in a variety of social situations that he had stopped attending due to communication difficulties.

VOCATIONAL APPLICATIONS

Many adults experience significant difficulties communicating in their workplaces, which can have an impact on opportunities for advancement and even on job retention. FM systems can be used in any situation, ranging from a corporate board meeting to the floor of a manufacturing plant, if the participants are willing to cooperate.

Figure 7 shows the audiogram of a woman who is a surgical assistant. She has excellent auditory skills and is able to communicate very well without visual cues, which is essential in the operating room where the mouth must be covered by a surgical mask. While a score of 80% on a word recognition test is excellent for someone with a 90 dB hearing loss, legitimate concerns were raised by her employer about the possibility of misunderstood information during a surgical procedure. The use of an FM system enabled her to hear the surgeon's instructions more easily and assisted her in maintaining her job.

While we normally think of the FM user as sitting passively in the audience of the classroom while the lecturer wears the transmitter/ microphone, the "reverse FM" strategy has been very successful in a variety of vocational settings. For example, a hearing-impaired college professor has his students pass the microphone around the classroom so that he can more easily field their questions. A physician can give the microphone to her patients so that she can be sure she is taking an accurate history. Employees who are required to attend staff meetings or training seminars can request FM amplification systems that may be provided as a *reasonable accommodation* to be in compliance with the American with Disabilities Act (ADA) (1990). According to the ADA, employers must "make existing facilities used by employees readily accessible to and usable by individuals with disabilities . . ." (Sec. 101).

Figure 8 is the audiogram of a 42-year-old attorney diagnosed as having retinitis pigmentosa. She was having increasing difficulty at

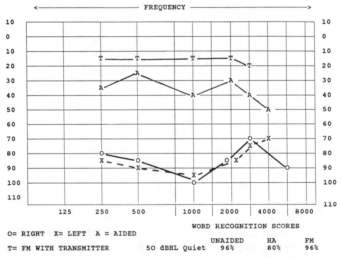

Figure 7. J.J. is a 26-year-old woman with a bilateral profound sensorineural hearing loss. She wears binaural Oticon E28P post auricular hearing aids and was fitted with a Phonic Ear System 4 FM system coupled to direct audio input boots, bilaterally.

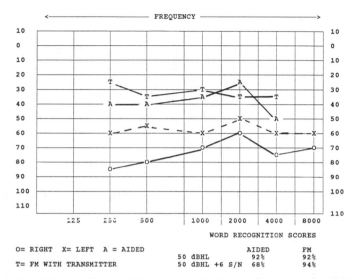

Figure 8. T.L. is a 42-year-old attorney who has a diagnosis of retinitis pigmentosa. She has a moderately severe sensorineural hearing loss in the left ear and a severe sensorineural hearing loss in the right ear. She wears binaural post auricular amplification. She was fitted with a Com Tek FM system with headphones, binaurally.

work, both in her office and in the courtroom. She is now using the FM system in her office in a "reverse" set-up, giving her clients the microphone during interviews. In the courtroom, where significant distances may separate the attorney and those speaking, she has a microphone set up on the witness stand; and while there are inherent limitations to the arrangement, (e.g., it is still very difficult to hear opposing counsel if he or she is not near the stand), the situation is better than it would be without the use of the FM system.

In addition to using the FM system for vocational purposes, this client uses the system at home with her large family. She has made the FM microphone part of a flower arrangement in the center of the table so that she can be a more active participant in the lively discussions taking place at dinner time.

This case illustrates that the FM system can be used by the same person for a variety of reasons. In addition to the vocational and social benefits that she derives from use of the system, there is the added factor of the visual impairment. The FM system provides her, according to her own report, with a sense of "connection" to the outside world, that was missing more and more as her visual impairment progressed. Clinical experience has shown this to be an important issue for many visually impaired clients who also have hearing impairments.

CONCLUSION

FM systems have been generally accepted as valid educational tools for children with hearing impairments. A creative audiologist should be able to see that there are potentially many more users and many more situations where FM amplification can be beneficial. While the cost of FM systems is an important consideration, their potential contribution is great. They can be extremely useful in an almost unlimited number of situations. We have seen FM systems used for horseback riding, skiing and bike riding lessons, in noisy vehicles, while watching television, and in noisy restaurants or at parties.

There is a need for a greater public acceptance of amplification in general and certainly a need for an easier acceptance of visible amplification, such as FM systems. As long as the emphasis is on "smaller is better," as is currently the trend with in-the-canal hearing aids *within* the profession, there is little hope that the public at large will come to accept something as visible as an FM transmitter and receiver. There is a behind-the-ear version of an FM unit currently being released on the market that may help this situation somewhat. Increased research, both into electronic advances and clinical usefulness, are needed to provide professionals and consumers with the best possible amplification systems.

REFERENCES

Americans with Disabilities Act. 1990.
Brackett, D., and Maxon, A. 1991. FM Systems for children with mild and moderate hearing losses. Paper presented to the 1991 SHHH Conference, Denver, Colorado.
Bess, F., Klee T., and Culbertson, J. L. 1986. Identification, assessment and management of children with unilateral sensorineural hearing loss. *Ear and Hearing* (7)1:43–51.
Blake, R., Torpey, C., and Wertz, P. 1986. Preliminary findings: Effect of FM auditory trainers on attending behaviors of learning disabled children. Rochester, MN: Telex Communications.
Cargill, S., and Flexer, C. 1989. Issues in fitting FM units to children with unilateral hearing losses: Two case studies. *Educational Audiology Monograph, Journal of the Educational Audiology Association* (1)1:30–47.
Flexer, C., Wray, D., Black, T., and Millin, J. 1987. Amplification devices: Evaluating classroom effectiveness for moderately hearing-impaired college students. *Volta Review* (89)7:347–57.
Loose, F. 1984. Learning disabled students use FM wireless systems. Rochester, MN: Telex Communications.
Stach, B. A., Loiselle, L. H., and Jerger, J. F. 1987. FM systems use by children with central auditory processing disorders. Paper presented at the annual

convention of the American Speech-Language-Hearing Association, New Orleans, LA, November.

Stach, B. A., Loiselle, L. H., Jerger, J. F., Mintz, S. L., and Taylor, C. D. 1987. Clinical experience with personal FM assistive listening devices. *The Hearing Journal* 40(5):24–30.

Index